CRISIS IN
URBAN PUBLIC FINANCE

CRISIS IN
URBAN PUBLIC FINANCE:
A Case Study of Thirty-Eight Cities

Pearl M. Kamer

PRAEGER

PRAEGER SPECIAL STUDIES • PRAEGER SCIENTIFIC

Library of Congress Cataloging in Publication Data

Kamer, Pearl M.
    Crisis in urban public finance.

    Includes index.
    Bibliography: p.
    1. Municipal finance—United States—Case studies.
I. Title.
HJ9145.K35   1983   336'.014'73   83-12168
ISBN 0-03-063942-5

Published in 1983 by Praeger Publishers
CBS Educational and Professional Publishing
a Division of CBS Inc.
521 Fifth Avenue, New York, NY 10175 USA

© 1983 by Praeger Publishers

3456789   052   987654321

Printed in the United States of America
on acid-free paper

To Frank and Anna Kamer

Contents

Foreword

The nation's cities, especially its largest ones, are experiencing growing fiscal stress. Reduced Federal aid to state and local governments is one cause. The long-simmering tax revolt is another factor. The cities have been adversely affected by the recent deep and protracted national recession, which eroded municipal revenues and boosted welfare-related municipal spending. Municipal fiscal problems also reflect basic economic and demographic changes that have been in motion for several decades. These include the movement of people and jobs from central cities to surrounding suburbs and the general shift of population and economic activity from "snowbelt" to "sunbelt." The selective nature of these processes drained northern cities of some of their most productive workers and eroded the municipal tax base. There is convincing evidence that a number of large sunbelt cities are also prone to fiscal stress. Many are highly dependent on Federal aid and ongoing aid cutbacks can have traumatic effects. Others face large unmet infrastructure needs. Still others are losing ground to their respective suburbs. This was once regarded as a malady affecting only northern cities. Clearly the problem is national in scope and requires national policy solutions.

It is apparent that tough fiscal decisions can no longer be postponed. Many of the nation's cities must prune back what some have described as their "overdeveloped" public sectors to levels that are consistent with slow-growing or diminishing resources. There is a great temptation to use a "meat-axe" approach, cutting programs across-the-board regardless of merit or need, to achieve retrenchment. A more rational approach is to determine the causes of fiscal stress in given cities and to tailor retrenchment policies to those causes. This goal presupposes some knowledge of the fiscal "pressure points" in given cities.

This book develops and applies a methodology to quantitatively analyze the magnitude of the fiscal problems faced by large cities. It uses a case-study approach to empirically determine the causes, manifestations, and relative degree of fiscal stress in thirty-eight of the nation's largest cities and evaluates the various policy options for retrenchment in the context of these findings. The indicators developed utilize regularly-published Census Bureau fiscal and economic data. It is anticipated that these indicators will be operationally useful to city and county administrators and legislative bodies in monitoring their own fiscal status on an ongoing basis.

I am grateful for the assistance of Dennis Young, a colleague at Harriman College, and Regina Armstrong, of the Regional Plan Association, who read sections of the initial draft and made many helpful suggestions. George Sternlieb, of the Rutgers Center for Urban Policy Research, was kind enough to review the major research findings. His perceptive comments helped to sharpen their focus. Xenia Duisin, the knowledgeable librarian at the Institute for Public Administration, provided invaluable assistance in locating various research materials. The staff of the Urban Institute made available several draft reports that helped to guide my choice of indicators. The staff of the Governments Division of the U.S. Bureau of the Census was most helpful in interpreting Census Bureau fiscal statistics and in providing special tabulations of unpublished data, where needed. I am particularly grateful to my colleagues at the Long Island Regional Planning Board, Lee Koppelman, Arthur Kunz, Edith Tanenbaum, and Israel Wilenitz, for their support and encouragement of this effort.

Effective urban policy decisions cannot be made in a vacuum. There is a pressing need to accurately define and measure urban fiscal stress. To date, most empirical research in this area has been fragmented both in terms of its geographic focus and in terms of the variables used to measure stress. In part, this reflects the lack of integration between empirical research and existing theories of urban fiscal stress. However, in large measure, it reflects the constraints imposed by the existing fiscal and economic data base. These constraints surface repeatedly throughout the analysis. In a sense, this study demonstrates what measures can be readily-developed from existing data. More definitive analysis awaits the development of a more detailed, consistent, and timely municipal data base. It is hoped that this study will stimulate efforts to achieve such a data base.

Pearl M. Kamer

List of Tables

List of Figures

CRISIS IN
URBAN PUBLIC FINANCE

1

Introduction

The nation's cities, particularly its large cities, are currently experiencing some degree of fiscal stress. Fiscal stress can range in severity from actual default, which is the inability to pay bills or to obtain financing in the bond markets, to the inability to sustain current services with available resources. Most cities are in the latter category.

It has become apparent that tough fiscal decisions can no longer be postponed. Many of the nation's cities must prune back their "over-developed" public sectors to levels consistent with slow-growing or diminishing resources. There is a great temptation to use a "meat-axe" approach, cutting programs across-the-board regardless of merit, to achieve retrenchment. A more rational approach is to determine the causes of fiscal stress in given cities and to develop retrenchment policies which address these causes.

This book develops and applies a methodology to quantitatively analyze the magnitude of the fiscal problems faced by large cities. It uses a case-study approach to empirically determine the causes of fiscal stress in 38 of the nation's largest cities and evaluates the various policy options for retrenchment in the context of these findings. The goal is to determine how municipal managers can best provide essential public services in a cost-effective manner, thereby reducing or at least stabilizing municipal spending. This goal presupposes some knowledge of the fiscal "pressure points" in given cities. The indicators developed as part of the analysis will also be operationally useful to city and county governments in monitoring their own fiscal status vis-à-vis that of other areas on a continuing basis.

THE CAUSES OF MUNICIPAL FISCAL STRESS

The causes of fiscal stress in U.S. cities are deep-seated and not easily reversible. Reduced Federal aid to state and local governments is one cause. In part, such cutbacks reflect the desire to balance the Federal budget, or at least to control the ballooning Federal deficit, and to satisfy expenditure priorities in other areas such as national defense. However, cutbacks in aid also reflect the Reagan Administration's philosophy that massive Federal assistance to the nation's cities is not equitable because it siphons resources from the nation-at-large to pay for programs that generally have a local impact. It is the Administration's position that programs with a local impact should be the responsibility of states and their respective local governments.

The supply-side approach to economic development has also worsened the fiscal problems of the nation's cities. The investment tax credit and the Accelerated Cost Recovery System (ACRS) for depreciation, enacted as part of the Economic Recovery Tax Act of 1981, implicitly encourage the movement of capital and labor from industries and areas of low profitability to industries and areas of high profitability. This works to the detriment of the nation's cities, particularly its older ones.

The cities have also suffered from the deep and protracted national recession, which significantly reduced municipal revenues and boosted welfare-related municipal spending. Northern cities, with their obsolete plants and aging public infrastructures, have been disproportionately hurt by recent recessions and have generally failed to share proportionately in ensuing recoveries. Worsening economic conditions also led to disarray in the municipal bond markets. Interest rates on municipal bonds recently reached historic levels, forcing many cities to postpone or cancel planned bond offerings, just at a time when their need for additional revenue had become acute. New tax-exempt instruments, such as industrial development bonds, also made municipal bonds less attractive as a tax shelter.

The current fiscal problems of the nation's cities also reflect basic economic and demographic changes which have been evident for several decades. They include the movement of people and jobs from central cities to surrounding suburbs and the general shift of population and economic activity from "snowbelt" to "sunbelt." These shifts reached a critical "tipping point" by the mid-1970s. Their selective nature drained northern cities of some of their most productive workers and eroded the municipal tax base. At the same time, the central-city population mix shifted toward high-cost citizens, those requiring extensive public services in order to survive in an urban environment. In some cities, the gap between needs and resources was widened by poor municipal management and by a large municipal bureaucracy that sought to perpetuate itself. In addition, many northern cities could not annex surrounding suburbs and thereby recapture taxable activity.

THE PRESENT STUDY IN THE CONTEXT OF CURRENT LITERATURE

There is a substantial body of literature that provides a theoretical framework for understanding urban fiscal stress. Irene Rubin summarized this literature in terms of three models; the migration and tax base erosion model, the bureaucratic growth model and the political vulnerability model.[1]

The migration and tax base erosion model attributes urban fiscal strain to population and job shifts and their impact on the municipal tax base. For example, the stream of migration from the rural south to the cities of the northeast, midwest, and far west imposed expenditure demands on these cities which severely strained their resources. These demands were concentrated in areas such as education, welfare, vocational training, and health care. The migration of middle and upper income residents and businesses from city to suburb compounded the problem by eroding the tax base needed to pay for these services. Attempts by cities to generate additional revenues through higher taxes generally backfired because they triggered a further exodus of middle income residents and businesses. Moreover, many suburban residents continued to work within their respective central cities and to utilize municipal facilities and services, thereby contributing to higher municipal spending.

The more recent stream of migration from snowbelt to sunbelt drained population and jobs from entire metropolitan regions. The nation's northern cities were most severely affected. The generalized decline of northern cities and states, which became apparent during the 1970s, was a product of urban congestion and attendant high rents, transportation bottlenecks, air and water pollution. It also reflected higher energy costs, greater unionization, and higher labor costs in the north. The move to the sunbelt was facilitated by changes in technology that reduced the advantages of locating in or near large urban centers. The rapidity with which technological changes influenced the economy largely nullified efforts by municipal officials in the north to preserve their respective tax bases.

The migration and tax base erosion model attributes urban fiscal stress to causes which are external to given cities. Equally valuable explanations of fiscal stress are embodied in the bureaucratic growth and political vulnerability models. Both relate fiscal stress to the internal functioning of cities. The basic premise of the bureaucratic growth model is that government grew too large too rapidly. Rubin suggests that if such growth reflects the legitimate demand for additional services for which citizens are willing to pay, it may not lead to overspending and fiscal stress. However, problems can arise when overspending by municipal government is part of an attempt by bureaucrats to perpetuate the municipal bureaucracy. The third model, the political vulnerability model, theorizes that the more vulnerable a city is to the demands of special interest groups, the greater the likelihood that overspending and fiscal stress will result. According to this theory, a mayor who lacks the plurality to keep him in office must satisfy the needs of a diverse array of interest groups, and in the process will tend to overspend.

The theoretical literature is complemented by a number of empirical studies which attempt to measure the degree of fiscal stress in given cities. Some of the major research efforts are summarized below.

Brookings Institution Indicators[2]

The Brookings Institution "Intercity Hardship Index" incorporated 1970 census information for 55 large cities. The variables included unemployment rates, dependency ratios, educational attainment, incidence of overcrowded housing, and poverty and per capita income. They were equally weighted and linked to form a single index number. A companion "Index of Intrametropolitan Hardship" for the same areas was designed to measure the need for burden-sharing arrangements between a city and its suburbs.

Congressional Budget Office Indicators[3]

The Congressional Budget Office developed measures of economic, social, and fiscal need for 45 large cities in connection with the renewal or adoption of several grant programs. Their Index of Social Need incorporated per capita income, unemployment rates, and measures of poverty, dependency, and overcrowded housing. Their Index of Economic Need incorporated age of housing as well as population, employment and income changes. Their Index of Fiscal Need measured tax effort and the size of the property tax base. It also incorporated a composite measure relating local public service needs to tax effort and fiscal capacity.

Treasury Department Indicators[4]

The U.S. Department of the Treasury developed an Index of Fiscal Strain for 48 large cities as part of its evaluation of the fiscal impact of the Economic Stimulus Package (ESP) on large urban governments. The variables used and their respective weights were as follows: population change (37), change in city per capita income relative to national per capita income (27), change in per capita own-source revenue relative to change in per capita income (12), change in per capita long-term debt relative to change in per capita income (12), and percent change in full market value of property (12). The variables were linked by means of standard (z) scores which were then weighted and summed to derive a total fiscal strain value. The cities were classified as low, moderate, or high strain types based on pre-selected cutoff points.

The H.U.D. Community Need Index[5]

The U.S. Department of Housing and Urban Development created a system for ranking cities which incorporated measures of municipal age, decline, density, and poverty. The age and decline variables included age of population and housing, population changes, and changes in number of retail establishments and retail sales. The density indicator incorporated measures of crime, population density, proportion of rental housing, changes in minority-group populations, and unemployment rates. The poverty indicator included the ratio of non-whites to the total population, the incidence of overcrowded and substandard housing, educational attainment, the proportion of families headed by females, and the proportion of families with incomes below pre-selected poverty thresholds.

There are also a number of studies that identify the sources of fiscal stress without empirically measuring them. For example, the Urban Institute has developed a list of indicators which appear to be associated with fiscal stress.[6] They include: substantial outmigration over a 10- to 15-year period or a sharp increase in net outmigration, defined as a population loss of 10% or more during a five-year period; an absolute loss in private employment or only minor employment gains during periods of national economic growth; a high local tax burden, defined as 7% or more of personal income, and a widening tax burden gap between the central city and its suburbs; an increasing proportion of the population comprised of low income households; substantially lower gains in per capita income than the metropolitan area or the state; the inability to annex, consolidate, or otherwise share in the regional tax base; high unemployment; a large concentration of employment in manufacturing; and, per capita long-term debt above or close to $1000. The Urban Institute has also prepared a report that demonstrates how to evaluate a city's economic base, tax capacity, expenditures, employment, short-run financial condition, dependence on outside aid, and pension liabilities.[7]

Based on a 1973 survey of 30 cities, the Advisory Commission on Intergovernmental Relations (ACIR) identified the following fiscal danger signals: an operating fund revenue-expenditure imbalance in which current expenditures significantly exceed current revenues in one fiscal period; a consistent pattern in which current expenditures exceed current revenues by small amounts for several years; an excess of current operating liabilities over current assets; short-term operating debt outstanding at the conclusion of a fiscal year; a high and rising rate of property tax delinquency; a sudden substantial decrease in assessed value for unexpected reasons; an under-funded, locally-administered retirement system; and, poor budgeting, accounting, reporting, and financial management techniques.[8]

Much of the empirical research to date has been fragmented both in terms of its geographic focus and in terms of the variables used to portray stress. This, in turn, reflects the fact that most empirical studies are not well integrated with existing theories of urban fiscal stress. In the absence of a theoretical focus, there is no logical basis for selecting the individual variables or for relating them in any systematic way to the incidence of fiscal stress.

This study attempts to more completely integrate empirical analysis with existing theory. It documents the social and economic changes suggested by the migration and tax base erosion model for each of 38 large cities, and systematically examines evidence of fiscal stress in each of these cities. While the case-study method is generally of limited usefulness in model testing, the cities profiled represent a sufficient cross-section of large cities in all regions to permit reasonable inferences concerning the validity of the migration and tax base erosion model as a predictor of fiscal stress. The case-study approach also makes it possible to document intercity differences in the causes of fiscal stress.

ORGANIZATION OF THE BOOK

This book contains seven chapters. The introductory chapter discusses the methodology and data sources, and summarizes the salient findings of succeeding chapters.

Chapter 2 analyzes economic and demographic changes within each of the sample cities in the context of the three streams of migration that have characterized the post-war period. That is, it documents the movement from the rural south the the urban north, the movement from city to suburb, and the movement from snowbelt to sunbelt. It compares central city and suburban population change, by race; it analyzes the changing central city share of metropolitan area retail sales, service-industry receipts, and manufacturing jobs; and, it compares central city and suburban crime rates. The final section develops an index of socio-economic stress by which individual cities are ranked. Chapter 2 sets the stage for systematically examining the fiscal consequences of the migration and tax base erosion model in large cities.

Chapters 3, 4, and 5 develop indicators of fiscal stress for each of the sample cities. Chapter 3 focuses on the revenue side of the fiscal equation. It attempts to relate revenue patterns in each city to the incidence of fiscal stress. The premise is that some cities are in trouble, not because their expenditures are too high in some absolute sense, but because their expenditures are high relative to their ability to generate public revenues. The mix of revenue sources in each city is analyzed as are changes in revenue mix during the fiscal 1969–79 decade. The analysis reveals the growing municipal dependence on Federal and state aid, evaluates the role of such aid in stabilizing municipal tax burdens, and demonstrates what proportion of each city's expenditures is being financed by "outside" revenue sources that are beyond its direct control. Chapter 3 also evaluates the relative strength of the tax base in each city. The property, sales, and income tax bases are examined separately to determine each city's potential for expanding locally-generated revenues. Property tax burdens in cities which levy an income and/or general sales tax are compared with property tax burdens in cities without these auxiliary taxes. Each city's reliance on user charges and fees is examined and the degree of fee intensity is related to municipal tax burdens. Measures of tax efficiency in providing basic municipal services are also computed. The final section develops an index of revenue stress by which the individual cities are ranked. The index attempts to identify those cities that are prone to fiscal stress because of the manner in which they raise public revenues.

Chapter 4 examines the expenditure side of the fiscal equation. Each city's revenue base is compared with its level of spending and rate of expenditure growth. Trends in operating and capital expenditures are examined separately to pinpoint the origins of expenditure stress in each city. Operating expenditures are disaggregated into "common function" and "all other" operating expenditures to demonstrate the impact of extensive functional responsibilities on overall spending.* Chapter 4 also analyzes the relationship between personnel costs and operating expenditures, and analyzes how much expenditure retrenchment has occurred in large U.S. cities in recent years. The final section develops an index of expenditure stress by which individual cities are ranked. The index seeks to identify those

---

*Common functions are those commonly performed by most cities. In this study they are defined as current spending for highways, police and fire protection, sanitation, parks and recreation, financial administration, and general control.

cities that are prone to fiscal stress by virtue of their unique expenditure patterns.

Chapter 5 analyzes the debt and liquidity positions of each city. It examines the use of short-term debt, evaluates changes in the volume of long-term debt, and analyzes the mix between newly-issued tax-supported and revenue debt in given cities. It links the volume of long-term debt issued during the fiscal 1969–79 period with the volume of capital spending in each city. Chapter 5 also analyzes changes in debt burdens over time and demonstrates how the need to service debt is a constraint on municipal spending in given cities. Each city's liquidity position is measured in terms of its available cash and securities less short-term debt. Evidence of retrenchment in terms of debt and liquidity is also presented. The final section develops two stress indexes, one for debt and one for liquidity, by which individual cities are ranked. This procedure identifies those cities which are prone to fiscal stress, either because they are characterized by an unfavorable debt position, or by an unfavorable liquidity position, or both.

Chapters 6 and 7 summarize the empirical findings and discuss the various policy options available to cities and other local governments. These options would allow them to remain solvent, to bring expenditures into line with available resources, and still provide a relatively diverse array of municipal services.

Chapter 6 attempts to pinpoint those cities that are currently experiencing fiscal stress or that are most vulnerable to fiscal stress. The indexes for revenues, expenditures, debt, and liquidity are integrated into an overall measure of fiscal stress using standard (z) scores. This measure is then compared with the index for socio-economic stress in each city to demonstrate the relationship between socio-economic conditions and the incidence of fiscal stress. Chapter 6 attempts to answer the following types of questions. Does erosion of the municipal tax base automatically result in fiscal stress? Do cities with strong private sector economies nevertheless experience fiscal stress? The results of this study are compared with those of related studies to test the consistency of the findings. Recent survey information concerning the fiscal status of large cities is also introduced in this chapter. The final section discusses the economic outlook for large cities in the context of Reaganomics, the new federalism, and the fiscal condition of the various states.

Chapter 7 focuses on the policy options available to large cities to help bring expenditures into line with revenues. It considers revenue options such as restructuring the municipal tax base and implementing metropolitan tax base sharing. Expenditure options such as turning over selected functions to the private sector, improving municipal management, and participating in joint public-private ventures are considered.

METHODOLOGY

Characteristics of the Sample Cities

Each of the 38 cities profiled in this book contained a 1980 population of 300,000 or more.* Only the largest cities were selected for analysis because the demographic and economic changes implicit in the migration and tax base erosion model have reached their most advanced stages in the largest cities.

The various stress measures were computed for both individual cities and for groups of cities. The sample cities were grouped by geographic region, population density, direction of population change, and differences in functional responsibilities. The existing literature suggests that these distinctions are correlated with the incidence of fiscal stress. For example, Thomas Muller found that population decline is associated with a loss of income which, in turn, limits the ability of cities to finance public services.[9] W. Patrick Beaton found that declines in population coincide with the abandonment of older physical plants which, in turn, causes higher expenditures for protection and control. Beaton also found that declining cities have large, costly, and well-entrenched bureaucracies which resist change.[10] Cities were grouped by region because the migration and tax base erosion model suggests that fiscal problems are likely to be most acute in northeastern and midwestern cities.

A number of criteria were used in grouping the sample cities. For example, cities were classified as "growing," "mixed," or "declining," based on population statistics from the 1960 and 1970 decennial censuses and preliminary population statistics from the 1980 census. Growing cities were those that gained population throughout the 1960–80 period; declining cities lost population throughout this period; mixed cities gained population between 1960 and 1970, but lost population between 1970 and 1980. Each city was classified geographically by assigning it to one of the four major census regions: the northeast, the north central (midwestern) states, the south, or the west. For purposes of analysis, the northeastern and north central states are defined as the "snowbelt," and the south and west comprise the "sunbelt." Cities were classified as "low," "medium," or "high" density based on preliminary 1980 population per square mile. Low-density cities contained fewer than 4000 persons per square mile; medium-density cities contained between 4000 and 8000 persons per square mile; high-density

---

*The only exception was Louisville which had a 1980 population of 298,000.

cities contained more than 8000 persons per square mile. Differences in functional responsibility were defined in terms of how many of the "least common" functions—education, health and hospitals, and public welfare—each city performed. Those cities that spent at least $40 per capita for a given least common function in fiscal year 1979 were classified as performing that function. Cities that spent at least $10 per capita for all three least common funtions combined were classified as performing "minimal amounts" of the least common functions. Five categories were used to denote levels of functional responsibility: the performance of three least common functions, two of them, one, minimal amounts, and none.

The sample cities and their respective groupings are shown in Table 1.1. Six of them, Chicago, Detroit, Houston, Los Angeles, New York, and Philadelphia, contained 1980 populations in excess of one million. At the opposite extreme, cities like Oakland, Newark, and Omaha contained fewer than 350,000 residents in 1980. One city, Indianapolis, is distinguished by an unusual form of countywide government. In 1970, the City of Indianapolis merged with all but three of its surrounding suburbs inside Marion County in an arrangement called "Uni-Gov." This occasionally distorts the various stress indexes because Indianapolis appears to have sustained an unusually rapid growth of revenues and expenditures.

It is apparent from Table 1.1 that the declining, northern, high-density cities that perform one or more of the least common functions are often one and the same. This is also true of the growing, low-density, southern and western cities with few responsibilities outside of the traditional common functions. It was expected that the former groups of cities would display similar fiscal profiles. The latter groups of cities were expected to display similar financial characteristics, and were also expected to display fewer symptoms of stress than their declining northern counterparts.

New York City, by virtue of its population size and the sheer magnitude of its ficsal variables, was considered separately throughout the analysis; otherwise, it would tend to distort the group findings.

The Measures of Socio-Economic and Fiscal Stress

Where possible, indicators of fiscal stress were computed from published Census Bureau statistics. This will enable other researchers to replicate the methodology in the future, and will allow municipal officials to evaluate their own city's relative fiscal position on an ongoing basis. The City Government Finance series, published annually by the Census Bureau, was the primary source of financial data.[11] A companion publication, Local Government Finances in Selected Metropolitan Areas and Large Counties, provides similar information for metropolitan areas and their component counties so that the stress-measures developed can be applied to counties and metropolitan areas as well.[12] The economic measures were derived from the 1967 and 1977 economic censuses including the Censuses of Manufactures, Retail Trade, and Selected Services.[13] Although more recent information is available for given cities, the economic censuses provide the only consistent source of data for all cities. Population and housing information for the sample cities was derived from the 1960, 1970, and 1980 decennial censuses of population and housing.[14] Information about municipal employment and earnings was obtained from the *City Employment* series which is also published annually by the Census Bureau.[15] Unpublished Census Bureau statistics and information from private sources were incorporated where necessary.

The various financial measures were computed for fiscal years 1969, 1975, 1979, and 1981. It should be noted that Census Bureau fiscal years are not coterminous with calendar years. For example, census statistics apply not to calendar year 1981 but to the fiscal 1980–81 period, which includes all fiscal years ending between July 1, 1980 and June 30, 1981. Most cities are on a calendar year basis and end their budget years on December 31st. The next most common fiscal period is the twelve months ending June 30th. For convenience, fiscal year 1969 will be used to denote the fiscal 1968–69 period, fiscal 1975 to denote the fiscal 1974–75 period, and so forth. The time series analysis covers the fiscal 1969–75, fiscal 1975–79, and fiscal 1979–81 periods.

The financial measures are expressed on a per capita basis. For the years between decennial censuses, the population estimates used to compute them were developed by the author. They therefore differ from those published in *City Government Finances* which incorporates less current population estimates. The use of the more current population estimates leads to higher per capita figures for declining cities and lower per capita figures for growing cities than the published version.

Per capita figures for each of the city groupings were computed from the raw data for individual cities within each group and do not represent a group mean. For example, instead of averaging per capita general revenues for the northeastern cities to develop a group measure, general revenues and total population were summed separately and revenues then divided by population. This tends to dilute the influence of extreme values within each group.

Standard (z) scores were used to compute the various stress indexes. Cities in the lowest 25% of the distribution, that is, having z scores of $-.675$ or less, were characterized as "distressed". Cities located between the 25th and 75th percentiles, that is, having z scores between $\pm.675$, were labeled as "moderately distressed." Cities falling within the top 25% of the distribution, that is, having z scores of $+.675$ or higher, were classified as "not distressed." The methodology is specifically designed to compare large cities

TABLE 1.1. Sample Cities, Grouped by Selected Variables

			Groupings		
Population Size	1980 Population	Population Change	Geographic Region	Population Density	Differences in Functional Responsibility
Over One Million	*(Thousands)*	*Growing*	*Northeast*	*Low*	*Three Functions*
New York	7,071	Columbus	Boston	Atlanta	New York
Chicago	3,005	Dallas	Buffalo	Dallas	*Two Functions*
Los Angeles	2,967	Honolulu	Newark	Ft. Worth	Baltimore
Philadelphia	1,688	Houston	Philadelphia	Honolulu	Boston
Houston	1,594	Los Angeles	Pittsburgh	Houston	Denver
Detroit	1,203	Oklahoma City	*No. Central*	Indianapolis	Indianapolis
700,000 to One Million		Phoenix	Chicago	Kansas City	Newark
Dallas	904	San Antonio	Cincinnati	Memphis	San Francisco
San Diego	876	San Diego	Cleveland	New Orleans	*One Function*
Phoenix	790		Columbus	Oklahoma City	Buffalo
Baltimore	787	*Mixed*	Detroit	Phoenix	Detroit
San Antonio	785	Atlanta	Indianapolis	San Diego	Memphis
Honolulu	763[a]	Denver	Kansas City	*Medium*	Philadelphia – health
Indianapolis	701	Ft. Worth	Milwaukee	Cincinnati	St. Louis
500,000 to 699,999		Indianapolis	Minneapolis	Cleveland	*Minimal Amounts*
San Francisco	679	Kansas City	Omaha	Columbus	Atlanta
Memphis	646	Long Beach	St. Louis	Denver	Chicago
		Memphis	Toledo	Long Beach	Cleveland
		Omaha	*South*	Los Angeles	
		Portland		Louisville	
		Toledo			

(margin annotation, top of last column: edn, health, public welfare)

		Declining	West		High		
Milwaukee	636			Atlanta		Milwaukee	Kansas City
Cleveland	574	Baltimore	Denver	Baltimore	Baltimore	Minneapolis	Long Beach
Columbus, OH	565	Boston	Honolulu	Dallas	Boston	Oakland	Los Angeles
Boston	563	Buffalo	Long Beach	Ft. Worth	Buffalo	Omaha	Louisville
New Orleans	557	Chicago	Los Angeles	Houston	Chicago	Pittsburgh	San Diego
		Cincinnati	Oakland	Louisville	Detroit	Portland	
Less Than 500,000		Cleveland	Phoenix	Memphis	Newark	St. Louis	*None*
Seattle	494	Detroit	Portland	New Orleans	Philadelphia	San Antonio	Cincinnati
Denver	491	Louisville	San Diego	Oklahoma City	San Francisco	Seattle	Columbus
St. Louis	453	Milwaukee	San Francisco	San Antonio		Toledo	Dallas
Kansas City	448	Minneapolis	Seattle		*High*		Ft. Worth
Atlanta	425	Newark	New York	*West*	Baltimore		Honolulu
Pittsburgh	424	New Orleans		Denver	Boston		Houston
Oklahoma City	403	Oakland		Honolulu	Buffalo		Milwaukee
Cincinnati	385	Philadelphia		Long Beach	Chicago		Minneapolis
Ft. Worth	385	Pittsburgh		Los Angeles	Detroit		New Orleans
Minneapolis	371	St. Louis		Oakland	Newark		Oakland
Portland, OR	366	San Francisco		Phoenix	Philadelphia		Oklahoma City
Long Beach	361	Seattle		Portland	San Francisco		Omaha
Buffalo	358			San Diego			Phoenix
Toledo	355	New York		San Francisco	New York		Pittsburgh
Oakland	339			Seattle			Portland
Newark	329						San Antonio
Omaha	312			New York			Seattle
Louisville	298[b]						Toledo

[a] Includes the combined City and County of Honolulu.
[b] Louisville was included because it maintained a population of at least 300,000 throughout most of the study period.
Source: U.S. Bureau of the Census

13

to one another. That is, it is designed to determine *relative* levels of stress. If all of the sample cities were fiscally distressed in an absolute sense, this methodology could fail to detect it.

The Data Constraints

There are a multitude of conceptual problems and data constraints that affect the findings. Intercity differences in functional responsibility are a major problem area. The assignment of government functions between a state and its local units varies from state-to-state, which can make simple intercity comparisons misleading. For example, services such as sewage, water supply, housing, and mass transit may be provided by the city itself, by special public districts, or by the private sector. Variations in the assignment of governmental responsibility for public assistance, health, hospitals, and public housing greatly affect the level of expenditures, revenue, and debt in given cities. Even where functional responsibilities are similar, financing arrangements can differ. That is, two cities can provide the same service at the same cost but one city might be more stressed than the other because it finances the service through local taxes while its neighbor relies on federal or state aid. This study circumvents the problem of intercity differences in assigned responsibilities to some extent by dividing current expenditures into "common function" spending and "all other" current expenditures. However, at best this procedure provides only an estimate of intercity cost differences in supplying generally similar services.

There are significant limitations in terms of the data base itself. Census Bureau financial and wage statistics are grossly inadequate in some respects. The Census Bureau handles the finances of city governments on an "all funds" basis. Philip Dearborn notes that by "forcing" financial information for each city into a uniform accounting system, the Census Bureau can aggregate trends in revenues and expenditures in a consistent manner.[16] However, he also notes that this process tends to obscure key data relationships. For example, it is impossible to determine the condition of the general fund alone or to relate sources and uses of revenue to each other. There are also major inadequacies in the debt statistics. For example, researchers cannot distinguish between general obligation and revenue-supported debt or between different types of short-term debt. Census Bureau statistics on municipal wages exclude non-wage benefits such as pension or health care plans. In recent years, such fringe benefits have grown more rapidly than wages and salaries; they have significantly inflated expenditures in some cities.

The demographic and economic information for individual cities is also inadequate and is seldom available in a timely manner. Researchers must rely almost entirely on the Censuses of Population and Housing for data on income, employment, unemployment, poverty, educational attainment, and housing. Such information becomes available only once every ten years. The economic censuses also provide valuable economic benchmarks but they are conducted only once every five years.

The manner in which some of the statistics are used can also be misleading. For example, the retail sales and income figures used to measure the strength of the sales and income tax bases are not totally comparable with those bases as defined by local sales and income tax laws. Income statistics describe the incomes of municipal residents when, in fact, some cities tax commuters. By excluding commuter incomes, the analysis overstates the tax and debt burdens placed upon city residents and understates the strength of the municipal tax base. By contrast, the retail sales figures include all retail sales when, in fact, some cities don't tax food or drugs. Therefore, retail sales tend to overstate the strength of the municipal sales tax base. The use of per capita statistics can also be misleading. For example, when expenditures are expressed on a per capita basis, it is implied that such spending is incurred on behalf of municipal residents. In fact, the business community is also served. Moreover, cities with a large commuter workforce also provide services to these "part-time" residents. Therefore, the size of the resident population may not be the best indicator of the level or cost of public services. The absence of detailed information about the condition of the public infrastructure in given cities makes it difficult to meaningfully evaluate capital spending statistics. Without measures of "capital need" it is impossible to say with certainty whether cities are overspending or underspending relative to their unique needs. Clearly fiscal research would benefit greatly from a more comprehensive and detailed municipal data base.

SUMMARY OF FINDINGS

The Causes of Municipal Fiscal Stress

The economic and fiscal difficulties of large cities reflect deep-seated changes in production processes and consumption patterns. These changes contributed to, and later reenforced, the migration of people and the movement of jobs from city to suburb and from north to south. The net effect was to erode the municipal tax base, particularly in northern cities, at a time when central cities faced additional expenditure demands for poverty-related services. These shifts affected the sample cities as follows.

- Of the 38 cities studied, 27 lost population between 1970 and 1980. Population losses were 20% or more in Buffalo, Cleveland, Detroit, and St.

Louis. In 1980, 30 of the 38 cities accounted for less than 50% of their respective metropolitan populations; 12 contained 30% or less.

- The residential housing stock in most northern cities either declined or expanded by less than 5% between 1970 and 1980. Buffalo, Chicago, Cincinnati, Cleveland, Detroit, Kansas City, Newark, Pittsburgh, and St. Louis lost housing units during the 1970s; Detroit lost 11% of its 1970 housing stock.

- The slow growth of the residential housing stock in northern cities affected the growth of property tax revenues; the parallel erosion of economic activity affected their sales and income tax bases. Between 1967 and 1977, virtually all of the sample cities experienced some erosion of retail sales, service industry receipts, and manufacturing employment. For example, Atlanta's share of metropolitan area retail sales declined from 58% to 28%; Detroit's share fell from 36% to 19%. In 1977, northern cities like Boston, Detroit, Minneapolis, Newark, and Pittsburgh accounted for less than 30% of all manufacturing jobs within their respective metropolitan areas.

Growth indexes, in which the average U.S. growth rate is the base of 100, underscore the dramatic shift of population and jobs to the sunbelt.

- During the 1970s, the index of population growth was 2 in the northeast and 35 in the midwest as compared with 174 in the south and 210 in the west. In effect, the rate of population growth in the northeast was equivalent to only 2% of the national average while the rate in the west was more than double the national average.

- During the 1970s, the index of employment growth was 34 in the northeast and 66 in the midwest as compared with 153 in the south and 171 in the west. Jobs in the northeast grew at only 34% of the national average; jobs in the west grew at 171% of the national average.

These selective patterns of migration helped to create the climate for fiscal distress, particularly in large, northern cities.

- Newark, Atlanta, St. Louis, Detroit, and Boston were found to be the most distressed cities studied in terms of the foregoing socio-economic variables.

- San Antonio, New York, Indianapolis, Honolulu, and Memphis were found to be the least distressed cities in terms of these variables.

Fiscal Stress: Revenues

Large cities may encounter fiscal difficulties not because their expenditures are too high in an absolute sense, but because their expenditures are high relative to their ability to generate public revenues.

This study found clearcut differences in revenue patterns and tax burdens between growing and declining cities, northern and southern cities, high- and low-density cities, and cities grouped by differences in functional responsibility.

- In fiscal 1979, the declining cities raised twice as much general revenue as the growing cities: $768 versus $416 per capita; per capita general revenues in the northeastern cities were 1.7 times those of cities located outside the northeast; per capita general revenues in the high-density cities were 1.8 times those of the low-density cities; per capita general revenues in cities which performed two least common functions were 2.6 times those of cities with no such responsibilities.
- Declining, northern cities raised more revenue in part because they received more intergovernmental aid, particularly state aid, than growing cities. In fiscal 1979, the declining cities received 4.3 times as much state aid as the growing cities; the northeastern cities received 3.2 times as much state aid as the southern cities; the high-density cities received 4.3 times as much state aid as the low-density cities; cities performing two least common functions received 7.8 times as much state aid as cities performing none.
- Despite large infusions of Federal and state aid, per capita taxes in the declining cities were 1.7 times those of the growing cities: $304 versus $177; taxes in the northeastern cities were more than double those of the southern cities; taxes in the high-density cities were almost double those of the low-density cities; taxes in cities performing two least common functions were more than double those of cities performing none.
- Fiscal 1979 tax burdens, defined as the ratio of taxes-to-personal income, were twice as high in the declining cities as in the growing cities: 4.53% versus 2.20%; tax burdens in the northeastern cities were 2.5 times those of the southern cities; tax burdens in the high-density cities were 2.1 times those of the low-density cities; tax burdens in cities performing two least common functions were 2.2 times those in cities performing none.
- Despite their disproportionately high tax burdens, the declining, northern cities were found to be less tax efficient in providing basic municipal services—highways, police and fire protection, sanitation, and parks and recreation—than their growing, sunbelt counterparts.

Evidence of revenue stress was also apparent in individual northern cities.

- In fiscal 1979, New York, Boston, San Francisco, Baltimore, and Boston were characterized by the highest per capita general revenues; New York Boston, Newark, Philadelphia and St. Louis also had the highest tax burdens.
- During the 1970s, intergovernmental aid, a highly variable and unpredictable revenue source, supplanted "own-source" revenues to some extent in each of the sample cities. The adjusted ratio of own-source revenue-to-intergovernmental aid was actually less than one in Buffalo, Memphis, and Minneapolis, indicating that these cities raised less revenue locally than they received in the form of Federal and state aid; Buffalo raised only 69¢ locally for every aid dollar it received in fiscal 1979.

- The adjusted ratio of outside aid-to-general expenditures also underscored the fragile revenue position of some large cities. In fiscal 1979, this ratio was 50% or more in Buffalo, Memphis, Baltimore, San Diego, Minneapolis, Milwaukee, Newark, Detroit, San Francisco, and New Orleans; it exceeded 70% in Buffalo and Memphis. In effect, 70% of Buffalo's expenditures were being financed by outside aid.
- The growing dependence on outside aid helped to mitigate the rise in tax burdens in large U.S. cities. In general, the higher the proportion of expenditure increases that were covered by increases in intergovernmental aid, the smaller the rise in tax burdens. Tax burdens actually declined in cities characterized by high ratios of aid-to-expenditure increases. Between fiscal 1969 and 1979, increases in intergovernmental aid were equivalent to at least 60% of increases in municipal spending in Milwaukee, Newark, Baltimore, Oakland, Detroit, Buffalo, and San Diego. Tax burdens declined in each of these cities except Detroit between fiscal 1969 and 1979.
- During the 1970s, the property tax became less important as a source of revenue in large U.S. cities. Whereas 28 of the 38 cities received at least half their tax revenues from the property tax in fiscal 1969, only 18 were dependent on property taxes for at least half their tax revenues a decade later; property taxes and tax burdens were perceptibly lower in cities that used general sales or income taxes in addition to the property tax.
- As of fiscal 1979, 11 northern cities, Boston, Detroit, Pittsburgh, St. Louis, Baltimore, Milwaukee, Newark, Philadelphia, Buffalo, Cleveland, and Chicago, demonstrated some weakness in their property, sales, and/or income tax bases, as defined in this study.
- Cities with weak tax bases also have the option of supporting selected public services through user charges. In fiscal 1979, the ratio of user fees-to-tax revenues was less than 25% in Buffalo, Baltimore, St. Louis, New York, Boston, Philadelphia, Chicago, Newark, and Pittsburgh. Virtually all are northern cities. Mean tax burdens in these "low fee intensity" cities were more than double tax burdens in the "high fee intensity" cities, many of which are located in the west and south.
- The growth of general revenues in large cities slowed dramatically between fiscal 1975 and fiscal 1979. This, in turn, reflected slower growth of intergovernmental aid. Own-source revenues grew even more slowly than intergovernmental aid between fiscal 1975 and fiscal 1979 because of slower growth of tax revenues; tax revenues declined in real terms in 17 of the sample cities during this period.
- Based on the foregoing analysis, New York, Boston, Newark, and Buffalo were found to be the most distressed cities in terms of their revenue profiles; Long Beach, Dallas, Houston, and Seattle were found to be the least distressed cities.

Fiscal Stress: Expenditures

Extensive and growing expenditure requirements can cause fiscal problems that are as severe as those created by difficulties in generating public revenues.

   This study revealed major differences in municipal expenditures, employment, and wage levels between growing and declining cities, northern and southern cities, high- and low-density cities, and cities grouped by differences in functional responsibility. The declining, high-density, and northeastern cities were characterized by consistently higher expenditures, employment levels, and wage costs than the other groups of cities.

- In fiscal 1979, general expenditures in the declining cities were double those of the growing cities: $727 versus $371 per capita; their operating expenditures were also twice as high, $554 versus $267 per capita. Per capita general spending by the northeastern cities was significantly above that of the western cities, $955 versus $493; per capita spending by the high-density cities was almost double that of the low-density cities; cities responsible for two least common functions spent almost 2.5 times as much as cities that performed none.
- In fiscal 1979, the declining cities spent 55% more than the growing cities for the designated common functions—highways, police and fire protection, sanitation, parks and recreation, financial administration, and general control. Within the common functions, the declining cities spent 66% more for police protection, 43% more for fire protection and more than twice as much for general control, as the growing cities. The declining cities spent almost three times as much for all other operating expenditures than the growing cities, $305 versus $106 per capita. This category includes the least common functions. Similar differences emerged when cities were grouped by region, by population density, and by differences in functional responsibility.
- The declining, northern cities employed significantly more municipal workers than their growing, sunbelt counterparts. In October 1979, full-time equivalent municipal employment per 10,000 residents was 82% higher in the declining than in the growing cities, 227 versus 125 employees; it was 76% higher in the northeastern than in the western cities; it was 67% higher in the high-density than in the low-density cities. Levels of municipal employment also increased consistently with the number of least common functions performed. Declining cities were also characterized by above-average municipal wages while the growing cities tended to pay below-average wages.

Evidence of expenditure stress was apparent in a number of individual cities.

- In fiscal 1979, Atlanta, Baltimore, Boston, Buffalo, Cincinnati, Detroit, Newark, Philadelphia, and St. Louis were characterized by above-average general spending, but by below-average personal income, which is a proxy for the strength of the local tax base. All except Atlanta were also characterized by above-average tax burdens.
- Expenditure increases for the common municipal functions did not appear to be a major source of expenditure stress during the 1970s. However,

increases in all other operating expenditures, a category that includes the least common functions, was a source of stress in many cities. In Boston, New York, Baltimore, Newark, and Buffalo, increases in all other operating expenditures accounted for more than 70% of the increase in total operating expenditures between fiscal 1969 and 1979.

- There are strong indications that escalating operating expenditures siphoned resources from capital spending in large cities during the 1970s. During the fiscal 1969–79 decade, capital spending averaged less than 15% of total general spending in Chicago, San Francisco, Boston, St. Louis, New York, and Newark. There was generally an inverse relationship between the ratio of capital-to-general spending and the overall level of operating expenditures. That is, the higher the ratio of capital-to-general spending, the lower the level of operating expenditures, and vice versa.

- In fiscal 1979, the ratio of wage and salary spending-to-operating expenditures exceeded 70% in New York, San Francisco, Memphis, Seattle, Chicago, Milwaukee, Los Angeles, Dallas, Ft. Worth, San Antonio, and San Diego. Levels of municipal employment varied widely by city, reflecting intercity differences in the scope of functional responsibilities. For example, Boston employed almost twice as many workers as Phoenix in the common functions and almost eight times as many in all other functions; Baltimore employed more than twice as many workers as Houston in the common functions and almost 11 times as many in all other functions; New York employed twice as many workers as San Diego in the common functions and almost 13 times as many in all other functions.

- There is convincing evidence of expenditure retrenchment in large cities between fiscal 1975 and 1979. The growth of operating expenditures slowed in virtually all of the sample cities and actually declined in real terms in New York, Newark, San Francisco, Cincinnati, and San Diego. Twenty-nine cities experienced real declines in wage and salary spending during the fiscal 1975–79 period. Between October 1975 and October 1979, the ratio of municipal employment-to-population declined in 15 of the sample cities: New York, Newark, Buffalo, Philadelphia, Cincinnati, Long Beach, Oakland, Minneapolis, Portland, Toledo, Milwaukee, Los Angeles, Omaha, Honolulu, and San Diego.

- Based on the foregoing analysis, Boston, Baltimore, Newark, New York, and Buffalo were found to be the most distressed cities in terms of expenditures; Long Beach and Oklahoma City were found to be the least distressed.

Fiscal Stress: Debt and Liquidity

In many states, the payment of interest and the repayment of principal on general obligation debt holds the highest claim on a city's fiscal resources. A number of debt indicators are useful in revealing the presence of fiscal stress. They include: per capita debt, the rate of growth of debt, debt burdens and debt-service payments. Likewise, a city's liquidity position, its excess of cash and securities over short-term debt, indicates its potential vulnerability to unforseen fiscal shocks.

There were major intergroup differences in the various debt measures.

- Between fiscal 1969 and 1979, declining, northern cities issued more tax-supported debt than their growing, sunbelt counterparts. The declining cities issued almost twice as much guaranteed debt as the growing cities, $404 versus $230 per capita; the northeastern cities issued 2.5 times as much guaranteed debt as the western cities. Many northern cities are prohibited from issuing revenue bonds.
- In fiscal 1979, the declining, northeastern, and high-density cities generally had higher debt burdens and were characterized by consistently higher debt-service payments than the other groups of cities. For example, the ratio of long-term general debt-to-income was 3.9% in the growing cities and 7.7% in the declining cities, 11.5% in the northeastern cities and 3.7% in the western cities, 8.1% in the high-density cities and 6.8% in the low-density cities, 10.4% in cities performing one least common function and 5.6% in cities performing none. In fiscal 1979, debt-service payments in the declining cities were 1.5 times those of the growing cities, $74 versus $48 per capita; debt-service in the northeastern cities was more than double that of the western cities. Nevertheless, debt-service was a greater constraint on general spending in growing than in declining cities because overall spending levels were so much higher in the declining cities.
- In fiscal 1979, declining northern cities had consistently lower net cash reserves than the other groups of cities. Net cash reserves were equivalent to only 45% of annual operating expenditures in the declining cities as compared with 99% in the growing cities, 31% in the northeastern cities and 100% in the southern cities, 34% in the high-density cities and 110% in the low-density cities.

A number of individual cities also appeared to be distressed in terms of their debt and/or liquidity positions.

- Atlanta, New York, San Francisco, San Antonio, Seattle, Boston, Oklahoma City, and Philadelphia were characterized by gross debt in excess of $1000 per capita. Debt levels in excess of this amount are widely regarded as burdensome. However, not all of this debt was tax-supported.
- Long-term debt accounted for virtually all of the outstanding debt in each of the sample cities except for Columbus and Toledo. These two cities were characterized by significant volumes of short-term debt in the form of bond anticipation notes.
- Cities which issued above-average amounts of long-term debt between fiscal 1969 and 1979 were generally characterized by above-average ratios of capital-to-general spending during the fiscal 1969–79 decade, and vice versa. Atlanta, San Antonio, Minneapolis, Seattle, Oklahoma City, Houston, Oakland, Louisville, and Phoenix issued above-average long-term debt and

were characterized by above-average ratios of capital-to-general spending; Cleveland, Newark, Buffalo, Detroit, Chicago, Pittsburgh, Baltimore, and St. Louis were characterized by below-average net additions to long-term debt and by below-average ratios of capital-to-general spending.

- Between fiscal 1969 and 1979, none of the long-term debt issued by Oakland or Long Beach was guaranteed by those cities. Less than half the debt issued by Atlanta, San Antonio, Louisville, Oklahoma City, Los Angeles, Seattle and St. Louis was guaranteed debt. By contrast, all of the long-term debt issued by Boston and Newark was guaranteed debt. At least 90% of the long-term debt issued by New York, San Francisco, Baltimore, Cincinnati, Indianapolis, Honolulu, and Pittsburgh was also guaranteed debt.

- Fiscal 1979 debt burdens, as measured by the ratio of long-term debt-to-income, exceeded 15% in Atlanta, New York, San Antonio, and Philadelphia. By contrast, the ratio of debt-to-income was less than 5% in San Diego, Long Beach, Chicago, Toledo, Honolulu, and Pittsburgh. Between fiscal 1969 and 1979, this ratio declined in 25 of the 38 cities.

- Unrestricted net cash reserves equalled or exceeded annual operating expenditures in Atlanta, Oklahoma City, Houston, Seattle, Long Beach, San Francisco, and San Diego. They were equivalent to 20% or less of annual operating expenditures in Boston, Chicago, Columbus, and New York. This ratio was negative in Toledo.

- There was significant debt retrenchment in individual cities, particularly after fiscal 1975. Between fiscal 1975 and 1979, long-term debt declined in real terms in 25 of the 38 cities; New York City's fiscal crisis also apparently jolted many large cities into reducing their reliance on short-term debt. Between fiscal 1975 and 1979, debt-service payments declined in constant dollars in 21 of the 38 cities.

- Many cities improved their liquidity positions during the latter part of the 1970s. Between fiscal 1975 and 1979, the ratio of unrestricted net cash reserves-to-annual operating expenditures improved in 20 of the 38 cities.

- Based on the foregoing analysis, New York City was found to be distressed in terms of debt. Toledo, Boston, Chicago, New York, Columbus, Detroit, Buffalo, Newark, and Cleveland were found to be distressed in terms of liquidity.

The 1980s: Continued Retrenchment

The latest available Census Bureau data indicate that the process of fiscal retrenchment first evident during the latter part of the 1970s carried over into the 1980s.

- Between fiscal 1979 and fiscal 1981, general revenues declined in constant dollars in 21 of the 38 sample cities. Nineteen cities experienced real declines in general spending and 24 were characterized by real declines in outstanding debt.

- Retrenchment was apparently spurred by significant reductions in inter-governmental aid, which declined in constant dollars in 27 of the 38 cities. Declines exceeded 10% in Boston, Buffalo, Cleveland, Atlanta, Oakland, Denver, New Orleans, San Francisco, Los Angeles, Portland, Louisville, Ft. Worth, Columbus, Dallas, Phoenix, Omaha, San Diego, Honolulu, and Oklahoma City. Between fiscal 1979 and 1981, 19 cities experienced real declines in state aid and 29 experienced real declines in Federal aid.
- Declines in outside aid apparently forced many cities to fall back upon their own resources. Between fiscal 1979 and 1981, own-source revenues increased in constant dollars in 22 of the sample cities. As a result, the ratio of intergovernmental revenue-to-total general revenue declined in 26 cities and the ratio of taxes-to-total general revenue increased in 22 cities. However, the relative importance of the property tax continued to diminish as large cities increasingly relied on general sales and income taxes.
- Between fiscal 1979 and 1981, operating expenditures declined in constant dollars in 28 of the 38 cities. Real wage and salary expenditures declined in 29 cities, often reflecting reductions in the size of the municipal workforce. Between October 1979 and October 1981, the ratio of full-time muncipal employment-to-population declined in 26 of the 38 cities.

By the early 1980s, large U.S. cities had apparently been forced to rely to a greater extent on locally-generated revenues. This led to a wave of tax increases and concomitant expenditure reductions. Recent survey evidence underscores the worsening fiscal plight of large cities and raises the possibility of even more drastic retrenchment ahead.

NOTES

1. Irene S. Rubin, *Running in the Red, The Political Dynamics of Urban Fiscal Stress* (Albany: State University of New York Press, 1982), pp. 5–9.
2. Richard P. Nathan and Charles Adams, "Understanding Central City Hardship," *Political Science Quarterly* 91(Spring, 1976):47–62. *Brookings Inst*
3. Peggy Cuciti, "City Need and the Responsiveness of Federal Grants Programs," Report for the U.S. House of Representatives Committee on Banking, Finance, and Urban Affairs, Subcommittee on the City, 95th Congress, 2nd Session, (Washington: U.S. Government Printing Office, 1978.)
4. U.S. Department of the Treasury, Office of State and Local Finances, *Report on the Fiscal Impact of the Economic Stimulus Package on 48 Large Urban Governments* (Washington: U.S. Government Printing Office, January 1978.)
5. For an analysis of the H.U.D. Index and other measures of urban strain see Robert W. Burchell, David Listokin, George Sternlieb, James W. Hughes, Stephen C. Casey, "Measuring Urban Distress: A Summary of the Major Urban Hardship Indices and Resource Allocation Systems," in *Cities Under Stress, The Fiscal Crisis of Urban America*. Robert W. Burchell and David Listokin (eds.) (Piscataway, N.J.: Rutgers University Center for Urban Policy Research, 1981), pp. 159–229.

6. Thomas Muller, *Growing and Declining Urban Areas: A Fiscal Comparison*, Draft report (Washington: The Urban Institute, 1976); U.S. Senate Subcommittee on Urban Affairs, *The Future of State and Local Government Finances*, Hearings, January 22 and 23, 1976 (Washington: U.S. Government Printing Office, 1977).

7. George E. Peterson, Henry L. Mortimer, Brian Cooper, Elizabeth Dickson, and George A. Reigeluth, *Urban Fiscal Monitoring*, Draft report (Washington: The Urban Institute, August 1978.)

8. Advisory Commission on Intergovernmental Relations, *City Financial Emergencies: The Intergovernmental Dimension* (Washington: U.S. Government Printing Office, July 1973.)

9. Muller, *Growing and Declining Urban Areas*, p. 4.

10. W. Patrick Beaton, "The Determinants of Police Protection Expenditures," *National Tax Journal* 27(June 1974):335–49.

11. The latest volume in this series is U.S. Bureau of the Census, *City Government Finances in 1980–81*, Series GF-81, No. 4 (Washington: U.S. Government Printing Office, 1982.)

12. The latest volume in this series is U.S. Bureau of the Census, *Local Government Finances in Selected Metropolitan Areas and Large Counties: 1979–80*, Series GF-80, No. 6 (Washington: U.S. Government Printing Office, 1981.)

13. U.S. Bureau of the Census, 1977. *Census of Retail Trade*, Geographic Area Series RC-77-A-52. United States, and selected state volumes; (Washington: U.S. Government Printing Office October, 1979) U.S. Bureau of the Census, *1977 Census of Service Industries* Vol. II, Geographic Area Statistics, Part 1, U.S. Summary, Alabama-Indiana, Part 2, Iowa-North Carolina, Part 3, North Dakota-Wyoming, (Washington: U.S. Government Printing Office, August, 1981); U.S. Bureau of the Census, *1977 Census of Manufactures*, Volume III, Geographic Area Statistics, Part I, General Summary, Alabama-Montana, Part 2, Nebraska-Wyoming, (Washington: U.S. Government Printing Office, August, 1981.)

14. U.S. Bureau of the Census, 1980 Census of Population, *Standard Metropolitan Statistical Areas and Standard Consolidated Statistical Areas: 1980*, PC 80-S1-5, (Washington: U.S. Government Printing Office, October, 1981.)

15. The latest volume in this series is U.S. Bureau of the Census, *City Employment in 1981*, Series GE-81, No. 2 (Washington: U.S. Government Printing Office, September 1982.)

16. Philip M. Dearborn, "Urban Fiscal Studies," in *Essays in Public Finance and Financial Management, State and Local Perspectives*. John E. Petersen and Catherine Lavigne Spain (eds.) (Chatham: N.J.: Chatham House Publishers, 1978), pp. 156–64.

2

The Underlying Causes of Municipal Fiscal Stress

The economic and fiscal difficulties of large cities, particularly those located in the northeast and midwest, reflect deep-seated changes in production processes and consumption patterns. These changes contributed to and later reenforced the mass movement of people and jobs from city to suburb and from north to south. Such shifts drained northern cities of some of their most productive workers and eroded the municipal tax base.

These streams of migration were a response to private market forces but were intensified by federal programs and policies and by recent recessions. This chapter analyzes post-war changes in the spatial distribution of people and jobs as a basis for understanding the fiscal problems of large cities.

THE DIMENSIONS OF THE MOVE TO THE SUBURBS

During the 1950s and 1960s, the problems of northern cities were viewed as part of a struggle between cities and their respective suburbs, with the suburbs cast as the villains. In the early post-war years, middle-income families moved from northern cities to surrounding suburbs in search of newer housing, better schools, and additional space. A home in the suburbs was part of the American dream. Rising personal incomes, widespread automobile ownership, the availability of cheap energy, and a plethora of Federal subsidy programs helped to make that dream a reality.

Those who migrated to northern cities during this period often came from the rural south and lacked the skills needed to compete successfully in an urban environment. Their presence contributed to the worsening unemployment and welfare problems of large northern cities. This situation triggered additional waves of outmigration. This time the outmigrants were fleeing from the decay, racial tensions, poverty, and rising crime rates which characterized many older industrial cities.

The selective outmigration of the white middle-class left northern cities with a high proportion of economically-disadvantaged residents, and the demand for welfare-related public services escalated. At the same time, the municipal tax base was eroded, not only by the exodus of the middle-class, but also by the loss of employment to surrounding suburbs. Manufacturing plants also moved to the suburbs. New production techniques required horizontal plant layouts, and older industrial cities lacked the space to accomodate such layouts. A recent study by the Congressional Budget Office illustrates this point. It found that developable land constituted less than ten percent of total land in one-third of those cities with populations of more than 100,000. Moreover, such land was found to be three to eight times more costly than comparable suburban land.[1] Other factors also encouraged manufacturers to move to the suburbs. The growing use of trucks to transport raw materials to plants and move finished goods to distributors underscored the disadvantages of a central city location in terms of street congestion and inadequate parking and loading facilities. The growing prominence of high-technology manufacturing industries, which required a skilled labor force and which were footloose in the sense that they no longer needed access to raw materials, also facilitated the shift to the suburbs. Moreover, the suburban workforce was widely perceived as more productive than its central city counterpart. Worker productivity is an important locational consideration. The Congressional Budget Office study found: "For every dollar of value added in the United States, 66 cents is spent on labor. This is nearly four times the expenditure on land, plant, and equipment combined."[2] Herrington Bryce and Seymour Sachs summed up the disadvantages of central cities for manufacturing as follows:

" . . . the kind of manufacturing industries that benefit most from the economic environment in which cities have a comparative advantage are not growing as rapidly as those that need the sort of environment in which outlying areas have a comparative advantage."[3]

During the 1960s and 1970s, trade and service industries also moved to the suburbs. Wholesalers need a location that minimizes distribution costs. Because of worsening road congestion, most cities were no longer least-cost distribution points for their regions. Wholesalers found that they could serve the metropolitan area most efficiently and economically from locations in nearby suburbs. Retailers moved to the suburbs to be closer to their customers. Shopping trips generally average less than five miles each, which is a shorter distance than for most other types of trips. Therefore, retailers cannot afford to locate too far from their customers, or they will lose sales to their competitors.

Until recently, it was assumed that central cities would continue to dominate their respective regions in terms of service-industry employment, and that the expansion of service jobs would offset employment losses in other industries. Large northern cities have been more successful in retaining service-industry employment than in retaining manufacturing, wholesaling, or retail jobs. However, much of the recent expansion in service jobs has occurred in consumer-related service industries, such as health care and education. These industry segments have also grown rapidly in the suburban portions of metropolitan areas. On balance, the growth of service-industry employment in central cities has not offset the loss of manufacturing jobs to the extent anticipated. Harvey Garn and Larry Ledebur, who studied employment changes in selected cities between 1967 and 1972, found that the growth of service employment " . . . in the relatively more distressed cities and those with poorer manufacturing performance . . . offset less than thirteen percent of the job losses in manufacturing, retail, and wholesale trade . . . ."[4] They concluded that the shift from manufacturing to services in distressed cities was more a product of declines in manufacturing employment than of the rapid growth of service jobs.

The negative consequences of suburban development were most evident in the northern cities. Unlike their southern and western counterparts, most northern cities were unable to recapture lost population and economic activity by annexing surrounding territory. An analysis of recent annexations by cities profiled in this book illustrates the problem. During the 1960s, the five northeastern cities studied failed to annex surrounding territory. However, seven of the ten southern cities and seven of the ten western cities did annex formerly-suburban territory and thereby gained 380,000 residents. During the 1970s, the northeastern cities again failed to annex surrounding territory, but the southern cities annexed approximately 360 square miles, thereby gaining more than 320,000 residents.[5]

Fixed boundaries are only one aspect of the problems facing northern cities. John Mollenkopf has cited a number of other factors that have a bearing on how given cities fare economically. These include: the city's role in the hierarchy of cities, the mix of industrial and service activities that the city inherited from the era in which it matured, and the extent to which the city developed in an environment of political conflict.[6] Mollenkopf says that Philadelphia, Boston, New York, Houston, Dallas, and similar "advanced service cities", continued to gain jobs and to successfully develop service-based economies because they "sit astride important market linkages." However, those industrial cities that are farther down in the urban hierarchy, which developed in the nineteenth century and which, as a consequence, are burdened by nineteenth-century industrial activities, have fared much worse. Most northern, industrial cities are in this category. By contrast, most sunbelt cities, which matured during the post-industrial era and could, therefore, develop a service-based economy from the very beginning, have fared the best. Mollenkopf also contends that cities with intense political conflicts have fared poorly because investors tend to shun areas of conflict. His model is presented as an alternative to the cost-of-production market model, which states that interregional differences in wages, productivity, unionization, market size, and similar factors determine which cities grow and prosper and which cities flounder.

Once cities lose ground to their respective suburbs or to non-urban areas, a self-reenforcing cycle may lead to further decline and decay. Katharine Bradbury, Anthony Downs, and Kenneth Small illustrate this process.[7] They have isolated seven processes of decline in central cities relative to their suburbs that tend to be "self-aggravating." They note, for example, that in cities with high concentrations of blacks, social discrimination leads to the withdrawal of whites. This, in turn, causes a further increase in the proportion of blacks. As population declines, the costs of government services for remaining residents can increase and, as a result, taxes can rise. This occurs because the costs of public services are not necessarily proportional to the population served. Higher taxes can trigger a further outmigration of people and jobs. Employment losses, in turn, reduce agglomeration economies for remaining firms causing additional job losses. Cultural activities, specialized retailing, and mass transit, each of which is characterized by decreasing costs to scale, suffer from reduced patronage in declining cities. As average costs for these services rise, prices must be raised and/or services curtailed. This further reenforces the decline. Physical blight becomes contagious because the value of housing reflects the condition of neighboring housing units. Moreover, as cities lose population, they tend to lose the political ability to obtain the outside assistance that is essential to their survival.

Information from the 1980 decennial census and from the 1977 economic censuses indicates the dimensions of recent city-to suburban population and job shifts. Between 1970 and 1980, the number of people residing within designated Standard Metropolitan Statistical Areas (SMSAs) increased from almost 140 million to almost 170 million, which represents a gain of 22%. The rate of suburban population growth exceeded that of central cities by a wide margin. For example, the number of persons living in central cities increased from 64 million to only 68 million between 1970 and 1980, a gain of about 6%. Those living in metropolitan suburbs increased from 75 million to more than 100 million, a gain of about one-third. As a result, the proportion of the nation's population living in suburban

TABLE 2.1. The Dimensions of City–Suburban Population Shifts, 1950 Through 1980

	Population (Millions)				Percent Distribution, By Race, 1980			
	1950	1960	1970	1980	Total	White	Black	Hispanic[a]
Total U.S. Population	151.4	179.3	203.2	226.5	100	100	100	100
Inside SMSAs	84.9	112.9	139.4	169.4	75	73	81	87
In Central Cities	49.7	58.0	63.8	67.9	30	25	58	50
Outside Central Cities	35.2	54.9	75.6	101.5	45	48	23	37
Outside SMSAs	66.5	66.4	63.8	57.1	25	27	19	13

[a] Persons of Spanish origin may be of any race.
Source: U.S. Bureau of the Census

areas increased from 37% to almost 45%. Suburban growth was accompanied by a decline in the number of persons living outside of metropolitan areas. This probably reflects the outward movement of SMSA boundaries and the incorporation of formerly rural areas into the suburban portions of metropolitan areas.

Not only did the central city population grow slowly during the 1970s, but its racial mix also changed, with blacks and Hispanics constituting increasingly larger proportions of the central city population. In 1980, 25% of the nation's white population lived within metropolitan central cities as compared with almost 58% of all blacks and 50% of all Hispanics. However, blacks and other minority groups remained underrepresented in the suburbs. In 1980, only 23% of the nation's black population and 37% of its Hispanic population lived in metropolitan suburbs; 48% of the nation's white population lived in metropolitan suburbs.

These findings are summarized in Table 2.1.

During the 1970s, population and housing growth in the sample cities was generally much slower than in surrounding suburbs. The northeastern and midwestern cities experienced large population losses. Such losses averaged 15% for the northeastern cities as a group and 13% for the midwestern cities. Both groups of cities also lost housing units, but the housing stock did not decline as precipitously as the population because of a general decline in average household size. This, in turn, reflected increases in the number of single-person households and childless couples. By contrast, the southern and western cities continued to grow. During the 1970s, the southern cities as a group experienced a 5% increase in population and a 24% increase in housing units; the western cities experienced a 6% increase in population and a 16% increase in housing units. Suburban population growth around growing, southern and western cities was also more rapid than around declining, northern cities.

There was a parallel erosion of economic activity that was especially pronounced in declining northern cities. Between 1967 and 1977, for example, the sample cities lost ground to their respective suburbs in terms of service-industry receipts, retail sales, and manufaturing employment. By 1977, the declining cities accounted for only 47% of metropolitan area service-industry receipts, 27% of metropolitan retail sales, and 35% of metropolitan manufacturing jobs. The northeastern cities accounted for 39% of metropolitan area service-industry receipts, 22% of metropolitan retail sales, and 26% of metropolitan manufacturing employment. By contrast, the southern cities accounted for 72% of metropolitan area service-industry receipts, 52% of metropolitan retail sales, and 59% of metropolitan manufacturing jobs.

These findings are summarized in Table 2.2.

THE DIMENSIONS OF THE MOVE TO THE SUNBELT

The fiscal consequences of suburbanization in large cities were exacerbated by the concomitant shift of people and jobs from the north to the south and west. In fact, by the early 1970s, the problems of large, northern cities came to be viewed as part of a larger struggle between north and south rather than as a localized contest between cities and their respective suburbs. The catalyst for these changed perceptions was the 1973 Arab oil embargo. The northeast, with its scarcity of readily-usable energy supplies and its disproportionate dependence on imported oil, was hard hit by the increases in energy prices. To make matters worse, during the 1960s, many northern industrial plants had switched from coal, which is abundant in the snowbelt, to oil and natural gas, which are abundant in the sunbelt. The increases in energy prices produced windfall profits for firms and individuals in the southwest, but siphoned much-needed capital from the northeast and midwest.

The energy situation was not the only factor favoring the growth of the sunbelt states. Advances in transportation and communications enabled southern cities to undercut the comparative advantages of northern cities in terms of transportation access and agglomeration economies. The north was also hurt by the slow growth of manufacturing relative to other industries, because manufacturing accounted for a large proportion of total employment in northern cities and states. By contrast, the south was not hampered by outmoded industrial plants and was able to shift relatively painlessly into high-technology manufacturing and services. Moreover, the south was able

TABLE 2.2. Central City–Suburban Population, Housing, and Employment Shifts For City Groupings

| City Grouping | Percent Change, 1970–80 | | | | Central City Share of SMSA | | | | | |
| | Population | | Housing Units | | Retail Sales | | Service-Industry Receipts | | Manufacturing Jobs | |
	City	Suburbs	City	Suburbs	1967	1977	1967	1977	1967	1977
By Population Change										
Growing	+14	+29	+30	+42	58	52	70	64	54	52
Mixed	− 5	+35	+11	+42	44	33	51	43	41	33
Declining	−14	+ 8	− 2	+28	42	27	65	47	43	35
By Geographic Region										
Northeast	−15	+*	−*	+17	34	22	53	39	35	26
North Central	−13	+11	− 1	+32	47	33	71	51	50	40
South	+ 5	+39	+24	+64	71	52	81	72	65	59
West	+ 6	+23	+16	+37	51	42	66	58	46	44
By Population Density										
Low	+ 9	+45	+29	+67	70	55	81	75	67	62
Medium	− 5	+12	+ 7	+30	45	34	63	50	45	40
High	−13	+ 7	− 2	+26	40	26	64	46	42	32
By Differences in Functional Responsibility										
Two Functions	− 9	+10	+ 5	+29	38	29	58	48	37	31
One Function	−16	+ 6	− 3	+26	40	27	62	39	41	34
Minimal Amounts	− 4	+16	+ 5	+32	50	38	70	57	51	43
None	+ 4	+24	+21	+45	56	43	70	61	52	47

*Less than 0.5%
Source: U.S. Bureau of the Census

to capture the dynamic growth industries that bypassed older industrial areas. The south's attractiveness as a location for industry has often been attributed to its low wages, weak unions, and low taxes. However, David Perry and Alfred Watkins underscore the fact that the south also captured high-wage industries, and that, between 1940 and 1960, almost 90% of the growth of southern manufacturing jobs was centered in rapidly-growing, high-wage industries.[8] They concluded:

> "Thus, it is misleading to attribute the emergence of the South simply to the relocation of low-paying industries from the Northeast to the Sunbelt. This factor may account for a significant share of the decline recently experienced in older metropolitan areas, but it does not account for the great bulk of southern manufacturing growth."[9]

As the south's economy matured and deepened, it developed those support services that were formerly imported from the north. Sophisticated advertising, legal, and health services became available in southern as well as northern cities. However, Robert Cohen makes the point that non-sunbelt firms still control a significant proportion of sunbelt investments, and that sunbelt firms continue to utilize the services of banks and law firms located in the north. He finds little basis for the contention that these has been "a fundamental realignment in the centers of corporate power" and continues to regard the south as a "dependent nation" whose finances are controlled by outsiders.[10]

The sunbelt's growing economic dominance was both a response to and a cause of rapid population growth. The south and west were widely perceived as offering better economic opportunities and a better quality of life than the northern states. Retirees, attracted by the warmer sunbelt climate, moved to the south and west in large numbers and brought their pensions with them. This process drained capital from northern cities and states. Economic stagnation, culminating in disproportionately high unemployment rates, ensued. *Business Week* summarized the situation as follows:

> "While production, population, and jobs are booming in the South and West, where energy and high-technology industries abound, they are plummeting in the old industrial Northeast and Midwest. So swift are the dislocations of labor and capital in the Northeast and Midwest that they are intensifying the social and political problems that high unemployment, urban decay, and eroding political power inevitably cause.
> "Meanwhile, the South and West have been winning the inter-regional battle for economic resources and are building an economic and political base that will almost ensure that booming growth will continue."[11]

Census data illustrate the dimensions of the shift to the sunbelt. Between 1970 and 1980, the nation's population increased from 203 million to 226 million; the southern and western states accounted for 90% of that growth. Between 1960 and 1970, by contrast, the south and west had accounted for only 60% of U.S. population growth. Growth indexes, in which the average U.S. growth rate serves as a base of 100, underscore the dramatic decline of the northern states. During the 1960s, the index of population growth was 73 in the northeast, 72 in the midwest, 107 in the south, and 181 in the west. In effect, population growth in the northeast was only 73% of the national average, while population growth in the west was equivalent to 181% of the national average. During the 1970s, these disparities widened perceptibly. The index of population growth fell to only 2 in the northeast and 35 in the midwest, but accelerated to 174 in the south and 210 in the west. In effect, the rate of population growth in the northeast was equivalent to only 2% of the national average, and the rate of population growth in the west was more than double the national average. As a result, the sunbelt's share of the nation's population increased from about 46% in 1960 to 52% in 1980. Census Bureau projections envision a U.S. population of about 260 million by the year 2000 with the sunbelt states accounting for 55% of the total. It therefore seems unlikely that sunbelt population gains will be reversed or even arrested during this century.

It is interesting to note that growing southern prosperity dramatically altered interregional migration patterns for blacks during the 1970s. Between 1960 and 1970, the south exported its black population to other regions. During the 1960s, the south's black population grew at a rate equal to only 30% of the U.S. growth rate for blacks, while the black population in the northeastern, midwestern, and western states grew at 221%, 166%, and 287% respectively of the U.S. average for blacks. During the 1970s, by contrast, the black population in the southern and midwestern states increased at a rate equal to the national rate of increase for blacks. In the west, the black population continued to increase at a rate almost double the national average for blacks. However, in the northeast, black population growth averaged only 67% of the U.S. average for blacks. The proportion of blacks within the northeastern states nevertheless continued to increase during the 1970s because of the continued outmigration of whites from the northeast. The number of whites residing in the northeast declined by almost 5% between 1970 and 1980. It is also noteworthy that in 1980, blacks remained a higher fraction of the total population in the south, 18.6%, than in other regions. Blacks remained underrepresented in the west, where they constituted only 5.2% of the population in 1980.

These findings are summarized in Table 2.3.

Interregional shifts in employment and economic activity have been equally dramatic. Between 1960 and 1970, U.S. non-farm wage and salary

TABLE 2.3. Interregional Population Shifts, by Race, 1960 Through 1980

Census Region	Total Population (millions)			Percent Black			Index of Change[a] 1960–70			Index of Change[a] 1970–80		
	1960	1970	1980	1960	1970	1980	Total	Whites	Blacks	Total	Whites	Blacks
Northeast	44.6	49.0	49.1	6.8	8.9	9.9	73	57	221	2	*	67
New England	10.5	11.8	12.3	2.3	3.3	3.8	95	93	305	37	28	128
Middle Atlantic	34.1	37.2	36.8	8.2	10.6	11.9	67	45	214	*	*	61
North Central	51.6	56.6	58.9	6.7	8.1	9.1	72	64	166	35	16	97
East North Central	36.2	40.3	41.7	8.0	9.6	10.9	83	73	174	31	*	101
West North Central	15.4	16.3	17.2	3.6	4.3	4.6	45	42	125	46	61	74
South	55.0	62.8	75.3	20.6	19.1	18.6	107	133	30	174	293	100
South Atlantic	26.0	30.7	36.9	22.5	20.8	20.7	136	168	47	178	327	114
East South Central	12.0	12.8	14.7	22.4	20.1	19.6	47	77	*	127	255	67
West South Central	17.0	19.3	23.7	16.3	15.6	14.8	105	120	45	200	266	99
West	28.1	34.8	43.2	3.9	4.9	5.2	181	181	287	210	186	192
Mountain	6.9	8.3	11.4	1.8	2.2	2.4	156	165	235	325	477	286
Pacific	21.2	26.5	31.8	4.5	5.7	6.3	189	187	294	174	90	181
U.S. Total	179.3	203.2	226.5	10.5	11.1	11.7	100	100	100	100	100	100

[a]Note: U.S. growth rate = 100

* denotes an absolute decline

Source: U.S. Bureau of the Census

employment increased from 54 million to almost 71 million jobs; the south and west accounted for 57% of that growth. Between 1970 and 1980, the number of wage and salary jobs increased from 71 million to almost 91 million; 72% of that growth occurred in the south and west.

Indexes of employment change underscore the economic decline of the north and the concomitant economic expansion of the sunbelt states. For the 1960–70 period, the index of employment change was 63 in the northeast, 84 in the midwest, 138 in the south, and 134 in the west. For the 1970–80 period, the index of employment change was only 34 in the northeast and 66 in the midwest as compared with 153 in the south and 171 in the west. During the 1970s, the rate of employment growth in the northeastern states was only 34% of the national average, while the rate of employment growth in the western states was 171% of the national average. As a result, the sunbelt's share of U.S. non-farm jobs increased from less than 42% in 1960 to more than 51% in 1980.

The northeast's poor employment performance was largely attributable to massive declines in manufacturing employment. During the 1970s, the underpinnings of the northeast's industrial base appeared to disintegrate. Rising energy costs rendered northern manufacturing plants obsolete at an increasingly rapid pace and forced many of them to close. Between 1960 and 1970, the nation gained 2.6 million wage and salary jobs in manufacturing, 70% of them in the south and west. Between 1970 and 1980, the nation gained only one million manufacturing jobs. However, whereas the south and west gained 1.7 million manufacturing jobs, the northeast and midwest collectively lost 680,000 such jobs. As a result, the sunbelt's share of U.S. manufacturing employment increased from 34% in 1960 to 45% in 1980. (See Table 2.4). Had employment in the northern states expanded at a rate equivalent to the national rate of increase between 1960 and 1980, the north would have gained an estimated 8.7 million additional jobs, including 2.3 million additional manufacturing jobs.

The general shift of economic activity toward the sunbelt states is also evident in other indicators. In 1972, the south and west accounted for less than 45% of U.S. capital investment in manufacturing; by 1977, their share had risen to almost 51%. In 1972, southern and western manufacturers accounted for less than 39% of U.S. value added in manufacturing; by 1977, the sunbelt states accounted for almost 42% of U.S. value added. The sunbelt's share of U.S. retail sales increased from 49% to almost 52% between 1972 and 1977; its share of U.S. service-industry receipts rose from 47% to 52%. (See Table 2.5)

Above-average rates of population and employment growth were accompanied by above-average rates of income growth in the south and west. These regions accounted for almost 48% of the increase in U.S. personal income during the 1960s and for more than 54% of total income growth

TABLE 2.4. Interregional Employment Shifts, 1960 Through 1980

Census Region	Total Employment[a] (thousands of jobs)			Manufacturing Employment (thousands of jobs)		
	1960	1970	1980	1960	1970	1980
Northeast	15,613	18,661	20,486	5,579	5,603	5,086
New England	3,699	4,544	5,474	1,452	1,456	1,523
Middle Atlantic	11,914	14,117	15,012	4,127	4,147	3,563
North Central	15,863	19,979	23,730	5,496	6,258	6,094
East North Central	11,659	14,611	16,827	4,495	5,032	4,715
West North Central	4,204	5,368	6,903	1,001	1,226	1,379
South	14,214	20,295	29,114	3,705	5,136	6,088
South Atlantic	7,180	10,504	14,625	2,041	2,695	3,042
East South Central	2,759	3,833	5,176	844	1,223	1,384
West South Central	4,275	5,958	9,313	820	1,218	1,662
West	8,341	11,790	17,547	1,974	2,369	3,125
Mountain	1,876	2,667	4,488	264	365	565
Pacific	6,465	9,123	13,059	1,710	2,004	2,560
U.S. Total	54,031	70,725	90,877	16,754	19,366	20,393

Census Region	Index of Change, 1960–70		Index of Change, 1970–80	
	Total Employment	Manufacturing Employment	Total Employment	Manufacturing Employment
Northeast	63	3	34	*
New England	74	2	72	87
Middle Atlantic	60	3	22	*
North Central	84	89	66	*
East North Central	82	77	53	*
West North Central	90	144	100	235
South	138	248	153	350
South Atlantic	150	206	138	243
East South Central	126	288	123	248
West South Central	127	311	198	688
West	134	128	171	602
Mountain	136	245	240	103
Pacific	133	110	151	523
U.S. Total	100	100	100	100

Note: U.S. Growth rate = 100
* denotes an absolute decline.
[a] denotes non-farm wage and salary jobs.
Source: U.S. Bureau of Labor Statistics

TABLE 2.5. Selected Economic Indicators, by Region, 1972, 1977 (Percent Distribution)

Census Region	New Capital Investment in Manufacturing		Manufacturing Value Added		Service-Industry Receipts		Retail Sales	
	1972	1977	1972	1977	1972	1977	1972	1977
Northeast	21.5	17.5	26.3	23.9	29.3	25.2	23.8	21.1
New England	5.2	4.5	6.4	6.2	5.1	5.2	6.1	5.6
Middle Atlantic	16.3	13.0	19.9	17.7	24.2	20.0	17.7	15.5
North Central	33.8	31.6	34.9	34.2	23.5	22.5	27.2	27.1
East North Central	28.1	26.1	28.2	27.4	17.4	16.4	19.6	19.3
West North Central	5.7	5.5	6.7	6.8	6.1	6.1	7.6	7.8
South	32.0	37.2	25.4	27.3	25.5	27.8	30.4	31.6
South Atlantic	16.0	12.7	12.5	12.3	14.0	14.6	15.6	15.7
East South Central	6.3	7.3	6.0	6.1	3.8	3.8	5.5	5.7
West South Central	9.7	17.2	6.9	8.9	7.7	9.4	9.3	10.2
West	12.7	13.7	13.4	14.6	21.7	24.5	18.6	20.2
Mountain	3.0	3.1	2.1	2.4	5.3	6.0	4.6	5.1
Pacific	9.7	10.6	11.3	12.2	16.4	18.5	14.0	15.1
U.S. Total	100.0	100.0	100.0	100.0	100.0	100.0	100.0	100.0

Source: U.S. Bureau of the Census

during the 1970s. During the 1960s, income growth in the northeast was equivalent to 89% of the U.S. average rate of increase; income growth in the south was equivalent to 120% of the national average. During the 1970s, disparities in the rate of income growth between north and south became even greater. As a result, the sunbelt states increased their share of U.S. personal income from 42% in 1960 to 51% in 1980.

The same trends are apparent when income is expressed on a per capita basis in order to standardize for differences in population size. Between 1970 and 1980, per capita income growth in the northeast was slightly below the U.S. average rate of increase, and per capita income growth in the south was slightly above the national average. This led to some interregional convergence in terms of income. (See Table 2.6).

The foregoing statistics clearly indicate that the sunbelt states made rapid economic strides during the past two decades and that growth disparities between the north and the south actually widened during the 1970s. Sometime during the 1970s, the sunbelt states for the first time accounted for more than half the nation's population, jobs, and total personal income. These shifts, coupled with the general movement of people and jobs to the suburbs, created the basis for fiscal stress in large cities.

TABLE 2.6. Total and Per Capita Personal Income, by Region

Total Personal Income (Billions of Current Dollars)

Census Region	Total Personal Income			Index of Change	
	1960	1970	1980	1960–70	1970–80
Northeast	112.9	214.0	489.2	89	76
New England	25.5	50.4	122.5	97	85
Middle Atlantic	87.4	163.6	366.7	87	73
North Central	117.0	223.1	562.7	90	90
East North Central	85.9	163.3	405.7	90	88
West North Central	31.1	59.8	157.0	92	96
South	96.3	211.8	643.6	120	121
South Atlantic	47.9	109.7	321.5	129	114
East South Central	18.0	37.7	108.8	109	112
West South Central	30.4	64.4	213.3	111	137
West	69.9	144.6	438.3	107	120
Mountain	14.2	29.7	101.1	109	142
Pacific	55.7	114.9	337.2	106	115
U.S. Total	396.1	793.5	2133.8	100	100

Per Capita Personal Income (Current Dollars)

Census Region	Per Capita Personal Income		Percent of U.S. Average	
	1970	1980	1970	1980
Northeast	4,367	9,963	112	105
New England	4,271	9,959	110	105
Middle Atlantic	4,398	9,965	113	105
North Central	3,942	9,553	101	101
East North Central	4,052	9,729	104	103
West North Central	3,669	9,128	94	97
South	3,373	8,547	87	90
South Atlantic	3,573	8,713	92	92
East South Central	2,945	7,401	76	78
West South Central	3,337	9,000	86	95
West	4,155	10,146	107	107
Mountain	3,578	8,868	92	94
Pacific	4,336	10,604	111	112
U.S. Average	3,893	9,458	100	100

Note: U.S. growth rate = 100
Source: U.S. Department of Commerce, Bureau of Economic Analysis.

GOVERNMENT POLICY AS A CAUSE OF POPULATION AND EMPLOYMENT SHIFTS

Federal programs and policies reenforced private-market decisions to move from city to suburb and from north to south. The national system of interstate highways, authorized by congress in the mid-1950s to meet the nation's defense needs, made the south accessible to other regions. Franklin James contends that by offering greater subsidies for the construction of new highways than for the maintenance of existing ones, the Federal government, in effect, forced " . . . built-up areas with established transport systems . . . to bear a higher proportion of the costs of their transportation."[12] These built-up areas were located primarily in the north.

Other Federal spending programs also helped the sunbelt states. Army Corps of Engineers' waterway projects opened southern cities to international trade. The proliferation of Federal defense installations in the south helped create new consumer and industrial markets there. Interregional shifts in defense procurement reenforced the ongoing population shift to the southern and western states.

Tax laws also facilitated industrial development in the sunbelt states. Accelerated depreciation for new industrial and commercial plants and the use of investment tax credits encouraged investment in new plants and equipment and discouraged investment in existing facilities. In effect, government tax policy encouraged business to invest in growing areas, such as the sunbelt states, and to withdraw from older, established northern industrial areas.

The Federal government also helped underwrite the costs of suburban development. Federally-subsidized highways enabled people to work in cities but live in adjacent suburbs. Construction of beltways around central cities permitted suburban residents to commute more easily to suburban jobs. Suburban businesses were thus able to compete with central city employers for the services of the suburban workforce. Federal grants for water and sewer systems facilitated suburban residential, commercial, and industrial development by reducing development costs and providing excess capacity for future development. Federal mortgage credit and insurance programs helped to finance the purchase of single-family homes, most of which were located in the suburbs. The Federal tax code indirectly encouraged homeownership by allowing deductions for mortgage interest and property taxes. Federal tax policy permitted more generous tax deductions for new construction than for rehabilitation of existing plants and equipment furthering the movement of jobs to the suburbs. Once again, business was encouraged to invest in growing areas at the expense of established areas such as older central cities. George Peterson contends that such incentives may not have altered the ultimate locational decisions of firms, but that they speeded the exodus of manufacturers from declining cities.[13] Roger Vaughan concurs:

"Federal policies have not been the root cause of decentralization. That role has been played by market forces—technological change, the secular rise in real incomes, and changes in world trade patterns. But federal policies have accentuated these forces, and for many cities, the increase in the speed and extent of decentralization may have been the straw that broke their fiscal backs."[14]

A number of other Federal programs probably affected the economic fortunes of large northern cities by impeding the operation of their labor markets. It is alleged that the expansion of Federal welfare programs helped to reduce labor force participation by low-income households. It is also thought that generous unemployment insurance payments boosted unemployment in some cities because job seekers could be more selective in accepting employment. Minimum-wage legislation may well have reduced the supply of available jobs, thereby creating a pool of surplus labor that enabled employers to discriminate more freely against minorities and young workers. More stringent Federal safety and health regulations coupled with increases in social security and unemployment insurance taxes raised the relative cost of employing labor and reduced the demand for labor, particularly unskilled labor. At the same time, tax breaks to capital reduced the relative cost of capital and encouraged industry to become more capital intensive. Therefore, Federal labor market policies tended to discourage labor force participation and limit employment opportunities for central city residents.

The cities themselves contributed to their own economic and fiscal decline. Tom Muller has demonstrated that declining cities are more likely than growing cities to have payroll or income taxes; types of taxes that businessmen find particularly burdensome.[15] Robert Schmenner found that businessmen resent the bureaucratic delays involved in obtaining zoning and building permits for plant changes within cities, and that they may opt to move to the suburbs to avoid such delays.[16]

It therefore appears that government policies at all levels of government reenforced decisions by firms and individuals to move to the suburbs and to the sunbelt states.

THE IMPACT OF INFLATION AND RECESSION

The foregoing migration patterns have been evident for several decades. However, the fiscal crisis of the cities assumed a new urgency in 1975 in the wake of New York City's serious fiscal problems. It appears that ongoing population and employment shifts reached a critical threshold, a tipping point, by the mid-1970s. Moreover, that tipping point was reached just as the nation was experiencing alternate bouts of recession and inflation that worked to the fiscal disadvantage of large northern cities.

Periods of inflation and recession widen the gap between revenues and expenditures. The process works as follows: Severe inflation erodes spendable income so that a given level of private income can purchase fewer and poorer quality goods and services. However, since public goods appear to be free, city residents often demand more of them. Inflation also triggers higher wage demands by municipal workers who seek to recapture lost purchasing power. Even a slight increase in the level of compensation for municipal workers can wreak havoc with municipal budgets because government is labor intensive and wages and salaries constitute a high proportion of total expenditures. This helps explain why government production costs tend to rise faster than comparable private-sector costs. During periods of inflation, the goods and services purchased by government also become more costly. It has been demonstrated, for example, that during the 1965–72 period, inflation accounted for 40% of the dollar increase in goods and services purchased by New York City and for 29% of the growth of total expenditures by the City.[17]

Municipal tax revenues often fail to increase as fast as the rate of inflation. This is because cities that are highly dependent on real-property taxes generally cannot reassess property frequently enough to fully capture the inflationary increase in property values. Moreover, in cities with severe population losses, real-property values may grow slowly or actually decline, even during periods of severe inflation.

Recessions are equally damaging to municipal finances. The nation's older cities contain a disproportionate share of marginal firms. Recessions speed up the closing of marginal plants and management channels capital into plants and equipment that will provide the best economic return once recovery begins. Such plants tend to be located in suburban areas or in newer sunbelt communities. Franklin James concludes:

> " . . . the investment opportunities foregone cannot be counted on to reappear when business conditions improve. By contrast, in growing cities, business retrenchment during recessions means that businesses defer taking advantage of investment opportunities, but when the economy improves, they again take advantage of them."[18]

To make matters worse, cities that lose older businesses and industries during recessions generally fail to replace them with new and expanding activities, such as offices and high-technology manufacturing. This is a serious blow to the central city economy. David Birch has found that it is the relatively new business establishments in their first four years of operation

TABLE 2.7. The Impact of Recent Recessions on Central City Employment, Eight Selected Cities

City	Percent Change, Private Employment[a]		Percent Change, Manufacturing	
	1969–71	1973–75	1969–71	1973–75
Indianapolis	−4.1	− 3.0	− 9.5	− 9.0
Baltimore	−2.0	−15.3	−12.2	−16.9
Denver	+5.4	−11.8	− 1.2	− 7.6
New Orleans	−0.3	−13.8	−15.3	−16.6
New York	−3.9	− 9.3	N.A.	N.A.
Philadelphia	−6.0	−11.0	−14.2	−23.2
San Francisco	−2.8	+ 9.4	− 6.0	−19.7
St. Louis	−7.6	−18.1	−53.3	−24.3
Mean—Eight Cities	−3.7	− 9.1	−23.7	−18.4
U.S. Average	−0.6	− 2.4	− 8.8	− 7.0

N.A.—Not available
[a] Excludes government and proprietorship employment
Source: County Business Patterns

that produce about 80% of all new jobs within central cities.[19] Recessions, therefore, erode economic activity and tax revenues, particularly in older industrial cities, just at a time when more revenue is needed to finance recession-induced expenditures.

Employment changes in eight of the cities profiled in this book illustrate the impact of the 1969–71 and 1973–75 national recessions on the economy of older cities. During the 1969–71 recession, employment declined by 0.6% nationally. In the eight sample cities, the mean rate of employment decline was 3.7%. During the 1973–75 recession, U.S. employment declined by 2.4%. In the eight sample cities, the mean rate of employment decline was 9.1%; in Baltimore and St. Louis, employment declines exceeded 15%.

The loss of manufacturing jobs was even more pronounced. During the 1969–71 recession, manufacturing employment declined by almost 9% nationally, but by an average of almost 24% in the eight sample cities. During the 1973–75 recession, manufacturing employment declined by 7% nationally, but by an average of more than 18% in the eight sample cities. In St. Louis, manufacturing employment declined by more than 50% during the 1969–71 recession and by about 25% during the 1973–75 recession. (See Table 2.7).

Research performed by Roy Bahl and David Greytak suggests that the loss of manufacturing jobs can cause a serious drain on the finances of some cities. They analyzed the fiscal impact of changes in employment mix in New York City and found:

" . . . the replacement of a manufacturing job requires the addition of 0.95 wholesale or retail trade jobs, 0.73 finance, insurance, and real estate jobs, 1.04 service jobs, and 1.25 government jobs."[20]

Government activity is not subject to property or business income taxes. Service industries generate relatively low tax receipts per employee because they pay relatively low wages and contain a high proportion of non-profit enterprises that are often exempt from property taxes. Therefore, large increases in government and service jobs are needed to compensate for the revenue losses caused by the loss of manufacturing jobs.

Information from the Current Population Survey provides useful insights into the spatial dynamics of economic recovery within large metropolitan areas.[21] The Survey provides information about employment changes within the central city and suburban portions of nine metropolitan areas during the 1975–79 period. This was the period of recovery from the 1973–75 national recession. Between 1975 and 1979, employment in the nine central cities grew by an average of only 3%, while employment growth in their respective suburbs averaged 18%. In three of these cities— Baltimore, New York and Philadelphia—central city employment continued to decline throughout the 1975–79 period despite the national recovery; employment remained unchanged in Chicago and increased by only 3% in Cleveland and Detroit during this period. Clearly, some of the nation's older cities failed to respond to the 1975–79 upturn. (See Table 2.8).

TABLE 2.8. The Dynamics of Economic Recovery, 1975–79, Cities versus Suburbs

	Central City Employment (Thousands of Jobs)			Suburban Employment (Thousands of Jobs)		
SMSA	1975	1979	Percent Change	1975	1979	Percent Change
Baltimore	307	291	− 5	553	671	+21
Chicago	1168	1168	0	1752	2019	+15
Cleveland	235	243	+ 3	583	613	+ 5
Dallas–Ft. Worth	386[a]	494[a]	+28	737	911	+24
Detroit	431	444	+ 3	1206	1465	+22
Houston	635	731	+15	373	562	+51
Milwaukee	273	288	+ 5	337	414	+23
New York	2775	2755	− 1	873	970	+11
Philadelphia	635	628	− 1	1213	1385	+14
Total	6845	7042	+ 3	7627	9010	+18

[a] Refers to employment for the City of Dallas
Source: U.S. Bureau of Labor Statistics

EVIDENCE OF SOCIO-ECONOMIC DISTRESS IN LARGE CITIES

It is alleged that the foregoing demographic and economic shifts have caused economic distress and deterioration of the social fabric in large U.S. cities. This section reviews recent economic and demographic changes in each of the sample cities, and relates such changes to evidence of socioeconomic distress.

Demography and Housing

Of the 38 cities studied, 27 lost population between 1970 and 1980. Population losses were 20% or more in Buffalo, Cleveland, Detroit, and St. Louis, and ranged from 10 to 20% in Atlanta, Boston, Chicago, Cincinnati, Kansas City, Louisville, Milwaukee, Minneapolis, Newark, New York, Omaha, Philadelphia, and Pittsburgh. The only "big gainers" were Houston, Phoenix, San Antonio, and San Diego, where population gains were 20% or more. In 1980, 30 of the 38 cities accounted for less than 50% of their respective metropolitan populations; 12 contained 30% or less of their metropolitan area population.

In most northern cities, the residential housing stock declined or expanded by less than 5% between 1970 and 1980. Buffalo, Chicago, Cincinnati, Cleveland, Detroit, Kansas City, Newark, Pittsburgh, and St. Louis lost housing units. Losses ranged from less than 1% of the housing stock in Cincinnati, to 11% in Detroit. The central city housing stock grew by less than 5% in Boston, Milwaukee, Minneapolis, New York, and Philadelphia between 1970 and 1980. Each of these cities also lost population during the 1970s. However, housing declines were more moderate than population declines because of a drop in average household size. For example, Pittsburgh's population declined by 18% between 1970 and 1980, but its housing stock declined by only 6%; Detroit lost 20% of its population, but its housing stock fell by only 11%; Cleveland's population declined by 24%, but its housing stock declined by only 9%. The relatively slow growth of the housing stock in declining, northern cities limited the growth of property tax revenues; those cities that were heavily dependent on property taxes were most severely affected. By contrast, a number of sunbelt cities experienced rapid growth of housing units during the 1970s. The housing stock in Columbus, Dallas, Honolulu, Houston, Oklahoma City, Phoenix, San Antonio, and San Diego expanded by 25% or more during this period.

These findings are summarized in Tables 2.9 and 2.10.

Economic Activity

Inroads into the residential housing stock of large northern cities during the 1970s limited the growth of revenues from real-property taxes. The parallel erosion of economic activity tended to weaken their sales and income tax bases also.

Between 1967 and 1977, virtually all of the sample cities experienced some decline in their share of metropolitan area retail sales as a result of the shift of retail activity to the suburbs. Cities with the steepest rates of decline included Atlanta, Detroit, Minneapolis, Newark, and St. Louis. Atlanta's share of metropolitan area retail sales fell from 58 to 28%, Detroit's share declined from 36 to 19%, and Newark's declined from 21 to 10%. In 1977, 11 cities—Atlanta, Boston, Buffalo, Cincinnati, Cleveland, Detroit, Minneapolis, Newark, Philadelphia, Pittsburgh, and St. Louis—accounted for less than 30% of total retail sales within their respective metropolitan areas.

Most of the sample cities also experienced declines in their share of metropolitan area service-industry receipts. However, large cities were generally more successful in retaining service-industry activity than in holding retail activity. Only 10 cities—Baltimore, Boston, Buffalo, Cleveland, Detroit, Minneapolis, Newark, Philadelphia, Pittsburgh, and St. Louis—accounted for 50% or less of service-industry receipts within their respective metropolitan areas in 1977.

The sample cities also lost ground to their suburbs in terms of manufacturing jobs. In 1977, northern cities like Boston, Detroit, Minneapolis, Newark, and Pittsburgh accounted for less than 30% of metropolitan area manufacturing jobs. By contrast, sunbelt cities like San Antonio, San Diego, Phoenix, Oklahoma City, Memphis, Houston, Honolulu, and Dallas continued to account for the majority of manufacturing jobs within their respective metropolitan areas.

These findings are summarized in Table 2.11.

As a result of the erosion of economic activity during the 1970s, many northern cities sustained disproportionately high unemployment relative to their suburbs. In 1979, unemployment rates averaged 12.6% for the City of Baltimore and 7.8% for the Baltimore SMSA; 9.6% for the City of Cleveland and 5.9% for the Cleveland SMSA; 11.8% for the City of Philadelphia and 7.5% for the Philadelphia SMSA. Unemployment rates for blacks residing in the central city were even higher: 17.9% in Baltimore, 13.8% in Cleveland, 18.0% in Detroit, and 19.0% in Philadelphia.[22]

The Social Consequences

The current literature suggests that these selective population and employment shifts have damaged the social fabric of declining cities, and that

TABLE 2.9. Central City–Suburban Population Shifts, by Race, 1970–80, Thirty-Eight Sample Cities

City	Percent Change in Total Population, 1970–80		Blacks as a Proportion of the Total Population, 1980	
	City	Suburbs	City	Suburbs
Atlanta	−14	+46	67	14
Baltimore	−13	+19	55	9
Boston	−12	− 3	22	2
Buffalo	−23	− *	27	2
Chicago	−11	+14	40	6
Cincinnati	−15	+ 9	34	4
Cleveland	−24	+ 1	44	7
Columbus, OH	+ 5	+11	22	2
Dallas	+ 7	+48	29	4
Denver	− 4	+60	12	2
Detroit	−20	+ 8	63	4
Ft. Worth	− 2	+48	23	4
Honolulu	+12	+30	1	3
Houston	+29	+71	28	7
Indianapolis	− 5	+24	22	1
Kansas City	−12	+15	27	6
Long Beach	+ 1	+ 7	11	10
Los Angeles	+ 6	+ 7	17	10
Louisville	−18	+20	28	6
Memphis	+ 4	+27	48	21
Milwaukee	−11	+11	23	1
Minneapolis	−15	+21	8	1
Newark	−14	− 2	58	14
New Orleans	− 6	+39	55	13
New York	−10	− 1	25	8
Oakland	− 6	+10	47	6
Oklahoma City	+10	+30	15	4
Omaha	−10	+32	12	2
Philadelphia	−13	+ 5	38	8
Phoenix	+31	+92	5	1
Pittsburgh	−18	− 2	24	4
Portland, OR	− 4	+40	8	1
St. Louis	−27	+ 6	46	11
San Antonio	+20	+22	7	5
San Diego	+26	+49	9	3
San Francisco	− 5	+10	13	6
Seattle	− 7	+26	10	1
Toledo	− 7	+15	17	1
Mean	− 5	+23	27	6

*Less than 0.5%

Note: No allowance has been made for changes in central city or SMSA boundaries between 1970 and 1980. There was a major change in SMSA definition in the New York area.

Source: U.S. Bureau of the Census

Central City Share of Metropolitan Area Population

City	1970	1980	1980, by Race		
			Whites	Blacks	Hispanics
Atlanta	31	21	9	57	25
Baltimore	44	36	22	77	36
Boston	22	20	16	79	54
Buffalo	34	29	23	84	59
Chicago	48	42	29	84	73
Cincinnati	33	28	21	75	38
Cleveland	36	30	20	73	69
Columbus	53	52	46	93	61
Dallas & Ft. Worth	52	43	35	84	64
Denver	42	30	26	76	53
Detroit	34	28	12	85	40
Honolulu	52	48	42	25	35
Houston	62	55	46	83	66
Indianapolis	66	60	54	97	70
Kansas City	40	34	28	71	46
Los Angeles & Long Beach	45	44	41	58	42
Louisville	42	33	27	71	37
Memphis	75	71	62	84	64
Milwaukee	51	46	38	98	76
Minneapolis	22	18	16	57	21
Newark	19	17	7	46	46
New Orleans	57	47	31	80	40
New York	79	78	70	92	94
Oklahoma City	53	48	45	78	61
Omaha	64	55	52	86	62
Philadelphia	40	36	26	72	55
Phoenix	60	51	49	78	58
Pittsburgh	22	19	15	58	27
Portland	38	30	27	83	32
St. Louis	26	19	13	51	25
San Antonio	74	73	71	79	88
San Diego	51	47	44	74	48
San Francisco & Oakland	35	31	22	63	33
Seattle	37	31	27	80	39
Toledo	50	45	40	91	54
Mean	45	40	33	75	51

TABLE 2.10. City–Suburban Shifts in Residential Housing Units, 1970–80

City	Percent Change in Housing Units, 1970–80	
	City	Suburbs
Atlanta	+ 5	+72
Baltimore	− 1	+41
Boston	+ 4	+14
Buffalo	− 6	+18
Chicago	− 3	+35
Cincinnati	− *	+28
Cleveland	− 9	+20
Columbus	+30	+29
Dallas	+29	+70
Denver	+17	+98
Detroit	−11	+29
Ft. Worth	+12	+70
Honolulu	+38	+53
Houston	+58	+99
Indianapolis	+12	+44
Kansas City	− *	+35
Long Beach	+ 6	+14
Los Angeles	+11	+14
Louisville	− 3	+44
Memphis	+23	+52
Milwaukee	+ 3	+32
Minneapolis	+ 2	+48
Newark	− 5	+10
New Orleans	+ 9	+67
New York	+ 1	+11
Oakland	+ 2	+30
Oklahoma City	+27	+50
Omaha	+ 5	+59
Philadelphia	+ 2	+24
Phoenix	+53	+151
Pittsburgh	− 6	+16
Portland	+11	+63
St. Louis	−15	+24
San Antonio	+37	+51
San Diego	+42	+81
San Francisco	+ 2	+30
Seattle	+ 4	+48
Toledo	+10	+38
Mean	+10	+45

City	Central City Share of Metropolitan Area Housing Units	
	1970	1980
Atlanta	33	23
Baltimore	46	38
Boston	25	23
Buffalo	38	33
Chicago	53	44
Cincinnati	38	32
Cleveland	39	33
Columbus	55	56
Dallas & Ft. Worth	55	47
Denver	47	35
Detroit	38	30
Honolulu	59	56
Houston	64	58
Indianapolis	68	63
Kansas City	43	36
Los Angeles & Long Beach	48	47
Louisville	46	37
Memphis	78	74
Milwaukee	55	49
Minneapolis	27	21
Newark	19	17
New Orleans	60	50
New York	82	80
Oklahoma City	56	52
Omaha	67	58
Philadelphia	44	39
Phoenix	61	49
Pittsburgh	24	20
Portland	42	33
St. Louis	30	22
San Antonio	75	73
San Diego	54	48
San Francisco & Oakland	40	35
Seattle	43	35
Toledo	53	47
Mean	49	43

*Less than 0.5%
Note: No allowance has been made for changes in central city or SMSA boundaries between 1970 and 1980.
Source: U.S. Bureau of the Census

TABLE 2.11. Central City Share of Metropolitan Area Economic Activity, 1967, 1977

City	Retail Sales		Service-Industry Receipts		Manufacturing Employment	
	1967	1977	1967	1977	1967	1977
Atlanta	58	28	77	51	46	31
Baltimore	50	30	74	49	51	44
Boston	30	20	50	40	25	19
Buffalo	39	25	56	45	38	33
Chicago	52	36	76	60	56	41
Cincinnati	45	29	70	53	51	40
Cleveland	40	24	65	50	56	46
Columbus	67	57	76	70	79	58
Dallas & Ft. Worth	69	54	79	74	78	62
Denver	53	33	71	59	55	40
Detroit	36	19	63	28	36	27
Honolulu	82	73	93	92	91	87
Houston	75	68	86	82	71	70
Indianapolis	60	74	76	85	64	73
Kansas City	60	36	80	65	50	44
Los Angeles & Long Beach	47	44	62	52	42	41
Louisville	57	36	77	63	58	57
Memphis	82	83	91	89	90	81
Milwaukee	58	41	72	57	55	45
Minneapolis	33	18	60	36	34	24
Newark	21	10	35	20	26	15
New Orleans	65	45	76	63	61	46
New York	65	69	90	86	78	76
Oklahoma City	71	60	87	78	90	81
Omaha	75	70	82	82	84	75
Philadelphia	40	29	59	44	46	35
Phoenix	68	53	74	70	71	69
Pittsburgh	34	20	60	42	29	23
Portland	60	38	77	63	51	43
St. Louis	33	18	60	34	33	37
San Antonio	90	84	91	87	90	81
San Diego	54	48	72	68	68	67
San Francisco & Oakland	43	33	64	58	41	36
Seattle	54	38	74	61	40	46
Toledo	62	47	79	61	76	59
Mean	55	43	72	60	57	50

Note: No allowance has been made for changes in central city or SMSA boundaries between 1967 and 1977.

Source: U.S. Bureau of the Census

this damage manifests itself in disproportionately high crime rates. In fact, however, the growing, sunbelt cities as a group were characterized by higher crime rates than the declining, northern cities. For example, in 1980, serious crimes per 100,000 residents averaged 8,297 for cities in the northeast as compared with 10,003 for the western cities. Crime rates per 100,000 residents averaged 8,777 for the declining cities and 9,457 for the growing cities. The "low-crime" cities were Indianapolis, Louisville, Milwaukee, and Philadelphia, where serious crimes per 100,000 residents averaged 5,311, 6,725, 6,514, and 5,991 respectively. The "high-crime" cities were Atlanta, Boston, Newark, and Oakland, where serious crimes per 100,000 residents averaged 13,974, 13,456, 12,936, and 13,013 respectively.[23] Thus, the relationship between population and job losses and the incidence of crime is somewhat tenuous. Thomas Muller explains the convergence in crime rates between growing and declining cities in terms of " . . . lower birth rates and fewer persons in the 14–24 age group residing in declining cities. Persons in this age group committed about 52% of all crimes in the nation based on arrest records. Changes in density as a result of population movement is an added factor, since high-density tends to correlate with crime activity."[24]

As expected, however, there were major differences in crime rates between central cities and their suburbs. This generalization applied regardless of region. For the 38 cities as a group, serious crimes per 100,000 residents averaged 9,694 in the central city and only 5,092 in adjacent suburbs. Crimes per 100,000 residents averaged 13,974 in Atlanta and only 5,792 in the Atlanta suburbs, 8,127 in Buffalo and 4,153 in the Buffalo suburbs, 11,726 in Dallas and 5,378 in the Dallas suburbs, 10,995 in Kansas City and 4,017 in its suburbs, 11,573 in Phoenix and 7,021 in its suburbs. The perception of lower crime rates just across the city line reenforced the exodus of middle-income residents and businesses from these cities.

The findings regarding crime rates in large cities and their suburbs are summarized in Table 2.12.

AN INDEX OF SOCIO-ECONOMIC STRESS

Based on the foregoing statistics, an index of socio-economic stress was developed for each of the sample cities. It incorporates the following variables: central city share of SMSA population, 1980; central city share of SMSA residential housing stock, 1980; central city share of SMSA retail sales, 1977; central city share of SMSA service-industry receipts, 1977; central city share of SMSA manufacturing employment, 1977; proportion of blacks in the central city population, 1980; and serious crimes per 100,000 residents, 1980. Conceivably other variables could also have been used.

TABLE 2.12. Serious Crimes per 100,000 Residents, 1980, Cities versus Suburbs

City	Crime Rates		City	Crime Rates	
	The City	Its Suburbs		The City	Its Suburbs
Atlanta	13,974	5,792	Milwaukee	6,514	4,372
Baltimore	9,749	6,133	Minneapolis	9,656	4,850
Boston	13,456	6,018	Newark	12,936	5,786
Buffalo	8,127	4,153	New Orleans	9,610	6,327
Chicago	6,542	5,058	New York	10,043	5,020
Cincinnati	8,557	4,653	Oakland	13,013	7,203
Cleveland	10,038	3,713	Oklahoma City	8,976	5,065
Columbus	9,801	654	Omaha	7,838	4,196
Dallas	11,726	5,378	Philadelphia	5,991	4,977
Denver	11,962	6,630	Phoenix	11,573	7,021
Detroit	10,589	6,402	Pittsburgh	7,171	2,628
Ft. Worth	12,591	5,378	Portland	11,145	5,658
Honolulu	7,574	N.A.	St. Louis	14,265	4,580
Houston	9,029	4,238	San Antonio	7,369	3,749
Indianapolis	5,311	6,995	San Diego	8,053	6,107
Kansas City	10,995	4,017	San Francisco	10,372	7,203
Long Beach	8,943	7,244	Seattle	10,792	6,271
Los Angeles	9,904	7,244	Toledo	9,601	4,234
Louisville	6,725	·4,961			
Memphis	7,878	3,056	Mean	9,694	5,092

N.A.—Not available
Source: U.S. Department of Justice

However, in the absence of more precise knowledge concerning which variables best portray socio-economic stress, it was decided to opt for simplicity.

The raw scores for each variable were first converted to standard (z) scores. Composite z scores were then computed for population and housing, economic activity, and social conditions. The composite z score for population and housing represents the simple average of the individual z scores for central city share of SMSA population and central city share of SMSA housing units. The composite z score for economic activity is the simple average of the z scores for central city share of SMSA retail sales, service-industry receipts, and manufacturing jobs. The composite z score for social conditions is the simple average of the individual z scores for crime rates and racial composition of the population. The three composite z scores were then averaged to develop an overall measure of socio-economic stress. This measure was interpreted as follows: a z score of $-.675$ or less indicated stress; a z score of $+.675$ or more indicated the relative absence of stress; z scores falling between $\pm.675$ indicated a moderate amount of stress. Scores

TABLE 2.13. An Index of Socio-Economic Stress for Large Cities

Rank	City	The Index	Composite z Scores		
			Population and Housing	Economic Activity	Social Conditions
1	Newark	−1.74	−1.66	−1.95	−1.60
2	Atlanta	−1.39	−1.33	−0.76	−2.08
3	St. Louis	−1.30	−1.20	−1.16	−1.54
4	Detroit	−1.17	−0.86	−1.43	−1.22
5	Boston	−1.12	−1.36	−1.32	−0.68
6	Minneapolis	−0.76	−1.50	−1.35	+0.56
7	Oakland	−0.74	−0.47	−0.46	−1.30
8	Pittsburgh	−0.66	−1.40	−1.22	+0.65
9	Cleveland	−0.62	−0.70	−0.59	−0.56
10	Baltimore	−0.56	−0.34	−0.54	−0.80
11	Buffalo	−0.43	−0.74	−0.90	+0.36
12	Cincinnati	−0.43	−0.80	−0.55	+0.06
13	Denver	−0.36	−0.64	−0.37	−0.06
14	Kansas City	−0.29	−0.47	−0.13	−0.28
15	San Francisco	−0.22	−0.47	−0.46	+0.26
16	Philadelphia	−0.16	−0.17	−0.81	+0.51
17	Portland	−0.12	−0.44	−0.15	+0.24
18	New Orleans	−0.11	+0.42	+0.02	−0.78
19	Seattle	−0.09	−0.40	−0.14	+0.26
20	Chicago	+0.04	+0.06	−0.28	+0.33
21	Los Angeles	+0.06	+0.22	−0.29	+0.26
22	Louisville	+0.07	−0.48	+0.06	+0.64
23	Ft. Worth	+0.11	+0.19	+0.67	−0.52
24	Dallas	+0.12	+0.19	+0.67	−0.50
25	Long Beach	+0.19	+0.22	−0.29	+0.64
26	Milwaukee	+0.33	+0.36	−0.18	+0.82
27	Toledo	+0.33	+0.42	+0.25	+0.32
28	Columbus	+0.41	+0.78	+0.33	+0.13
29	Phoenix	+0.58	+0.81	+0.70	+0.22
30	San Diego	+0.64	+0.48	+0.54	+0.89
31	Houston	+0.76	+0.95	+1.20	+0.12
32	Oklahoma City	+0.79	+0.68	+1.18	+0.52
33	Omaha	+1.14	+1.24	+1.32	+0.85
34	Memphis	+1.20	+2.00	+1.79	−0.19
35	Honolulu	+1.22	+0.65	+1.78	+1.22
36	Indianapolis[a]	+1.27	+1.28	+1.42	+1.12
37	New York[a]	+1.28	+2.43	+1.41	−0.01
38	San Antonio	+1.64	+2.06	+1.77	+1.10

[a] Boundary changes may be partly responsible for these favorable results. In 1972, suburban Nassau and Suffolk Counties were removed from the New York, N.Y. SMSA. Bergen County, New Jersey was transferred to the reconstituted New York–N.J. SMSA. In 1970, the City of Indianapolis merged with most of its surrounding suburbs inside Marion County.

of −.675 or less include cities in the bottom 25% of the distribution; scores of +.675 or more include cities in the top 25%. The methodology is designed to establish *relative* stress levels in large U.S. cities. However, if all of the sample cities were distressed in absolute terms, this methodology could fail to detect it.

Seven cities ranked as socio-economically "distressed" in terms of the foregoing variables. They included: Atlanta, St. Louis, Newark, Detroit, Boston, Minneapolis, and Oakland. Eight cities were classified as "not distressed." They included: San Antonio, New York, Indianapolis, Honolulu, Memphis, Omaha, Oklahoma City, and Houston. Each of the remaining cities ranked as "moderately distressed."

The findings regarding socio-economic stress in large cities are summarized in Table 2.13.

NOTES

1. Congress of the United States, Congressional Budget Office, *Barriers to Urban Economic Development* (Washington: U.S. Government Printing Office, May, 1978), p. 5.

2. Ibid., p. 7.

3. Herrington J. Bryce and Seymour Sachs, "Trends in Central City Employment," in *Revitalizing Cities*, ed. Herrington J. Bryce (Lexington, Mass: Lexington Books, 1979), p. 10.

4. Harvey A. Garn and Larry Clinton Ledebur, "The Economic Performance and Prospects of Cities," in *The Prospective City*, ed. Arthur P. Solomon (Cambridge, Mass: The MIT Press, 1980), p. 251.

5. See U.S. Department of Commerce, Bureau of the Census, *Boundary and Annexation Survey, 1970–79.* GE 30-4, (Washington: U.S. Government Printing Office, December, 1980.)

6. John H. Mollenkopf, "Paths Toward the Post-Industrial Service City: The Northeast and the Southwest," in *Cities Under Stress, The Fiscal Crisis of Urban America*, eds. Robert W. Burchell and David Listokin (Piscataway, N.J.: Rutgers University Center for Urban Policy Research, 1981), pp. 77–112.

7. Katharine L. Bradbury, Anthony Downs, and Kenneth A. Small, "Some Dynamics of Central City–Suburban Interactions," *The American Economic Review* 70(May, 1980):410–14.

8. David C. Perry and Alfred J. Watkins, "Regional Change and the Impact of Uneven Urban Development," in *The Rise of the Sunbelt Cities*, eds. David C. Perry and Alfred J. Watkins, Vol. 14, Urban Affairs Annual Reviews (Beverly Hills, CA: Sage Publications, 1977), pp. 19–54.

9. Ibid., pp. 42–3.

10. Robert B. Cohen, "Multinational Corporations, International Finance, and the Sunbelt," in *The Rise of the Sunbelt Cities*, pp. 211–26.

11. "Dislocations that May Deepen", *Business Week*, Special Issue, No. 2690 June 1, 1981, p. 62. By special permission.

12. Franklin J. James, "Economic Distress in Central Cities," in *Cities Under Stress*, p. 46.

13. George E. Peterson, "Federal Tax Policy and Urban Development," in *Central City Economic Development*, ed. Benjamin Chinitz (Cambridge, Mass: Abt Books, 1979), pp. 67–78.

14. Roger J. Vaughan, "The Impacts of Federal Policies on Urban Economic Development," in *The Prospective City*, ed. Arthur P. Solomon, (Cambridge, Mass: MIT Press, 1980), p. 393.

15. Thomas Muller, "Central City Business Retention: Jobs, Taxes, and Investment Trends," Paper prepared for the Department of Commerce Urban Roundtable, February 22, 1978; revised June 1978.

16. Robert W. Schmenner, *The Manufacturing Location Decision: Evidence from Cincinnati and New England* (Cambridge, Mass: The Harvard–MIT Joint Center for Urban Studies, March 1978.)

17. See David Greytak, Richard Gustely, and Robert J. Dinkelmeyer, "The Effects of Inflation on Local Government Expenditures," *National Tax Journal* 27(1974):583–98.

18. James, "Economic Distress in Central Cities", p. 29.

19. David L. Birch, "The Processes Causing Economic Change in Cities," Paper presented to the Department of Commerce Roundtable on Business Retention and Expansion, February 22, 1978; revised September 1978.

20. Roy W. Bahl and David Greytak, "The Response of City Government Revenues to Changes in Employment Structure," *Land Economics* 52(November, 1976): 429.

21. See U.S. Department of Labor, Bureau of Labor Statistics, *Geographic Profile of Employment and Unemployment, 1979*, Report 619, (Washington: U.S. Government Printing Office, 1980) U.S. Department of Labor, Bureau of Labor Statistics, *Geographic Profile of Employment and Unemployment, 1975*, Report 481, (Washington: U.S. Government Printing Office, 1977).

22. See U.S. Department of Labor, *Geographic Profile of Employment and Unemployment, 1979*, Report 619 (Washington: U.S. Government Printing Office, 1980).

23. U.S. Department of Justice, FBI Uniform Crime Reports, *Crime in the United States*, (Washington: U.S. Government Printing Office, September 1981.)

24. Thomas Muller, "Changing Expenditure and Service Demand Patterns of Stressed Cities" in *Cities Under Stress*, p. 292.

3

Fiscal Stress in Large Cities: Revenues

Until recently, researchers specializing in municipal finance focused their attention and research efforts on the levels and determinants of municipal spending.[1] The revenue side of the equation was largely ignored. Today it is recognized that large cities may be in fiscal difficulty not because their expenditures are too high in an absolute sense, but because their expenditures are high relative to their ability to generate public revenues. Susan MacManus notes: "It is far easier for municipalities to spend money than it is to obtain money in the first place. Fiscal irresponsibility occurs when governments spend money . . . without properly analyzing the wheres and whens of revenue accumulation."[2] The rapid growth of federal and state aid during the past decade increased opportunities for fiscal irresponsibility by further separating the burden of raising revenue from the responsibility for spending it. The pleasure of spending had, in effect, been divorced from the pain of taxation.

This chapter analyzes the revenue positions of each of the sample cities as of fiscal year 1979, and examines changes in the composition of their revenue mix during the fiscal 1969–79 decade.

THE SOURCES OF MUNICIPAL REVENUE

The major sources of revenue for local governments are intergovernmental aid, local tax revenues, and locally-generated non-tax revenues, such

55

as user charges and fees. This section discusses the characteristics, advantages, and disadvantages of each major revenue source.

Intergovernmental Aid

During the 1970s, intergovernmental aid was the fastest-growing revenue source for most U.S. cities. George Break makes a persuasive case for intergovernmental aid to local governments. He says that such aid is needed to mitigate the consequences of benefit spillovers, to redress fiscal imbalances, to satisfy the unmet needs of lower-income groups, to decentralize political power, to encourage consumption of "merit" goods, to promote innovation and experimentation, and to help stabilize the economy.[3]

It is argued that benefit spillovers lead to an underallocation of resources to collective consumption. Spillovers occur when the results of municipal spending transcend a city's boundaries. As a result, the benefits of a given program are realized by both insiders who pay for it and outsiders who don't. The latter are "free riders". Significant spillovers are associated with transportation programs, environmental control services, and services associated with human resource development. Current technology in the areas of transportation and environmental control is not sophisticated enough to confine costs and benefits to small areas. Services connected with human resource development have relatively large spillovers because people are mobile. Well-educated people confer positive spillovers, sometimes called externalities, upon the communities to which they migrate and vice versa.

The existence of spillovers prevents cities from reaping the full benefits of their expenditures. They will therefore expand programs with spillovers only to the point at which the marginal benefits of such programs equal their marginal tax costs. George Break notes that the "socially optimal" point is that at which total marginal benefits equal total marginal costs. Otherwise, resources will be inefficiently distributed.[4]

To assure that sufficient resources are allocated to local programs with benefit spillovers, Federal grants are used to reduce program costs to insiders until such costs are roughly equivalent to the program benefits that insiders enjoy. This can be accomplished by means of an open-ended matching grant whose size is equal to the benefits received by outsiders. Benefit spillovers can be mitigated in other ways, but none is entirely satisfactory. For example, programs with spillovers can be shifted to higher levels of government. However, many programs, such as education, are best performed locally so that their content can be tailored to local tastes and preferences. Another alternative is to enlarge the jurisdiction until most benefit spillovers are eliminated. This, however, is rarely feasible.

Intergovernmental grants are also needed to redress various fiscal imbalances. In recent years, there has been a growing vertical imbalance between different levels of government—Federal, state, and local. This imbalance reflects the fact that the Federal government uses a progressive income tax, which responds readily to economic growth, as its major revenue source. State and local governments, which are responsible for most domestic expenditures, rely on less income-elastic property and sales taxes. The individual income tax is estimated to have an elasticity coefficient of 1.65, indicating that tax receipts rise more rapidly than incomes; the general sales tax is estimated to have a coefficient of 1.00, indicating that taxes rise proportionately to incomes; the local property tax has an estimated elasticity coefficient of only 0.80, indicating that tax receipts rise more slowly than incomes.[5] During the late 1960s and early 1970s, Federal income tax revenues were growing so rapidly that it was feared that the overflowing treasury would cause "fiscal drag," thereby slowing the economy. The need for "balancing grants" to mitigate vertical fiscal imbalances between levels of government was the basis for the general revenue sharing program which was first enacted in 1972.

Intergovernmental grants are also needed to redress horizontal fiscal imbalances between governments in the same tier. The fact that cities with inadequate tax bases provide inferior services at exorbitant tax rates, while their more affluent counterparts can offer quality services with only a modest tax effort has long been regarded as inequitable. In recent years, intergovernmental grants to large cities have also been used to achieve national economic stability. The Intergovernmental Anti-Recession Act of 1977 provided countercyclical aid to offset revenue losses resulting from the 1973–75 national recession. Such aid is a form of "pump-priming" that is designed to facilitate national economic recovery.

Although there are numerous justifications for intergovernmental aid, such aid also has major disadvantages. Aid formulas are often complex and sometimes favor less-distressed cities over their more-distressed counterparts. Intergovernmental aid can distort local spending priorities by stimulating spending in functional areas supported by grant money rather than in functional areas that satisfy local priorities. Substitution of intergovernmental aid for local taxes can also make local officials less accountable to their constituents in their spending decisions. Extensive reliance on intergovernmental aid makes cities vulnerable to sudden and unpredictable legislative changes in aid formulas and programs that can throw their budgets into disarray. George Break notes: " . . . many cities have become so dependent on federal aid that many experts doubt their ability to free themselves of his dependency or to survive without it."[6] Perhaps the most telling criticism of intergovernmental grants is that they may not achieve the goals set for them. Break's analysis of the price effects of intergovernmental grants raises this possibility. He notes that an open-ended matching grant under which the grantor provides $1 for every $2 spent by the grantee, a 50%

"match," provides an effective price reduction of 33%. This means that the grantee can purchase $1 of program benefits using only 67¢ of its own funds. If the grantee spends less of its money on the aided program than before, funds will be available for other uses, but the grant will have failed to achieve its purpose.[7]

The Advisory Commission on Intergovernmental Relations suggests that a well-rounded system of Federal aid should contain three elements: categorical grants to stimulate and support programs in specific areas of national interest, block grants to give states and localities more flexibility in satisfying their needs in broad functional areas, and general support grants, such as revenue sharing, to reduce intergovernmental fiscal disparities and give states and cities the opportunity to develop unique solutions to their distinctive problems.[8]

Categorical grants are one element in the tripartite system of Federal grants. Until 1972, virtually all Federal grants were categorical grants. Such grants are targeted to specific programs and come with stringent expenditure guidelines and performance standards. Categorical grants may be awarded on a formula or a project basis. Formula grants are used when there is a definable target population whose needs can be objectively measured. Formula grants are relatively automatic once the formula has been agreed upon, but such agreements are often preceded by intense debate regarding the variables to be incorporated. The procedure for awarding project grants is somewhat different. States and localities are invited to apply for funding for individual projects in some area of public service. The distribution of project grants can be arbitrary, reflecting the "grantsmanship" of local agency personnel or the whims of Federal program managers.

Categorical grants may be of the matching or non-matching variety. Matching grants require some expenditure by the recipient government; non-matching grants do not. Medicaid and aid to families with dependent children (AFDC) are examples of open-ended matching grants. Until recently, it was assumed that non-matching grants have the same impact on local public spending as a net increase in private income. However, it has been demonstrated that non-matching grants stimulate more local spending per dollar received than an increase in private income, because it is easier for cities to spend grant money and to forego tax cuts than it is for them to raise taxes as private incomes rise.[9]

General revenue sharing (GRS) is the second element in the tripartite system of Federal grants. First enacted in 1972, the revenue-sharing legislation sought to reduce Federal involvement in domestic problems, to involve local citizens in governmental decision-making to a greater extent, to provide local tax relief, and to improve the quantity and quality of local public services. General revenue sharing is an unrestricted grant program. Participation is universal and automatic for "general purpose" units of government. Revenue sharing funds are distributed by formula and must be spent in certain designated priority categories. These include: ordinary and necessary maintenance and operating expenses for public safety, environmental protection, public transportation, health, recreation, libraries, social services for the poor and aged, financial administration, ordinary and necessary capital expenditures authorized by law, and debt retirement.[10]

The revenue sharing legislation was last renewed for three years beginning October 1, 1980. However, Congress suspended the state portion, amounting to $2.3 billion, as of fiscal year 1981. The move to cut state revenue sharing was prompted by growing Federal deficits at a time when many states had large budget surpluses. Elimination of the state portion and inflationary erosion of the purchasing power of revenue sharing dollars has limited the fiscal benefits from this form of Federal aid.[11]

Block grants are the third major component of the Federal grant system. They are cash transfers from the Federal government to lower levels of government which are related to income or wealth rather than to the performance of a specific function or service. Their use reflects widespread disenchantment with categorical grants as well as a desire to decentralize Federal activities. Recipient governments are given wide latitude in identifying problems and developing solutions and there are few Federally-imposed expenditure guidelines.

Consolidation of nine categorical grants into the Partnership for Health program in 1966 (PL 89-749) and enactment of the Omnibus Crime Control and Safe Streets Act of 1968 (PL 90-351) represented the first major use of block grants. These programs were followed by the Comprehensive Employment and Training Act (CETA) of 1973, which encompassed seventeen categorical programs, and the Housing and Community Development Act of 1974, which included the following urban aid programs: urban renewal, neighborhood development, model cities, water and sewer facilities, neighborhood and public facilities, open space–urban beautification–historic preservation, and rehabilitation loans. The Public Works Employment Act of 1976, which funded state and local capital projects, was also a block grant program.

The CETA legislation sought to improve the utilization of the nation's human resources by providing job training and employment assistance to the economically disadvantaged, unemployed, and underemployed.[12] The Housing and Community Development Act of 1974 authorized a program of community development block grants to localities based on a formula that incorporated level of poverty, age of the housing stock, and population growth lag.[13] Ann Markusen notes that the Act was an outgrowth of President Nixon's "new federalism" strategy, and that it was actually an attempt to wrest control of a number of categorical programs from the HUD bureaucracy so as to spread funds to more local governments.[14]

Under the Reagan Administration, the number of block grant programs has increased dramatically. Pursuant to the Omnibus Reconciliation Act of 1981, seventy-seven categorical grant programs were consolidated into nine new block grants, bringing the number of Federal block grant programs to eleven. Of the nine new "blocks," four were earmarked for health services, three for social services and cash payments to the poor, one for education, and one for community development. All go directly to the states, but certain funds are earmarked for passthrough to local governments.

Despite the recent proliferation of Federal grants, state aid continues to exceed Federal aid in many large cities. In fiscal 1980, the largest U.S. cities, those with populations of 300,000 or more, collectively received 39% of their intergovernmental revenues from the Federal government and 58% of the total from their respective states. This situation exists because state grants-in-aid are earmarked principally for education, public welfare, and general support; the largest U.S. cities often perform one or more of these "least common" functions. State aid may take the form of grants-in-aid or shared taxes. Grants-in-aid can represent a direct appropriation by the state legislature or may constitute a passthrough of Federal aid. Whereas the Federal government utilizes project grants to a great extent, state grants-in-aid are generally allocated by formula. Few state grants have formal matching provisions. However, states frequently reimburse their local governments for an agreed upon proportion of local program costs in specific functional areas.

Local Tax Revenues

Local taxes can be levied on property, retail sales, and/or income. The mix selected often determines the viability of the local tax base. Ideally, the local tax system should satisfy a number of economic criteria. George Break suggests that the ideal revenue system should achieve horizontal and vertical equity, should promote fiscal and economic efficiency, should be sufficiently flexible to meet changing revenue demands, and should be sensitive to economic growth.[15] Horizontal equity is satisfied when people in similar circumstances are treated similarly. That is, those who enjoy equal amounts of local government services and who own equal amounts of property should be taxed equally. Vertical equity is satisfied by a revenue system which treats people in different economic circumstances differently. That is, tax burdens should vary in some measurable and systematic manner to account for different circumstances. A revenue system is "fiscally efficient" if administrative costs are reasonable and it is readily understood by taxpayers. A revenue system is "fiscally flexible" if at least one major revenue source can be varied annually to meet changing revenue demands. Economic efficiency refers to the impact of given taxes on decisions to consume, save, work, and invest. A good tax system accomplishes its objectives but is neutral with respect to such private-sector economic decisions. A revenue system possesses growth sensitivity if the increase in receipts is at least proportionate to rising employment, prices, and personal income. Glenn Fisher suggests several additional political tests. He would consider the effects of a given revenue system on the structure of government, particularly on the vertical balance between levels of government. He also suggests that the revenue system selected must be acceptable to the general public.[16]

In fiscal 1980, real-property taxes generated 47% of local tax revenues in the largest U.S. cities, those with populations of 300,000 or more. The remainder came from general sales and gross receipts taxes, 16 percent; selective sales and gross receipts taxes on items such as alcoholic beverages, motor fuels, and tobacco, 10 percent; local income taxes, 21 percent; and miscellaneous tax sources, 6 percent.

Property taxes may be applied to real-property including land, improvements, and structures, and to personal-property, both tangible and intangible. Local zoning laws generally specify several categories of real-property, such as single- and multi-family residential, industrial, commercial, and agricultural. The value of each type of property for tax purposes is determined by a local assessor, who may use one or more of the following yardsticks: recent sales of comparable property, the cost of reproducing the property, and the income derived from the property. Most states assess property on a fractional basis; the assessed value being expressed as a percentage of the property's actual value. Property taxes may also be levied on tangible personal property such as machinery, furniture, cars, clothing, and jewelry, and on intangible personal property, such as stocks, bonds, savings accounts, and money. However, such items are less readily identifiable for tax purposes and are more mobile than real-property. Taxes on personal property are not widely used because they can be easily evaded.

The benefit principle supposedly justifies the widespread use of the property tax. That is, since property owners benefit from public services, they should be required to pay for them. However, the benefit principle applies only to a narrow range of services, such as street lighting and refuse collection. These services confer measurable benefits upon specific property owners. The relationships between real-property and services such as education and environmental protection, are much more tenuous. The property tax has also been criticized for allegedly penalizing those who improve their properties; improvements cause higher assessments and lead to higher taxes. This, in turn, may have impeded the reconstruction of the nation's older cities.

The real-property tax if often poorly and inequitably administered. Real-property changes hands infrequently so that it is difficult to establish its true market value. Assessment ratios and tax rates can differ even between neighboring jurisdictions, thereby causing economically inefficient locational decisions. The real-property tax has also proved an unsatisfacttory revenue source in northern cities characterized by depressed property values and in cities with large amounts of tax exempt property.

Perhaps the most serious criticism of the property tax is that it is regressive with respect to income, consuming a higher fraction of the incomes of the poor than of the wealthy. However, even this claim has been challenged. Henry Aaron contends that this criticism is based on the false assumption that the property tax is an excise tax on those who use the commodities produced by taxable real-property. According to this thinking, renters bear the taxes levied on their residences and automobile owners bear the taxes levied on automobile factories. However, Aaron contends that the property tax is a tax on capital and that the burden of the tax is shared by all owners of capital. He reasons: "Since the ownership of capital, or net worth, is progressively distributed with respect to income, the property tax on balance is a progressive, not a regressive, tax."[17] Aaron also suggests that the practice of determining the incidence of the property tax in relation to annual income is erroneous and that when household income is averaged for periods exceeding one year, the property tax is actually proportional or progressive for most income classes.

Despite the criticisms surrounding the property tax, it is still widely used, because for many governments, it may be the only broad-based tax for which institutional tools are available and an adminstrative bureaucracy is already in place. Its supporters also contend that it is a good way of taxing unrealized capital gains.[18]

In recent years, attacks on the real-property tax have taken the form of tax rate and tax levy limitations. Tax rate limits set the maximum rate that can be applied against the assessed value of property without approval by the electorate. Tax levy limits establish the maximum amount of revenue to be raised through the property tax.

Two of the best known property tax initiatives are California's Proposition 13 and Massachusetts' Propositon 2½. Proposition 13, enacted in June, 1978, provides that real-property be taxed at 1% of its estimated 1975–76 market value plus 0.25%, which is the estimated rate needed to service any bonded indebtedness approved by California voters prior to fiscal year 1978/79. Moreover, assessed values cannot be increased by more than 2% annually unless the property is sold, at which time it can be reassessed to reflect its market value. Proposition 13 also specified that no local tax can be increased or a new tax imposed without approval by two-thirds of the qualified voters; state tax increases must be approved by at least two-thirds of both houses of the state legislature. Of the initial reduction in property taxes, an estimated 33% went to homeowners, 17% to owners of rental property, 27% to owners of commercial and industrial property, 13% to owners of agricultural property, and 9% to the State of California. Calfornia cities lost 15% of their total revenues and California counties and school districts each lost 29% of their revenues.[19]

Massachusetts' Proposition 2½, enacted in November 1980, restricted property taxes to 2.5% of market value. Cities and towns that exceed the 2.5% limit must reduce total property taxes by 15% annually until the limit is reached. After that, property taxes may not rise by more than 2.5% annually, regardless of new development or the increase in property values. Individual towns and cities can override Propositon 2½ by a two-thirds vote.

Partly in response to recent attacks on the property tax, more and more cities are diversifying their tax bases and adopting income and/or general sales taxes. Income taxes can be levied on individuals and/or corporations. However, unlike the Federal government, individual cities cannot use even moderately-progressive income taxes because of the potential locational consequences for individuals and firms. Consequently, when used, municipal income taxes are proportional, flat-rate taxes. Since an income tax can be applied both to city residents and to suburban residents who work in the city, it enables cities to tap a relatively wide tax base. However, the heavy use of the personal income tax by the Federal government restricts its use by local governments. Moreover, the income elasticity of the personal income tax can be a liability during recessions when incomes grow slowly.

Sales taxes may be applied to all items or only to selected categories of goods and services. The former is called a general sales tax and is widely used by large U.S. cities. Unlike the personal income tax, the sales tax can be inequitable because it fails to allow for variations in personal circumstances. Unless home-consumed food is excluded, a general sales tax can be regressive. However, if food is exempted and services are taxed, a general sales tax is proportional for most income classes. This is because food constitutes a high proportion of the expenditures of low-income families and services are more prominently represented in the budgets of high-income households. The regressive nature of the sales tax can also be altered by giving consumers a specified tax-free allowance before the tax is imposed. However, the sales tax cannot be pushed to excessive rates in declining cities or retail activity will flee to adjacent, lower-taxed suburbs.

Non-Tax Revenue Sources

Non-tax revenues include both user charges and miscellaneous revenues from interest on assets, from fines and forfeits, from receipts from the sale of property and from special assessments. User charges are the most significant component of non-tax revenues. User charges put public prices on public products. They apply to those who voluntarily consume public services or use public facilities such as schools, highways, hospitals, parks, and airports. They are favored by economists not only because they raise additional revenues, but also because they can lead to a more efficient allocation of resources and a more equitable distribution of public services. Efficiency is served because user charges provide a price signal as to what goods should be produced and at what levels. Equity is served because only those who benefit from a service actually pay for it. User charges can reduce congestion by rationing scarce facilities to those who place the highest value on access to them. User charges can also provide the capital needed to maintain or expand existing public facilities. For example, a user charge imposed on motorists who travel on major highways during peak rush hours can reduce highway congestion while, at the same time, generating the capital needed for highway improvements. Since user charges are site-specific and are applied regardless of where the user lives, there is no problem of benefit spillovers to non-residents.

Like other revenue sources, user charges also have a number of limitations. They are not differentiated according to ability-to-pay and can be disproportionately burdensome to the poor. Moreover, user charges are appropriate only for those services with clearly-identifiable beneficiaries and where non-payers can be readily excluded. In additon, collection costs must be reasonable and the collection process easy to administer. While user charges can be applied to public golf courses, they are not applicable to pure public goods such as national defense. The nation's defense umbrella is collectively consumed and non-payers cannot be excluded. User charges are also inappropriate for redistributive services such as health care, or merit goods such as education, because the primary goal is to assure an adequate level of consumption. User charges would defeat this goal.

One stumbling block in applying user charges is the difficulty inherent in setting them at appropriate levels. Local governments rarely have adequate information to compute optimum prices. Moreover, the substitution of user charges for tax revenues could reduce local revenue sharing entitlements which are based, in part, on tax effort. Greater reliance on user charges could also lead to higher tax burdens for municipal residents because, unlike taxes, user charges are not deductible in calculating Federal income tax liabilities.

The foregoing analysis suggests that each major revenue source has distinct advantages and limitations. The mix chosen should reflect a city's revenue needs as well as the unique strengths and weaknesses of its tax base. Subsequent sections explore this subject more fully.

REVENUE USAGE: GROUPS OF CITIES

This section analyzes patterns of revenue usage for broad groups of cities. It attempts to answer the following types of questions: How do taxes and tax burdens differ by region? Do declining cities receive proportionately more outside aid than growing cities? To what extent do differences in revenue mix reflect differences in the scope of functional responsibilities? Are declining northern cities less tax efficient than growing southern cities?

Four revenue measures are used to answer these questions: per capita revenue levels, patterns of revenue reliance, tax burdens, and coefficients of tax efficiency. These measures were used by Susan MacManus in her analysis of revenue patterns in U.S. cities and suburbs.[20]

The findings show clearcut distinctions in revenue patterns and tax burdens between growing and declining cities, northern and southern cities, high- and low-density cities and cities grouped by differences in functional responsibility. As expected, the declining, northern, high-density cities, many of which perform one or more of the "least-common" functions, were characterized by similar revenue profiles as were the growing, low-density, southern and western cities whose responsibilities are largely confined to the basic municipal functions. The former groups of cities exhibited considerably more "revenue stress" than the latter. Despite large infusions of state aid, residents of declining, northern cities continued to bear tax burdens that were roughly double those of growing, southern cities. Moreover, declining, northern cities were relatively inefficient in providing basic municipal services, so that the disadavantage of high taxes and tax burdens was not offset, at least in part, by efficiently-provided public services. This situation helps to explain the recent exodus of households and firms from the nation's declining, northern cities.

Revenue Levels, Revenue Reliance, Fiscal Year 1979

In fiscal 1979, the declining cities as a group raised twice as much general revenue as the growing cities: $768 versus $416 per capita. There were similar intergroup differences for the other groups of cities. For example, per capita general revenues in the northeastern cities were 1.7 times those of cities located outside the northeast; per capita general revenues in the high-density cities were 1.8 times those of the low-density cities: $863 versus $470; per capita general revenues in cities that performed two least common functions were 2.6 times those of cities with no such responsibilities: $1143 versus $447.

The declining, northern cities raised more money largely because they received more intergovernmental aid, and particularly more state aid, than the growing, sunbelt cities. The declining cities received 4.3 times as much states aid as the growing cities: $175 versus $41 per capita; the northeastern cities received 3.2 times as much state aid as the southern cities: $273 versus $85 per capita; the high-density cities received 4.3 times as much state aid as the low-density cities: $223 versus $52 per capita; those cities performing two least common functions received 7.8 times as much state aid as cities performing none: $357 versus $46 per capita. The clearest intergroup differences emerged when cities were classified by differences in functional responsibility. This is because state aid is targeted to the least common functions.

Declining, northern cities also received more Federal aid than growing, southern cities but the differences were not as great as for state aid. For example, the declining cities received 1.7 times as much Federal aid as the growing cities: $156 versus $94 per capita; the northeastern cities received approximately the same level of Federal aid as the southern cities: $125 versus $120 per capita; and, cities performing two least common functions received almost twice as much Federal aid as cities performing none: $204 versus $109 per capita.

These distinctive aid patterns are reflected in distinctive patterns of revenue reliance for each group of cities. In fiscal 1979, the ratio of state aid-to-general revenue was 23% in declining cities and 10% in growing cities; it was 28% in the northeastern cities as compared with between 15% and 17% for cities in other regions; it was 26% in the high-density cities and 11% in the low-density cities; it was 31% in cities performing two least common functions and 10% in cities performing none. However, the growing, low-density, sunbelt cities were generally more dependent on Federal than state aid. Therefore, ongoing reductions in Federal aid could be more traumatic for growing cities than for declining ones.

Despite large infusions of state and Federal aid, per capita taxes in declining cities were 1.7 times those of growing cities: $304 versus $177; taxes in northeastern cities were more than double those of southern cities: $431 versus $210 per capita; taxes in high-density cities were almost double those of low-density cities: $348 versus $191 per capita; taxes in cities performing two least common functions were more than double those of cities performing none: $397 versus $187 per capita. These differences were apparent for both property and non-property taxes. Disproportionately high taxes in declining, northern cities reflect both their extensive functional responsibilities and the underutilization of non-tax revenue sources such as user charges. For example, non-tax revenues accounted for 24% of general revenues in the growing cities as compared with 15% in the declining ones, for 24% in the western cities as compared with only 12% in the northeastern ones, and for 23% in the low-density cities as compared with only 14% in the high-density cities.

New York City was analyzed separately because it is unique among large cities in terms of the size and complexity of its economy and the magnitude of its fiscal variables. For purposes of analysis, New York's revenue profile was compared with those of the declining, northeastern, and high-density cities. New York City fared poorly even when compared with these relatively distressed groups of cities. In fiscal 1979, New York's general revenues were more than double those of each of these groups. New York received 4.3 times as much state aid as the declining cities: $746 versus $175 per capita. State aid accounted for 37% of New York's general revenues as compared with only 23% in the declining cities, 28% in the northeastern cities, and 26% in the high-density cities. New York was the only city studied that performed all three least common functions. This accounts for its disproportionate reliance on state aid. In fiscal 1979, New York City received $155 per capita in Federal aid, about the same as for the declining cities. Federal aid accounted for only 8% of New York's general revenues as compared with 20% in the declining cities. Despite the well-publicized Federal bailout of New York City during the mid-1970s, it would appear that New York is not excessively dependent on Federal aid. If anything, it would appear that by fiscal 1979, New York City had become dependent on the generosity of New York State's administrators and legislators for its fiscal wellbeing.

Despite large amounts of state aid, New York City's per capita taxes were almost triple those of the declining cities: $865 versus $304. New York's property taxes were $446 per capita as compared with $151 for the declining cities; its non-property taxes were $419 per capita as compared with $153 for the declining cities. User charges in New York City were double those of the declining cities: $173 versus $79 per capita.

The findings suggest that as of fiscal 1979, New York City was pushing hard on the full range of revenue sources available to it in order to satisfy its large expenditure requirements. These findings are summarized in Tables 3.1 and 3.2.

Tax Burdens versus Tax Efficiency, Fiscal Year 1979

The bottom line in any analysis of revenues and taxes is whether the taxpayer feels that he's getting his money's worth for his tax dollars. According to Charles Tiebout, the residents of given areas are footloose and tend to "vote with their feet" in order to satisfy their unique preferences for public goods.[21] Consequently, the tradeoff between taxes paid and services received is a significant one. In order to evaluate that tradeoff, tax burdens in each group of cities were compared with measures of tax efficiency. Tax

TABLE 3.1. Revenue Levels for Major City Groupings, Fiscal Year 1979 ($ Per Capita)

Type of Revenue	By Population Change			By Region			
	Growing	Mixed	Declining	Northeast	No. Central	South	West
Total General Revenue	416	593	768	959	565	552	583
Intergovernmental Revenue	138[a]	234[a]	343[a]	413[a]	234[a]	222[a]	234[a]
Federal	94	124	156	125	138	120	129
State	41	86	175	273	86	85	100
Own-Source Revenue	278	359	425	546	331	330	349
Taxes	177	207	304	431	232	210	205
Property Taxes	80	104	151	245	101	117	85
Non-Property Taxes	97	103	153	186	131	93	120
Non-Tax Revenues	101	152	121	115	99	120	144
Current Charges	56	99	79	67	68	73	84
Miscellaneous	45	53	42	48	31	47	60

Type of Revenue	By Population Density			By Differences in Functional Responsibility				
	Low	Medium	High	Three[b] Functions	Two Functions	One Function	Minimal Amounts	None
Total General Revenue	470	527	863	2010	1143	819	502	447
Intergovernmental Revenue	170[a]	200[a]	396[a]	906[a]	564[a]	361[a]	185[a]	160[a]
Federal	105	122	161	155	204	134	121	109
State	52	71	223	746	357	186	59	46
Own-Source Revenue	300	327	467	1104	579	458	317	287
Taxes	191	199	348	865	397	328	207	187
Property Taxes	102	77	183	446	285	121	75	97
Non-Property Taxes	89	122	165	419	112	207	132	90
Non-Tax Revenues	109	128	119	239	182	130	110	100
Current Charges	66	77	79	173	126	84	65	59
Miscellaneous	43	51	40	66	56	46	45	41

[a] Includes interlocal revenues
[b] Denotes New York City
Source: Computations based on Census Bureau data.

69

TABLE 3.2. Patterns of Revenue Reliance for Major City Groupings, Fiscal Year 1979 (Percents)

Type of Revenue	By Population Change			By Region			
	Growing	Mixed	Declining	Northeast	No. Central	South	West
Total General Revenue	100	100	100	100	100	100	100
Intergovernmental Revenue	34[a]	39[a]	45[a]	43[a]	41[a]	40[a]	40[a]
Federal	23	21	20	13	24	22	22
State	10	14	23	28	15	15	17
Own-Source Revenue	66	61	55	57	59	60	60
Taxes	42	35	40	45	41	38	36
Property Taxes	19	18	20	26	18	21	15
Non-Property Taxes	23	17	20	19	23	17	21
Non-Tax Revenues	24	26	15	12	18	22	24
Current Charges	13	17	10	7	12	13	14
Miscellaneous	11	9	5	5	6	9	10

	By Population Density			By Differences in Functional Responsibility				
Type of Revenue	Low	Medium	High	Three[b] Functions	Two Functions	One Function	Minimal Amounts	None
Total General Revenue	100	100	100	100	100	100	100	100
Intergovernmental Revenue	36[a]	37[a]	46[a]	45[a]	49[a]	44[a]	37[a]	36[a]
Federal	22	23	19	8	18	16	24	25
State	11	13	26	37	31	23	12	10
Own-Source Revenue	64	63	54	55	51	56	63	64
Taxes	41	38	40	43	35	40	41	42
Property Taxes	22	15	21	22	25	15	15	22
Non-Property Taxes	19	23	19	21	10	25	26	20
Non-Tax Revenues	23	25	14	12	16	16	22	22
Current Charges	14	15	9	9	11	10	13	13
Miscellaneous	9	10	5	3	5	6	9	9

[a] Includes interlocal revenues
[b] Denotes New York City
Source: Computations based on Census Bureau data.

burdens are expressed in terms of the ratio of per capita taxes to per capita personal incomes. Ratios in excess of 7% are regarded as burdensome. Coefficients of tax efficiency relate per capita expenditures for given functions to tax burdens. The higher the coefficient, the greater the presumed degree of efficiency and the higher the presumed level of taxpayer satisfaction. However, these coefficients can be distorted by intergovernmental aid. Such aid can inflate expenditures relative to tax burdens thereby causing higher coefficients. Nevertheless, it could be argued that taxpayers are concerned not with the origin of funds spent on their behalf, but only with the level of spending per se. Moreover, expenditures are not necessarily a valid indicator of the quality of local public services, so that the coefficients of tax efficiency may not be accurate proxies for service quality.

In fiscal 1979, tax burdens in the declining cities were double those of the growing cities: 4.53% versus 2.20%; tax burdens in the northeastern cities were 2.5 times those of the southern cities: 7.10% versus 2.89%; tax burdens in the high-density cities were 2.1 times those of the low-density cities: 5.28% versus 2.46%; tax burdens in cities performing two least common functions were 2.2 times those in cities perfoming none: 5.51% versus 2.45%. Tax burdens in New York City were 11.88%, well above the 7% danger threshold. However, this figure somewhat overstates the actual tax burden imposed upon New York City residents, because non-residents employed in New York City pay a commuter tax and their incomes are not reflected in the computations.

Both property and non-property tax burdens were higher in declining, northern cities than in growing, sunbelt cities. However, the intergroup disparities were greatest for property tax burdens. For example, property tax burdens in cities that performed two least common functions were triple those of cities that performed none; non-property tax burdens were only 1.3 times as high.

The relevant question is whether high tax burdens in declining, northern cities have been offset to any extent by efficiently-provided public services. The coefficients of tax efficiency suggest that this was not the case. Coefficients were computed for all municipal functions and for five basic municipal services—highways, fire protection, police protection, sanitation, and parks and recreation. The declining cities were less tax efficient than either the growing or mixed cities on an overall basis and in terms of four of the five specific functions. For example, the coefficient for parks and recreation was 9.3 in the growing cities, 10.6 in the mixed cities, and 5.7 in the declining cities. The northeastern cities were less tax efficient than cities in other regions for all functions studied. The coefficient for police protection was 15.1 in the northeastern cities, 27.8 in the midwestern cities, 19.7 in the southern cities, and 28.9 in the western cities. The high-density cities were less tax efficient than the low- and medium-density cities for all functions studied. The efficiency coefficient for parks and recreation was 9.4 in the low-density cities, 9.7 in the medium-density cities, and 4.6 in the high-density cities. Cities that performed two least common functions scored well on an overall basis, probably because they received large amounts of intergovernmental aid. However, they generally scored poorly for each of the basic municipal services.

New York City provides an interesting contrast between tax burdens and levels of tax efficiency. The City was characterized by disproportionately high property and non-property tax burdens. Yet, New York's coefficients of tax efficiency were well below those for the declining cities, for the northeastern cities, and for the high-density cities, groups which have already been shown to have disproportionately low coefficients themselves. New York's coefficient for fire protection was 3.6 as compared with 9.5 for the declining cities, 7.3 for the northeastern cities, and 8.3 for the high-density cities. Its coefficient for police protection was 8.0 as compared with 22.2 for the declining cities, 15.1 for the northeastern cities, and 21.6 for the high-density cities. Thus, despite New York City's substantial reliance on state aid, despite its high taxes and tax burdens, the City scored poorly in terms of tax efficiency. It should be noted, however, that New York City provides all three least common functions—education, health and hospitals, and public welfare—and may have found it necessary to divert funds from basic municipal services in order to finance these added functional responsibilities. These findings are summarized in Table 3.3.

Changes in Revenue Usage: Fiscal Years 1969–79

Revenue measures for a given point in time provide a "snapshot" of intergroup differences in patterns of revenue usage. Equally significant is the manner in which the revenue mix has changed over time. This section analyzes changes in revenue usage during the fiscal 1969–79 decade. For purposes of analysis, per capita revenues for fiscal years 1969, 1975, and 1979 were converted to constant 1972 dollars by applying the implicit GNP deflator for state and local government purchases for each of these years. Average annual rates of change in revenues from each major revenue source were then computed for the fiscal 1969–75 and fiscal 1975–79 periods.

The findings indicate that intergovernmental revenue grew significantly faster than locally-generated "own-source" revenue in all groups of cities between fiscal 1969 and 1979. Average annual rates of growth for intergovernmental aid were about 23% in the growing and low-density cities, 12% in the northeastern cities, 10% in the western cities, and 9% in the

TABLE 3.3. Tax Burdens versus Tax Efficiency for Major City Groupings, Fiscal Year 1979 (Percents)

	By Population Change			By Region			
	Growing	Mixed	Declining	Northeast	No. Central	South	West
Total Tax Burdens	2.20	2.77	4.53	7.10	3.39	2.89	2.47
Property Tax Burdens	0.99	1.39	2.25	4.04	1.48	1.61	1.02
Non-Property Tax Burdens	1.21	1.38	2.28	3.06	1.91	1.28	1.45
Coefficients of Tax Efficiency							
All Functions	169.0	211.0	160.0	134.0	160.0	188.0	200.0
Highways	6.9	9.1	4.6	2.7	7.4	5.2	7.1
Fire Protection	13.8	14.2	9.5	7.3	10.8	11.8	14.8
Police Protection	27.7	21.2	22.2	15.1	27.8	19.7	28.9
Sanitation	6.9	6.7	5.7	4.6	7.0	6.8	5.6
Parks & Recreation	9.3	10.6	5.7	3.4	6.2	8.4	11.7

	By Population Density			By Differences in Functional Responsibility				
	Low	Medium	High	Three[a] Functions	Two Functions	One Function	Minimal Amounts	None
Total Tax Burdens	2.46	2.65	5.28	11.88	5.51	5.36	2.76	2.45
Property Tax Burdens	1.31	1.02	2.78	6.13	3.96	1.98	1.01	1.27
Non-Property Tax Burdens	1.15	1.63	2.50	5.75	1.55	3.38	1.75	1.18
Coefficients of Tax Efficiency								
All Functions	182.0	184.0	155.0	142.0	192.0	149.0	164.0	176.0
Highways	6.9	8.0	3.9	1.7	3.9	4.2	6.7	7.7
Fire Protection	12.8	14.4	8.3	3.6	9.5	7.4	12.5	14.4
Police Protection	22.0	27.2	21.6	8.0	15.9	20.6	32.2	23.1
Sanitation	7.0	6.8	5.3	3.3	3.3	5.6	7.5	7.5
Parks & Recreation	9.4	9.7	4.6	1.5	6.2	5.9	6.3	9.8

[a] Denotes New York City

Source: Computations based on Census Bureau data

declining and high-density cities. During the same period, own-source revenues grew by less than 1% annually in the growing, declining, and high-density cities and by about 2% annually in the low-density and northeastern cities; own-source revenues declined in real terms in the western cities. As a result, all groups of cities relied more extensively on Federal and state aid in fiscal 1979 than in fiscal 1969. During the 1970s, Federal aid to large cities grew significantly faster than state aid. This was particularly evident in growing, southern, and low-density cities which had received relatively little Federal aid in fiscal 1969.

Own-source revenues grew more slowly than intergovernmental aid in part because of widespread real declines in property tax revenues. For example, the ratio of property taxes-to-total taxes declined from 37% to 19% in the growing cities, from 34% to 20% in the declining cities, from 41% to 26% in the northeastern cities, from 33% to 21% in the southern cities, and from 36% to 21% in the high-density cities. Real declines in property tax revenues during the 1970s were partly offset by real increases in non-property taxes and user charges. These findings are summarized in Tables 3.4 and 3.5.

Conclusions

It is now possible to answer some of the questions posed at the beginning of this section. Do taxes and tax burdens differ by region? The northeastern cities clearly had higher taxes and tax burdens than their counterparts in other regions. Declining and high-density cities and those performing one or more least common functions were also characterized by disproportionately high taxes and tax burdens. Do declining cities receive proportionately more outside aid than growing cities? The declining cities were heavily dependent on outside aid, particularly state aid. The same generalization applies to the northeastern cities, the high-density cities, and those with relatively extensive functional responsibilities. To what extent do differences in revenue mix reflect differences in the scope of municipal responsibilities? There was a direct and positive relationship between the scope of responsibilities and the degree of dependence on state aid. Are declining, northern cities less tax efficient than growing, sunbelt cities? The results suggest that declining cities are less tax efficient, as defined in this study, both in terms of total spending and in terms of spending for basic municipal services.

The patterns of revenue usage in declining, northern cities show that high taxes and tax burdens have been compounded by low coefficients of tax efficiency. There is, therefore, a real possibility that these cities will experience further outmigration of people and jobs and continued erosion of the municipal tax base.

TABLE 3.4. Changing Patterns of Revenue Usage for Major City Groupings, Fiscal 1969–79 (Per Capita Revenue in Constant 1972 Dollars)

	By Population Change			By Region				
	Growing	Mixed	Declining	Northeast	No. Central	South	West
General Revenue							
Fiscal 1969	175	209	339	386	235	239	282
Fiscal 1975	212	303	427	495	310	319	311
Fiscal 1979	243	346	449	560	330	323	341
Intergovernmental Revenue							
Fiscal 1969	25	48	104	109	60	73	68
Fiscal 1975	54	108	176	203	111	138	94
Fiscal 1979	80	137	200	241	137	130	137
Own-Source Revenue							
Fiscal 1969	150	161	235	277	176	166	214
Fiscal 1975	158	196	251	292	199	181	216
Fiscal 1979	162	210	248	319	193	193	204
Taxes							
Fiscal 1969	107	97	174	226	126	113	144
Fiscal 1975	107	116	179	229	138	119	138
Fiscal 1979	103	121	178	252	136	123	120

| | By Population Density | | | By Differences in Functional Responsibility | | | | |
	Low	Medium	High	Three[a] Functions	Two Functions	One Function	Minimal Amounts	None
General Revenue								
Fiscal 1969	173	241	374	1017	512	315	222	196
Fiscal 1975	239	287	478	1360	673	406	270	242
Fiscal 1979	275	308	504	1175	668	479	293	262
Intergovernmental Revenue								
Fiscal 1969	30	56	121	473	189	89	41	46
Fiscal 1975	77	92	204	714	316	168	78	77
Fiscal 1979	99	117	231	530	329	211	108	94
Own-Source Revenue								
Fiscal 1969	143	185	253	544	323	226	180	151
Fiscal 1975	163	196	273	646	357	238	192	165
Fiscal 1979	175	191	273	645	339	268	185	168
Taxes								
Fiscal 1969	96	121	199	458	252	167	127	100
Fiscal 1975	107	121	207	517	253	175	132	104
Fiscal 1979	112	116	203	505	232	192	121	109

[a] Denotes New York City

Source: Computations based on Census Bureau data.

77

TABLE 3.5. Patterns of Revenue Reliance for Major City Groupings, Fiscal Years 1969 and 1979 (Percent of General Revenues Derived from Each Source)

	By Population Change			By Region			
	Growing	Mixed	Declining	Northeast	No. Central	South	West
Intergovernmental Revenue							
Fiscal 1969	14	23	30	28	25	31	24
Fiscal 1979	34	39	45	43	41	40	40
State Aid							
Fiscal 1969	10	15	19	19	12	23	16
Fiscal 1979	10	14	23	28	15	15	17
Federal Aid							
Fiscal 1969	3	3	8	7	9	4	6
Fiscal 1979	23	21	20	13	24	22	22
Own-Source Revenue							
Fiscal 1969	86	77	70	72	75	69	76
Fiscal 1979	66	61	55	57	59	60	60
Taxes							
Fiscal 1969	61	46	52	59	54	47	52
Fiscal 1979	42	35	40	45	41	38	36
Property Taxes							
Fiscal 1969	37	29	34	41	32	33	32
Fiscal 1979	19	18	20	26	18	21	15

	By Population Density			By Differences in Functional Responsibility				
	Low	Medium	High	Three[a] Functions	Two Functions	One Function	Minimal Amounts	None
Intergovernmental Revenue								
Fiscal 1969	17	24	32	47	36	29	19	23
Fiscal 1979	36	37	46	45	49	44	37	36
State Aid								
Fiscal 1969	10	14	22	45	30	17	9	12
Fiscal 1979	11	13	26	37	31	23	12	10
Federal Aid								
Fiscal 1969	3	5	9	2	6	7	8	6
Fiscal 1979	22	23	19	8	18	16	24	25
Own-Source Revenue								
Fiscal 1969	83	76	68	53	64	71	81	77
Fiscal 1979	64	63	54	55	51	56	63	64
Taxes								
Fiscal 1969	56	50	53	45	50	53	57	51
Fiscal 1979	41	38	40	43	35	40	41	42
Property Taxes								
Fiscal 1969	37	29	36	27	42	27	31	34
Fiscal 1979	22	15	21	22	25	15	15	22

[a] Denotes New York City

Source: Computations based on Census Bureau data.

REVENUE USAGE: INDIVIDUAL CITIES

This section analyzes patterns of revenue usage within individual cities. It demonstrates their growing reliance on intergovernmental aid and illustrates the impact of such aid on municipal tax burdens. It also evaluates the vulnerability of given cities to potential cutbacks in outside aid. The strengths and weaknesses of each city's tax base are examined to determine the ease with which large cities can generate additional own-source revenues. This is particularly crucial given current reductions in Federal aid. Each city's use of current charges is examined and the utilization of such charges is related to local tax burdens. The goal is to evaluate the ability of large U.S. cities to withstand any revenue "crunch" likely to result from the sudden withdrawal of Federal and state aid.

The Basic Stress Indicators, Fiscal Year 1979

A number of revenue configurations appear to be associated with fiscal stress. High and rapidly-rising general revenues may indicate that a city is tapping all available revenue sources to meet it expenditure requirements. Cities characterized by disproportionately high taxes and tax burdens, but which receive a relatively small proportion of their revenues from taxes, may also be in trouble. This configuration suggests that a city is using all available resources, including outside aid, but has nevertheless had to push hard on taxes. High and rising tax burdens accompanied by low coefficients of tax efficiency also suggest problems on the horizon. This configuration is associated with taxpayer dissatisfaction, with the outmigration of people and jobs, and with the attendant erosion of the local tax base. Above-average levels of intergovernmental aid accompanied by extensive reliance on such aid may also be a sign of difficulty. Cities in this situation are highly vulnerable to aid cutbacks and/or changes in aid formulas.

For purposes of analysis, each city has been ranked on a scale of one to 38 in terms of the basic stress indicators: revenue levels, intergovernmental aid, taxes, and tax burdens. The lower the ranking the greater the presumed degree of stress. For example, New York City ranked "first" in terms of per capita taxes; its fiscal 1979 taxes were $864 per capita. By contrast, San Antonio ranked 38th with per capita taxes of only $90. Indexes of change for the fiscal 1969–79 period were computed by dividing relative changes for each city by the average change for the distribution. Index numbers above one hundred indicate above-average rates of change and vice versa.

In fiscal 1979, per capita general revenues ranged from a low of $279 in San Antonio to a high of $2010 in New York City; the mean for the distribution was $685. New York, San Francisco, Baltimore, and Cincinnati were characterized by relatively high revenues in fiscal 1979 but experienced relatively slow revenue growth during the fiscal 1969–79 period. Conversely, a number of cities with disproportionately low fiscal 1979 revenue levels experienced relatively rapid growth of revenues during the 1970s. San Antonio, Ft. Worth, Dallas, Houston, Phoenix, and Omaha were in this category. Therefore, there was a process of convergence, albeit a modest one, between the high-revenue and low-revenue cities.

Those cities characterized by above-average revenue levels and above-average revenue growth would appear to be most prone to fiscal stress. Eight cities—Boston, Newark, Buffalo, Denver, Detroit, Philadelphia, St. Louis, and Atlanta—were characterized by above-average revenue levels in fiscal 1979 and by above-average revenue growth during the fiscal 1969–79 period. Buffalo's fiscal 1979 general revenues were $1071 per capita, well above the 38-city mean; during the fiscal 1969–79 decade, Buffalo's general revenues grew 14% faster than the average rate of growth for the sample cities. Denver's fiscal 1979 general revenues were $912 per capita; during the 1970s, they increased 29% faster than the average for the sample cities.

In fiscal 1979, taxes ranged from a low of $90 per capita in San Antonio to a high of $864 in New York City; the mean for the distribution was $258. Once again, some of the high tax cities experienced relatively slow tax growth. San Francisco, Baltimore, and Newark exemplify this group of cities. San Francisco's fiscal 1979 taxes were $402 per capita; between fiscal 1969 and 1979, they increased at only 44% of the mean rate for the sample cities. Newark's fiscal 1979 taxes were $367 per capita; during the 1970s, they increased at only 27% of this mean. By contrast, a number of cities with relatively low taxes experienced relatively rapid growth of tax revenues between fiscal 1969 and 1979. San Antonio, Phoenix, and Ft. Worth typify this group of cities. In fiscal 1979, municipal taxes in Phoenix were only $138 per capita; between fiscal 1969 and 1979, they increased 10% faster than the 38-city mean. Ft. Worth's fiscal 1979 taxes were only $158 per capita; they increased 30% faster than the 38-city mean.

Those cities characterized by above-average taxes and by above-average tax growth are of concern to fiscal analysts. Seven cities—New York, Boston, Philadelphia, St. Louis, Denver, Kansas City and Cincinnati—exhibited both stress criteria. In fiscal 1979, Boston's taxes were $768 per capita; they increased 19% faster than the average for the sample cities. Philadelphia's fiscal 1979 taxes were $430 per capita; their rate of increase exceeded the 38-city mean by 55%.

In fiscal 1979, the ratio of taxes to personal income ranged from a low of 1.40% in San Diego to a high of 11.88% in New York City; the group mean was 3.74%. Tax burdens in New York, Boston, Newark, Philadelphia, St. Louis, Baltimore, Detroit, Kansas City, San Francisco, Cincinnati, Buffalo, and Denver exceeded this mean; tax burdens in New York, Boston, Newark, and Philadelphia exceeded the 7% stress threshold. However, tax burdens in several high-tax cities—including Newark, Baltimore, San Francisco, and Buffalo—actually eased during the fiscal 1969–79 decade. Tax burdens in Newark declined from almost 11% to about 8%; San Francisco's tax burden declined from 6% to 4%. However, the remaining eight cities were characterized by above-average tax burdens in fiscal 1979 and by above-average increases in tax burdens during the fiscal 1969–79 period; most were also characterized by below-average coefficients of tax efficiency.

In fiscal 1979, per capita intergovernmental aid ranged from a low of $62 in Houston to a high of $906 in New York City; the mean for the distribution was $295. It is apparent that tax burdens eased in some cities, not because expenditure pressures abated, but because intergovernmental aid took up the slack during the 1970s. In fiscal 1979, Newark received intergovernmental aid of $737 per capita; such aid accounted for 64% of Newark's general revenues. Buffalo received per capita aid of $732, which was equivalent to 68% of its general revenues. Four cities—Newark, Buffalo, Detroit, and Minneapolis—were characterized by above-average intergovernmental aid in fiscal 1979 and by above-average aid growth during the fiscal 1969–79 decade.

Based on the above findings, it is possible to draw some tentative conclusions concerning revenue stress in given cities. For example, San Francisco, Baltimore, Newark, and Detroit were characterized by above-average taxes and tax burdens, by below-average reliance on taxes, and by above-average reliance on intergovernmental aid. These cities have apparently pushed hard on taxes but are still heavily dependent on outside aid to finance their expenditures. Boston, New York, Philadelphia, Kansas City, and St. Louis were characterized by high and rapidly-rising taxes and tax burdens and by below-average coefficients of tax efficiency. This combination is likely to arouse taxpayer discontent and to lead to further erosion of the municipal tax base. These findings are summarized in Figure 3.1 and Table 3.6.

The Growing Role of Intergovernmental Aid

This section evaluates the impact of intergovernmental aid on the revenue positions of large cities. It analyzes the new mix of outside aid and locally-generated revenue; it determines what proportion of total expenditures in given cities were being financed by outside aid as of fiscal 1979; and, it demonstrates how tax burdens were affected by recent increases in intergovernmental aid.

Intergovernmental aid is a highly variable and unpredictable revenue source. The amounts of aid available and the timing of aid payments are subject to changes in aid formulas, aid legislation, and administrative

A. Level and Growth of Taxes versus Tax Reliance

Index of Tax Change, FY 69–79	Per Capita Taxes, Fiscal Year 1979		
	Above Average	Below Average	
Above Average	Boston Cincinnati Denver Kansas City New York Philadelphia St. Louis	Atlanta Chicago Columbus Dallas Ft. Worth Houston Indianapolis	Louisville Seattle Minneapolis Oklahoma City Omaha Phoenix Portland San Antonio
Below Average	Baltimore Detroit Newark San Francisco	Buffalo Cleveland Honolulu Long Beach Los Angeles Memphis Milwaukee	New Orleans Oakland Pittsburgh San Diego Toledo

Tax Reliance FY 1979	Per Capita Taxes, Fiscal Year 1979		
	Above Average	Below Average	
Above Average	Boston Cincinnati Kansas City New York Philadelphia St. Louis	Chicago Dallas Ft. Worth Honolulu Houston Los Angeles	Oklahoma City Omaha Pittsburgh Portland Seattle
Below Average	Baltimore Denver Detroit Newark San Francisco	Atlanta Buffalo Cleveland Columbus Indianapolis Long Beach Louisville Memphis	Milwaukee Minneapolis New Orleans Oakland Phoenix San Antonio San Diego Toledo

FIGURE 3.1.

(continued on next page)

B. Tax Burdens versus Coefficients of Tax Efficiency

Percent Change in
Tax Burdens
FY 69–79 — Tax Burdens, 1979

	Above Average	Below Average	
Above Average	Boston Cincinnati Denver Detroit Kansas City New York Philadelphia St. Louis	Atlanta Chicago Columbus Dallas Ft. Worth Houston Indianapolis	Louisville Minneapolis Oklahoma City Omaha Seattle
Below Average	Baltimore Buffalo Newark San Francisco	Cleveland Honolulu Long Beach Los Angeles Memphis Milwaukee New Orleans Oakland Phoenix	Pittsburgh Portland San Antonio San Diego Toledo

Tax Burdens, 1979

Coefficient of
Tax Efficiency, 1979

	Above Average	Below Average	
Above Average	Detroit	Cleveland Columbus Dallas Indianapolis Long Beach Los Angeles Memphis Milwaukee	Minneapolis Oakland Phoenix Pittsburgh Portland San Antonio San Diego Seattle Toledo
Below Average	Baltimore Boston Buffalo Cincinnati Denver Kansas City Newark New York Philadelphia San Francisco St. Louis	Atlanta Chicago Ft. Worth Honolulu Houston Louisville New Orleans Oklahoma City Omaha	

FIGURE 3.1 *(cont'd)*

C. Level and Growth of Intergovernmental Aid versus Aid Reliance

Index of Change in Intergovernmental Aid, FY 69–79	Per Capita Intergovernmental Aid, Fiscal Year 1979			
	Above Average		Below Average	
Above Average	Buffalo Detroit Minneapolis Newark		Atlanta Cleveland Columbus Dallas Ft. Worth Honolulu Houston Indianapolis Kansas City Long Beach Los Angeles Louisville	New Orleans Oakland Oklahoma City Omaha Philadelphia Phoenix Pittsburgh Portland San Antonio San Diego St. Louis Toledo
Below Average	Baltimore Boston Memphis New York San Francisco		Cincinnati Chicago Denver Milwaukee Seattle	

Aid Reliance, FY 1979	Per Capita Intergovernmental Aid, Fiscal Year 1979			
	Above Average		Below Average	
Above Average	Baltimore Boston Buffalo Detroit Memphis Minneapolis	Newark New York San Francisco	Cleveland Indianapolis Milwaukee New Orleans Omaha Phoenix Pittsburgh	San Diego Toledo
Below Average			Atlanta Chicago Cincinnati Columbus Dallas Denver Ft. Worth Honolulu Houston Kansas City Long Beach	Los Angeles Louisville Oakland Oklahoma City Philadelphia Portland San Antonio Seattle St. Louis

FIGURE 3.1 *(cont'd)*

TABLE 3.6. The Basic Stress Indicators: Revenue Levels, Intergovernmental Aid, Taxes, Tax Burdens

	General Revenue				Intergovernmental Aid			
Rank	City	Per Capita General Revenue FY 79	Index of Change FY 69–79	Rank	City	Per Capita Intergovernmental Aid, FY 79	Index of Change FY 69–79	Aid Reliance (%)
1	New York	$2010	77	1	New York	$906	42	45
2	Boston	1624	103	2	San Francisco	755	75	51
3	San Francisco	1470	78	3	Newark	737	195	64
4	Baltimore	1207	70	4	Buffalo	732	102	68
5	Newark	1155	103	5	Baltimore	698	52	58
6	Buffalo	1071	114	6	Boston	676	88	42
7	Denver	912	129	7	Detroit	423	156	49
8	Detroit	860	129	8	Memphis	403	73	61
9	Philadelphia	811	119	9	Minneapolis	309	147	51
10	St. Louis	758	121	10	Cincinnati	291	12	40
11	Cincinnati	721	27	11	Denver	287	82	32
12	Atlanta	708	163	12	New Orleans	271	289	45
13	Memphis	665	93	13	Louisville	266	101	40
14	Louisville	659	85	14	Philadelphia	254	119	31
15	Kansas City	656	142	15	Cleveland	249	420	43
16	Minneapolis	611	126	16	Indianapolis	244	656	47

Left ranking:

Rank	City		
17	New Orleans	596	125
18	Oakland	584	84
19	Cleveland	580	133
20	Long Beach	576	79
21	Seattle	559	88
22	Portland	522	105
23	Indianapolis	517	290
24	Oklahoma City	497	159
25	Los Angeles	486	83
26	Milwaukee	476	68
27	Chicago	463	90
28	Omaha	450	189
29	Honolulu	427	70
30	Pittsburgh	419	82
31	Toledo	414	113
32	Phoenix	407	115
33	Columbus	403	125
34	Dallas	390	123
35	Houston	377	154
36	Ft. Worth	365	134
37	San Diego	363	94
38	San Antonio	279	174
	Mean	685	100

Right ranking:

Rank	City			
17	St. Louis	238	337	31
18	Milwaukee	237	53	50
19	Oakland	236	129	40
20	Atlanta	233	213	33
21	Phoenix	196	119	48
22	Long Beach	194	189	34
23	Portland	188	153	36
24	Omaha	186	307	41
25	Los Angeles	178	147	37
26	Kansas City	178	386	27
27	Pittsburgh	173	117	41
28	Chicago	173	93	37
29	Seattle	173	38	31
30	Toledo	169	162	41
31	Honolulu	160	225	38
32	Oklahoma City	158	197	32
33	San Diego	152	183	42
34	Columbus	144	146	36
35	Ft. Worth	110	744	30
36	San Antonio	106	598	38
37	Dallas	67	817	17
38	Houston	62	471	16
	Mean	295	100	41

(continued on next page)

TABLE 3.6 *(cont'd)*

		Taxes					Tax Burdens versus Tax Efficiency		
Rank	City	Per Capita Taxes FY 79	Index of Change FY 69–79	Tax Reliance (%)	Rank	City	Tax Burden, 1979 (%)	Percent Change 1969–79	Coefficient of Tax Efficiency[a] 1979
1	New York	$864	111	43	1	New York	11.88	+21	3.61
2	Boston	768	119	47	2	Boston	11.72	+17	5.05
3	Philadelphia	430	155	53	3	Newark	8.12	−26	5.66
4	San Francisco	402	44	27	4	Philadelphia	7.10	+46	6.69
5	St. Louis	395	125	52	5	St. Louis	6.72	+18	6.36
6	Baltimore	384	71	32	6	Baltimore	6.54	− 8	7.01
7	Newark	367	27	32	7	Detroit	4.54	+10	12.47
8	Denver	338	157	37	8	Kansas City	4.48	+49	8.99
9	Kansas City	335	190	51	9	San Francisco	4.34	−29	9.55
10	Detroit	282	92	33	10	Cincinnati	4.11	+19	10.56
11	Cincinnati	282	130	39	11	Buffalo	4.01	−13	9.01
12	Chicago	239	106	51	12	Denver	3.95	+22	10.26
13	Buffalo	238	64	22	13	Atlanta	3.52	+46	9.32
14	Atlanta	230	163	33	14	Louisville	3.45	+14	10.58
15	Dallas	223	131	57	15	Chicago	3.44	+14	11.85
16	Honolulu	222	59	52	16	Cleveland	3.26	−13	12.75
17	Seattle	220	172	39	17	New Orleans	3.06	−13	9.05
18	Louisville	217	115	33	18	Pittsburgh	3.03	−16	12.52
19	Pittsburgh	207	70	49	19	Honolulu	2.80	−24	9.60

20	Houston	207	159	55	20	Minneapolis	2.74	+18	13.70
21	Oklahoma City	207	197	42	21	Omaha	2.63	+42	8.68
22	Minneapolis	206	125	34	22	Oklahoma City	2.60	+39	10.00
23	Portland	202	105	39	23	Dallas	2.59	+12	12.16
24	New Orleans	200	90	34	24	Portland	2.50	*	15.76
25	Omaha	198	182	44	25	Seattle	2.37	+37	17.25
26	Cleveland	188	63	32	26	Houston	2.35	+11	10.31
27	Los Angeles	188	50	39	27	Memphis	2.33	− 5	15.33
28	Oakland	173	40	30	28	Oakland	2.25	−30	17.43
29	Indianapolis	161	157	31	29	Los Angeles	2.24	−24	14.19
30	Ft. Worth	158	130	43	30	Milwaukee	2.22	−17	14.88
31	Milwaukee	158	69	33	31	Columbus	2.17	+28	15.70
32	Toledo	152	94	37	32	Ft. Worth	2.16	+16	10.81
33	Memphis	151	99	23	33	Toledo	2.15	*	15.40
34	Columbus	147	151	36	34	Indianapolis	2.12	+34	12.94
35	Long Beach	142	59	25	35	Phoenix	1.83	+ 2	17.25
36	Phoenix	138	110	34	36	Long Beach	1.70	−18	27.58
37	San Diego	112	74	31	37	San Antonio	1.59	+ 6	13.79
38	San Antonio	90	119	32	38	San Diego	1.40	−17	16.70
	Mean	258	100	38		Mean	3.74	+ 7	11.86

[a] Represents the average coefficient for the following functions: Highways, Fire Protection, Police Protection, Sanitation, Parks and Recreation.

*Less than 0.5%

Source: Computations based on Census Bureau data.

regulations. Coefficients of dispersion illustrate the wide variability of Federal and state aid. During the fiscal 1969–79 period, the mean coefficient of dispersion for Federal aid to the sample cities was 1.18; the mean coefficient for state aid was 1.37. By contrast, the mean coefficient of dispersion for own-source revenues was only 0.68 and the coefficient for general expenditures was 0.71. These lower coefficients indicate considerably less variability.

During the 1970s, intergovernmental aid supplanted own-source revenues to some extent in each of the sample cities. At the same time, the Federal government supplanted the states as the dominant source of aid in all but a few large cities. In fiscal 1969, 31 of the 38 cities received more aid from their respective states than from the Federal government. A decade later, 28 of them received more Federal than state aid. State aid continued to predominate only in Baltimore, Buffalo, Boston, Memphis, Milwaukee, Newark, New York, Philadelphia, Pittsburgh, and San Francisco. Six of these cities have dependent school systems that receive state support.

Although most large cities received more Federal than state aid in fiscal 1979, the growing dependence on Federal aid was especially pronounced in cities like Denver and San Diego. Denver received almost 16 times as much state aid as Federal aid in fiscal 1969; in fiscal 1979, Federal aid exceeded state aid to the City by 22%. San Diego received almost 10 times as much state aid as Federal aid in fiscal 1969; it received 25% more Federal aid in fiscal 1979. Even in cities where state aid continued to predominate, the ratio of state-to-Federal aid declined sharply during the fiscal 1969–79 decade. For example, New York City received almost 27 times as much state aid as Federal aid in fiscal 1969, but less than five times as much a decade later.

These findings are summarized in Table 3.7.

In fiscal 1979, per capita Federal aid to the sample cities ranged from a low of $48 in Newark to a high of $302 in San Francisco; the mean for the distribution was $140 per capita. Per capita state aid ranged from a low of $4 in Ft. Worth to a high of $747 in New York City; the mean was $142 per capita.

In fiscal 1979, seven cities—Buffalo, Cleveland, New Orleans, Honolulu, Minneapolis, Kansas City, and Oklahoma City—were characterized by above-average amounts of Federal aid and by above-average reliance on Federal aid; during the fiscal 1969–79 decade, each also experienced above-average growth of Federal aid. In fiscal 1979, Newark, San Francisco, Boston, Detroit, Philadelphia, and Minneapolis received above-average amounts of state aid; each experienced above-average growth of state aid during the fiscal 1969–79 decade; each was also highly dependent on state aid. Dallas and Houston were virtually the only large cities to remain relatively independent of both Federal and state aid. In fiscal 1979, Dallas received 16% of its general revenues from the Federal government and 1%

TABLE 3.7. The Ratio of State-to-Federal Aid, Fiscal Years 1969 and 1979 (Percents)

		Ratio				Ratio	
Rank	City	FY 1969	FY 1979	Rank	City	FY 1969	FY 1979
1	Buffalo	31.47	1.72	21	Portland	1.95	0.32
2	New York	26.73	4.83	22	San Francisco	1.86	1.49
3	Long Beach	20.98	0.59	23	Detroit	1.80	0.99
4	Baltimore	17.86	1.75	24	Atlanta	1.65	0.75
5	Newark	15.76	14.10	25	Phoenix	1.49	0.81
6	Denver	15.68	0.82	26	Cincinnati	1.24	0.30
7	Memphis	15.27	2.24	27	Kansas City	1.24	0.18
8	San Diego	9.76	0.80	28	Omaha	1.17	0.34
9	New Orleans	9.20	0.27	29	Dallas	1.09	0.09
10	Indianapolis	7.05	0.97	30	Philadelphia	1.04	1.81
11	Minneapolis	6.70	0.95	31	Toledo	1.03	0.25
12	Milwaukee	5.63	2.48	32	Pittsburgh	0.96	1.29
13	Cleveland	5.18	0.27	33	Oakland	0.74	0.48
14	Los Angeles	5.00	0.70	34	Oklahoma City	0.64	0.06
15	Seattle	4.17	0.54	35	Chicago	0.41	0.42
16	Honolulu	3.66	0.11	36	Louisville	0.20	0.08
17	Columbus	3.18	0.34	37	Ft. Worth	0.18	0.04
18	Boston	3.17	1.70	38	Houston	0.10	0.09
19	St. Louis	2.85	0.64				
20	San Antonio	2.67	0.09				

Source: Computations based on Census Bureau data.

from the State of Texas. By contrast, Minneapolis, a city that was heavily dependent on outside aid, received 25% of its general revenues from the Federal government and 24% from the State of Minnesota.

Ratios of own-source revenues-to-outside aid and outside aid-to-general expenditures provide additional evidence of how dependent large cities have become on intergovernmental aid.* For example, the adjusted ratios of own-

---

*The census statistics used in these ratios were partly standardized to reflect intercity differences in the mix of functions performed. Intergovernmental aid for education and welfare was subtracted from the aid totals; expenditures for education and welfare were subtracted from general expenditures; and current charges for education were subtracted from own-source revenues. A number of inconsistencies nevertheless remain. For example, states may assist their cities by financing a given municipal function or by performing that function directly. State aid would be lower in the latter case than in the former.

source revenue-to-intergovernmental aid were actually less than one in Buffalo, Memphis, and Minneapolis. Buffalo raised only 69¢ locally for every aid dollar it received; Memphis and Minneapolis raised 96¢ and 97¢ respectively for every dollar of intergovernmental aid. Although own-source revenue exceeded outside aid on an adjusted basis in each of the remaining cities, Baltimore, Phoenix, New Orleans, Cleveland, San Diego, Milwaukee, and Detroit raised relatively small amounts of locally-generated revenue— ranging from $1.01 to $1.39—for every aid dollar. Between fiscal 1969 and 1979, Baltimore raised only an additional 69¢ for every added aid dollar; locally-generated revenue in Buffalo increased by only 41¢ for every added dollar of aid.

By contrast, a number of large cities including New York, Kansas City, St. Louis, Denver, Dallas, and Houston, enjoyed a relatively healthy relationship between own-source revenue and outside aid. On an adjusted basis, Denver generated $3.18 from its own sources for every aid dollar it received; Dallas raised $4.80 locally for every dollar of outside aid. Between fiscal 1969 and 1979, Denver raised an additional $2.62 for every added dollar of outside aid; Dallas raised an additional $3.24.

The adjusted ratio of outside aid-to-general expenditures also under-scores the fragile revenue positions of several large cities. In fiscal 1979, the adjusted ratio of outside aid-to-general expenditures was 50% or more in Buffalo, Memphis, Baltimore, San Diego, Minneapolis, Milwaukee, New-ark, Detroit, San Francisco, and New Orleans; it exceeded 70% in Buffalo and Memphis. Equally significant is the fact that in 20 of the 38 cities, aid increases between fiscal 1969 and 1979 were equivalent to at least half the total increase in general spending. These cities included: Buffalo, Memphis, Baltimore, San Diego, Minneapolis, Milwaukee, Newark, Detroit, San Francisco, New Orleans, Los Angeles, Phoenix, New York, Oakland, Honolulu, Indianapolis, Omaha, Chicago, Cleveland, and Portland. The adjusted ratio of aid-to-expenditure increases was 92% in Buffalo, 84% in Memphis, and 89% in San Diego. In effect, 92% of expenditure increases in Buffalo were covered by increases in intergovernmental aid.

Most of the remaining cities exhibited a healthier relationship between outside aid and expenditures. In fiscal 1979, outside aid was equivalent to less than one-third of general spending, on an adjusted basis, in Kansas City, Ft. Worth, Philadelphia, Columbus, St. Louis, Atlanta, Denver, Dallas, and Houston. The adjusted ratio of aid-to-expenditure inreases for the fiscal 1969–79 period was 23% in Houston, 25% in Dallas, 32% in Atlanta, and 33% in Columbus. These cities appear to be better insulated against possible reductions in intergovernmental aid.

The above findings are summarized in Figure 3.2 and Table 3.8.

Thus far, the analysis has focused on the negative consequences of the growing municipal dependence on intergovernmental aid. However, there have also been a number of positive by-products. For example, the infusion of large amounts of intergovernmental aid into large U.S. cities has helped to stabilize and, in some cases, to reduce municipal tax burdens. A number of researchers have demonstrated the beneficial impact of outside aid on local taxes. Steven Gold, who studied the distribution of funds under the General Revenue Sharing (GRS) program, the Comprehensive Employment and Training Act (CETA), the Community Development Block Grant (CDBG) program, and the Anti-Recession Fiscal Assistance (ARFA) program, estimated that between 50% and 70% of GRS, ARFA, and CETA funds, and 85% of CDBG funds resulted in higher local spending. He also found that:

> "Approximately three-fourths of revenue sharing funds which did not result in higher spending went into tax reduction, with the other fourth leading to lower borrowing ... intergovernmental aid has been far more important than any other mechanism for relieving property taxes."[22]

Patrick Larkey studied the budgetary impact of general revenue sharing in five U.S. cities—Albuquerque, New Mexico; Ann Arbor, Michigan; Cincinnati, Ohio; Detroit, Michigan; and Worcester, Massachusetts—and came to a similar conclusion. He found:

> "Where fiscal pressure exists, GRS funds tend to be merged with other general operating funds and used to support recurrent expenditure obligations. ..."[23]

However, Larkey noted that in the absence of fiscal pressures, GRS funds were sometimes used to displace local revenues, a process that can lead to reduced taxes.

This study found that, in general, the higher the proportion of expenditure increases that were covered by increases in intergovernmental aid, the smaller the rise in tax burdens. In fact, tax burdens actually declined in cities characterized by high ratios of aid-to-expenditure increases. Between fiscal 1969 and fiscal 1979, the adjusted ratio of aid-to-expenditure increases was 60% or more in Oakland, San Francisco, Newark, Los Angeles, Honolulu, Milwaukee, San Diego, Buffalo, New Orleans, Baltimore, and Memphis. Tax burdens declined in each of these cities between fiscal 1969 and 1979. Declines ranged from 5% in Memphis to 30% in Oakland. By contrast, the adjusted ratio of aid-to-expenditure increases was less than 40% in Philadelphia, Atlanta, Oklahoma City, Seattle, Columbus, and Denver. Tax burdens in each of these cities increased substantially between fiscal 1969 and 1979. It should be kept in mind, however, that there were other influences on taxes and tax burdens in given cities in addition to the level and rate of increase in intergovernmental aid.

A. Relationship Between Aid Growth and Aid Reliance: Federal Aid

Index of Change in Federal Aid FY 1969–79	Per Capita Federal Aid, Fiscal Year 1979			
	Above Average		Below Average	
Above Average	Baltimore, Buffalo, Cleveland, Denver, Honolulu, Kansas City	Minneapolis, New Orleans, New York, Oklahoma City, St. Louis	Atlanta, Columbus, Dallas, Ft. Worth, Houston, Indianapolis	Long Beach, Los Angeles, Memphis, Omaha, Portland, San Antonio, San Diego, Seattle
Below Average	Boston, Detroit, Cincinnati, Louisville, Oakland, San Francisco		Chicago, Milwaukee, Newark, Philadelphia, Phoenix	Pittsburgh, Toledo

Reliance on Federal Aid, FY 1979	Per Capita Federal Aid, Fiscal Year 1979			
	Above Average		Below Average	
Above Average	Buffalo, Cincinnati, Cleveland, Detroit, Honolulu, Kansas City	Louisville, Minneapolis, New Orleans, Oakland, Oklahoma City	Chicago, Columbus, Ft. Worth, Indianapolis, Omaha, Phoenix	Portland, San Antonio, San Diego, Toledo
Below Average	Baltimore, Boston, Denver, New York, San Francisco, St. Louis		Atlanta, Dallas, Houston, Long Beach, Los Angeles, Memphis, Milwaukee	Newark, Seattle, Philadelphia, Pittsburgh

FIGURE 3.2. *(continued on next page)*

B. Relationship Between Aid Growth and Aid Reliance: State Aid

Index of Change in State Aid FY 1969–79	Per Capita State Aid, Fiscal Year 1979			
	Above Average		Below Average	
Above Average	Boston Detroit Minneapolis Newark Philadelphia San Francisco		Atlanta Chicago Cleveland Dallas Ft. Worth Houston Indianapolis	Kansas City San Diego Long Beach St. Louis Los Angeles Oakland Omaha Phoenix Pittsburgh
Below Average	Baltimore Buffalo Memphis Milwaukee New York		Cincinnati Columbus Denver Honolulu Louisville New Orleans	Oklahoma City Portland San Antonio Seattle Toledo

Reliance on State Aid FY 1979	Per Capita State Aid, Fiscal Year 1979		
	Above Average		Below Average
Above Average	Baltimore Boston Buffalo Detroit Memphis Milwaukee	Minneapolis Newark New York Philadelphia San Francisco	Indianapolis Pittsburgh Phoenix San Diego
Below Average			Atlanta Long Beach Chicago Los Angeles Cincinnati Louisville Cleveland New Orleans Columbus Oakland Dallas Omaha Denver Oklahoma City Ft. Worth San Antonio Honolulu Seattle Houston St. Louis Kansas City Portland Toledo

FIGURE 3.2 (cont'd)

TABLE 3.8. Selected Measures of Aid Reliance

		Federal Aid					State Aid		
Rank	City	Per Capita Federal Aid FY 1979	Index of Change FY 69–79	Aid Reliance, FY 79 (%)	Rank	City	Per Capita State Aid FY 1979	Index of Change FY 69–79	Aid Reliance FY 79 (%)
1	San Francisco	$302	31	21	1	New York	$747	53	37
2	Baltimore	252	182	21	2	Newark	683	351	59
3	Boston	250	54	15	3	San Francisco	451	109	31
4	Buffalo	234	544	22	4	Baltimore	440	41	36
5	Louisville	228	40	35	5	Boston	425	115	26
6	New Orleans	212	902	36	6	Buffalo	403	97	38
7	Detroit	191	86	22	7	Detroit	190	206	22
8	Cleveland	189	765	33	8	Memphis	185	92	28
9	Cincinnati	187	33	26	9	Milwaukee	166	67	35
10	Denver	158	349	17	10	Philadelphia	160	259	20
11	Oakland	156	59	27	11	Minneapolis	147	129	24
12	Minneapolis	156	253	25	12	Denver	129	41	14
13	New York	155	107	8	13	Indianapolis	120	590	23
14	Kansas City	151	265	23	14	Pittsburgh	94	233	22
15	Oklahoma City	148	110	30	15	Atlanta	93	291	13
16	St. Louis	145	294	19	16	St. Louis	93	279	12
17	Honolulu	144	357	34	17	Phoenix	86	148	21

18	Portland	134	129	26
19	Omaha	133	252	30
20	Toledo	131	99	32
21	Atlanta	124	146	18
22	Indianapolis	123	955	24
23	Chicago	121	33	26
24	Long Beach	115	1173	20
25	Phoenix	106	65	26
26	Columbus	104	189	26
27	Seattle	103	124	18
28	Los Angeles	103	226	21
29	Ft. Worth	102	405	28
30	San Antonio	95	768	34
31	Philadelphia	88	27	11
32	Memphis	83	190	12
33	San Diego	80	405	22
34	Pittsburgh	73	33	17
35	Milwaukee	67	45	14
36	Dallas	61	1419	16
37	Houston	55	234	15
38	Newark	48	83	4
	Mean	140	100	22

18	Oakland	75	165	13
19	Los Angeles	72	109	15
20	Long Beach	68	111	12
21	San Diego	64	114	18
22	New Orleans	58	81	10
23	Cincinnati	56	1	8
24	Seattle	56	34	10
25	Cleveland	51	145	9
26	Chicago	51	164	11
27	Omaha	45	313	10
28	Portland	43	61	8
29	Columbus	36	54	9
30	Toledo	33	79	8
31	Kansas City	27	139	4
32	Louisville	18	46	3
33	Honolulu	16	3	4
34	Oklahoma City	9	2	2
35	San Antonio	8	70	3
36	Dallas	5	503	1
37	Houston	5	1052	1
38	Ft. Worth	4	417	1
		142	100	16

(continued on next page)

97

TABLE 3.8 *(cont'd)*

	Own-Source Revenue versus Outside Aid[a]				Outside Aid versus Expenditures[a]		
Rank	City	Own-Source Revenue/Outside Aid, FY 1979	Change in Own-Source Revenue/Outside Aid, FY 1969–79	Rank	City	Outside Aid/General Expenditures, FY 79	Change in Outside Aid/General Expenditures, FY 1969–79
1	Buffalo	0.69	0.41	1	Buffalo	0.74	0.92
2	Memphis	0.96	0.72	2	Memphis	0.72	0.84
3	Minneapolis	0.97	0.69	3	Baltimore	0.59	0.71
4	Milwaukee	1.01	0.77	4	San Diego	0.56	0.89
5	Detroit	1.04	0.74	5	Minneapolis	0.56	0.65
6	Baltimore	1.07	0.69	6	Milwaukee	0.55	0.69
7	Phoenix	1.08	0.79	7	Newark	0.54	0.80
8	New Orleans	1.21	0.72	8	Detroit	0.53	0.61
9	Cleveland	1.33	0.80	9	San Francisco	0.51	0.62
10	San Diego	1.39	0.80	10	New Orleans	0.50	0.67
11	Indianapolis	1.40	1.11	11	Los Angeles	0.49	0.72
12	San Francisco	1.41	0.90	12	Phoenix	0.47	0.51
13	Newark	1.41	0.48	13	New York	0.47	0.59
14	Omaha	1.41	1.08	14	Cincinnati	0.46	0.32
15	Pittsburgh	1.42	0.87	15	Oakland	0.45	0.61
16	Toledo	1.45	0.99	16	Honolulu	0.44	0.81
17	Cincinnati	1.48	1.84	17	Indianapolis	0.44	0.52
18	Louisville	1.48	1.11	18	Omaha	0.44	0.55
19	Oakland	1.48	0.87	19	Louisville	0.41	0.43
20	San Antonio	1.64	1.13	20	Chicago	0.40	0.54

Rank	City	Ratio	Rank	City	Ratio	Ratio	Ratio
21	Honolulu	1.66	21	Cleveland	0.73	0.39	0.52
22	Chicago	1.73	22	Boston	1.30	0.38	0.45
23	Los Angeles	1.73	23	Pittsburgh	1.03	0.38	0.46
24	Portland	1.77	24	Portland	1.22	0.37	0.51
25	Columbus	1.80	25	Toledo	1.39	0.37	0.48
26	Long Beach	1.98	26	Seattle	1.09	0.36	0.30
27	Atlanta	2.06	27	San Antonio	1.65	0.35	0.46
28	Oklahoma City	2.15	28	Long Beach	1.74	0.34	0.44
29	Boston	2.22	29	Oklahoma City	1.73	0.34	0.39
30	Seattle	2.23	30	Kansas City	2.64	0.32	0.46
31	Ft. Worth	2.31	31	Ft. Worth	1.49	0.32	0.42
32	Philadelphia	2.38	32	Philadelphia	1.93	0.31	0.36
33	New York	2.58	33	Columbus	2.08	0.29	0.33
34	Kansas City	2.69	34	St. Louis	1.91	0.28	0.38
35	St. Louis	2.72	35	Atlanta	1.82	0.28	0.32
36	Denver	3.18	36	Denver	2.62	0.27	0.34
37	Dallas	4.80	37	Dallas	3.24	0.17	0.25
38	Houston	5.06	38	Houston	3.83	0.17	0.23
	Mean	1.85		Mean	1.34	0.42	0.53

[a]Note: These ratios have been adjusted to reflect intercity differences in the mix of functions performed.
Source: Computations based on Census Bureau data.

The relationship between expenditure increases, aid increases, and tax burdens is shown in Table 3.9.

It is clear that increases in Federal and state aid helped to stabilize and in some cases to reduce tax burdens in large U.S. cities. However, such aid appears to have been a temporary palliative that masked fundamental weaknesses in the tax bases of large U.S. cities and delayed much-needed fiscal adjustments.

Tax Base Strengths and Weaknesses

Given current budgetary crises at the Federal and state levels, it seems likely that many cities will be thrown back on their own resources in the near future. The strength of their respective tax bases will be crucial to their ability to remain solvent and to maintain essential public services. The viability of the municipal tax base is a function of its size, its relative diversity, and its responsiveness to economic growth. The size of the local tax base is generally expressed in terms of taxable property values, incomes, and/or retail sales and is measured on a per capita basis. Collectively, these measures indicate the potential for generating local public revenues. The higher the value of each tax base, the lower the tax effort needed to generate the target level of revenues. Also important is the capacity of the tax base to expand. Cities that possess a rapidly-growing tax base have less need to periodically increase tax rates. A related consideration is the diversity of the municipal tax base. Diversity is needed because each particular tax base responds differently to cyclical upswings and downturns. Sales and income taxes are more income elastic than property taxes; they can rise relatively rapidly during upturns but may also plunge relatively steeply during recessions. A major advantage of a general sales or income tax in addition to a tax on real-property is that sales and income taxes allow cities to tap the wealth of non-residents who work or shop in the city.

Whereas 28 of the 38 cities received at least half their tax receipts from the property tax in fiscal 1969, only 18 were dependent on property taxes for at least half their tax revenues a decade later. As of fiscal 1979, only Boston, Buffalo, Indianapolis, and Milwaukee continued to rely almost exclusively on the property tax. Boston received 99% of its tax revenues from the property tax, which helps to explain the climate leading to enactment of Massachusetts' Proposition 2½. In most large cities, however, the ratio of property taxes-to-total taxes declined sharply during the fiscal 1969–79 decade; from 70% to 36% in Cleveland, from 61% to 28% in Oakland, from 94% to 57% in San Antonio, and from 81% to 46% in San Francisco.

General sales taxes were enacted in a number of large cities during the 1970s, thereby helping to stem the rise in property taxes and property tax burdens. Between fiscal 1969 and 1979, Kansas City, Omaha, San Antonio,

TABLE 3.9. The Relationship Between Expenditure Increases, Aid Increases, and Tax Burdens, Fiscal 1969–79

Rank	City	Percent Change in Tax Burdens	Ratio of Aid-to-Expenditure Increases	Rank	City	Percent Change in Tax Burdens	Ratio of Aid-to-Expenditure Increases
1	Oakland	−30	0.61	21	Dallas	+12	0.25
2	San Francisco	−29	0.62	22	Louisville	+14	0.43
3	Newark	−26	0.80	23	Chicago	+14	0.54
4	Los Angeles	−24	0.72	24	Ft. Worth	+16	0.42
5	Honolulu	−24	0.81	25	Boston	+17	0.45
6	Long Beach	−18	0.44	26	St. Louis	+18	0.38
7	Milwaukee	−17	0.69	27	Minneapolis	+18	0.65
8	San Diego	−17	0.89	28	Cincinnati	+19	0.32
9	Pittsburgh	−16	0.46	29	New York	+21	0.59
10	Buffalo	−13	0.92	30	Denver	+22	0.34
11	Cleveland	−13	0.52	31	Columbus	+28	0.33
12	New Orleans	−13	0.67	32	Indianapolis	+34	0.52
13	Baltimore	−8	0.71	33	Seattle	+37	0.30
14	Memphis	−5	0.84	34	Oklahoma City	+39	0.39
15	Portland	0	0.51	35	Omaha	+42	0.55
16	Toledo	0	0.48	36	Atlanta	+46	0.32
17	Phoenix	+2	0.51	37	Philadelphia	+46	0.36
18	San Antonio	+6	0.46	38	Kansas City	+49	0.46
19	Detroit	+10	0.61				
20	Houston	+11	0.23				

Note: The ratio of aid-to-expenditure increases has been adjusted to reflect intercity differences in the mix of functions performed.
Source: Computations based on Census Bureau data.

Seattle, and St. Louis enacted a general sales tax. As of fiscal 1979, 19 of the 38 cities used a general sales tax; 14 of them are located in the south or west, where municipal boundaries remain sufficiently flexible to allow the annexation of surrounding suburbs. Otherwise retailers would move beyond the city's reach to less heavily-taxed suburbs.

In fiscal 1979, 12 of the 38 cities utilized a local personal income tax, the same number as in fiscal 1969. Ten of the 12 are located in the northeast or midwest; most are impacted by surrounding suburbs and cannot use a general sales tax for fear of losing retail activity. Three cities—Kansas City, St. Louis, and New York—used both a general sales tax and an income tax in addition to the property tax.

Not only did large cities diversify their tax bases during the 1970s, but those cities that levied an income or general sales tax in both fiscal 1969 and 1979 relied more heavily on these taxes in fiscal 1979 than they did a decade earlier. For example, the ratio of sales taxes-to-total taxes rose from 5% to 24% in Dallas, from 36% to 45% in Denver, from 6% to 28% in Ft. Worth, from 12% to 28% in Houston, from 25% to 31% in Long Beach, and from 37% to 58% in Oklahoma City. The ratio of income taxes-to-total taxes increased from 27% to 60% in Cleveland, from 43% to 71% in Cincinnati, from 53% to 62% in Louisville, from 17% to 23% in New York, and from 49% to 65% in Philadelphia.

Some caution is needed in interpreting these statistics. The ratio of income tax revenues to total tax revenues was 19% in Baltimore and 65% in Philadelphia. However, unlike Philadelphia, Baltimore has a dependent school district which, like most school districts, is financed through property taxes. If school district revenues were included for Philadelphia as they are for Baltimore, Philadelphia's reliance on income taxes would also appear to be much lower.[24] Therefore, intercity differences in functional responsibilities can have a major bearing on the results.

Property taxes and tax burdens were perceptibly lower in cities that used general sales or income taxes in addition to the property tax. In fiscal 1979, Atlanta, Boston, Buffalo, Honolulu, Indianapolis, Memphis, Milwaukee, Minneapolis, Newark, and Portland used neither a general sales nor an income tax. The mean per capita property tax for these cities (excluding Boston) was $171; the mean property tax burden was 2.66%. Baltimore, Cincinnati, Cleveland, Columbus, Detroit, Louisville, Philadelphia, Pittsburgh, and Toledo levied a local income tax in addition to the property tax. Property taxes in these cities averaged only $94 per capita and the mean property tax burden was 1.51%. Chicago, Dallas, Denver, Ft. Worth, Houston, Long Beach, Los Angeles, New Orleans, Oakland, Oklahoma City, Omaha, Phoenix, San Antonio, San Diego, San Francisco, and Seattle levied a general sales tax in addition to the local property tax. Property taxes in these cities averaged only $84 per capita and the mean tax burden was only 1.05%.

In fiscal 1979, property taxes in cities with neither an income nor a general sales tax were approximately double property taxes in cities that levied either of these taxes. Property tax burdens in cities without an income or general sales tax were 1.8 times those of cities with an income tax and 2.5 times those of cities with a general sales tax.

These findings are summarized in Table 3.10.

The need to draw upon more than one tax base becomes clear when recent growth rates for the property, sales, and incomes tax bases of large U.S. cities are examined. The per capita market value of taxable property was computed for 18 of the 38 cities. Market values in each city were determined by applying the mean ratio of assessed-to-market value to the assessed value of real-property less partial exemptions. The mean ratio of assessed-to-market value was obtained from the 1967 and 1977 Censuses of Governments.[25] Market value is a better yardstick than assessed value for measuring the property tax base because it represents the total base subject to taxation. Moreover, intercity comparisons based on assessed values are not valid because different cities assess real-property at different fractions of market value.

In 1976, the latest year for which market values can be computed, the per capita market value of taxable property ranged from a low of $6584 in Pittsburgh to a high of $29,498 in San Francisco. There was, in effect, a 448% range between the high and low values. Between 1966 and 1976, the nominal increase in property values ranged from a low of 4% in St. Louis to a high of 184% in Denver. In constant 1967 dollars, this was equivalent to a decline of 39% in St. Louis and an increase of 64% in Denver.* Between 1966 and 1976, property values declined in real terms in St. Louis, Detroit, Pittsburgh, Baltimore, Milwaukee, Boston, Oakland, and San Francisco. Cities with slowly-growing or declining property tax bases must continually increase property tax rates or resort to auxiliary taxes in order to generate needed revenues; this could be a problem if those cities are operating at or near authorized tax rate ceilings.

The sales tax base of each city has been expressed in terms of per capita retail sales. In 1977, per capita sales ranged from a low of $1985 in Newark to a high of $4895 in Oklahoma City. This represents a range of 247%, narrower than that for property values. Between 1967 and 1977, nominal increases in retail sales ranged from a low of 20% in Newark to a high of 163% in Indianapolis. In constant 1967 dollars, this was equivalent to a 35% decline in Newark and a 49% increase in Indianapolis.** Nineteen of

---

*Nominal values were expressed in constant 1967 dollars by applying the appropriate Consumer Price Index for each metropolitan area. If no specific index existed, the index for the closest metropolitan area was used.

**A 1970 consolidation between Indianapolis and many of its surrounding suburbs undoubtedly boosted retail sales and caused this strong showing.

TABLE 3.10. Property Taxes and Tax Burdens for Individual Cities by Mix of Tax Revenues

Cities Without an Income or General Sales Tax

City	Per Capita Property Taxes, FY 79	Property Tax Burdens, FY 79	Property Taxes/ Total Taxes	
			FY 69	FY 79
Atlanta	$136	2.08%	59%	59%
Boston[a]	760	11.60	98	99
Buffalo	224	3.78	92	94
Honolulu	180	2.28	76	81
Indianapolis	154	2.03	99	96
Memphis	109	1.68	73	72
Milwaukee	152	2.13	96	96
Minneapolis	174	2.32	91	84
Newark	262	5.80	90	71
Portland	147	1.82	80	73
Mean	171	2.66		

Cities Which Levy an Income Tax

City	Per Capita Property Taxes, FY 79	Property Tax Burdens, FY 79	Property Taxes/ Total Taxes		Income Taxes/ Total Taxes	
			FY 69	FY 79	FY 69	FY 79
Baltimore	$255	4.33%	76%	66%	14%	19%
Cincinnati	62	0.90	49	22	43	71
Cleveland	68	1.18	70	36	27	60
Columbus	16	0.24	21	11	73	84
Detroit	133	2.15	59	47	39	41
Louisville	67	1.07	40	31	53	62
Philadelphia	110	1.81	39	25	49	65
Pittsburgh	109	1.59	63	53	20	21
Toledo	24	0.34	20	16	75	77
Mean	94	1.51				

[a] Boston and New York were not included in the group means because of their extreme values.

Source: Computations based on Census Bureau data.

TABLE 3.10 *(continued)*

Cities Which Levy a General Sales Tax

City	Per Capita Property Taxes, FY 79	Property Tax Burdens, FY 79	Property Taxes/ Total Taxes		General Sales Taxes/ Total Taxes	
			FY 69	FY 79	FY 69	FY 79
Chicago	$103	1.48%	57%	43%	14%	14%
Dallas	132	1.53	83	59	5	24
Denver	124	1.45	54	37	36	45
Ft. Worth	94	1.28	85	59	6	28
Houston	119	1.35	77	57	12	28
Long Beach	33	0.40	58	23	25	31
Los Angeles	61	0.73	51	32	28	27
New Orleans	60	0.91	43	30	41	47
Oakland	49	0.63	61	28	23	29
Oklahoma City	63	0.78	49	30	37	58
Omaha	110	1.46	81	56	0	33
Phoenix	48	0.63	40	34	49	44
San Antonio	52	0.91	94	57	0	34
San Diego	32	0.40	54	29	32	45
San Francisco	185	2.00	81	46	15	16
Seattle	77	0.83	54	35	0	17
Mean	84	1.05				

Cities Which Levy An Income and A General Sales Tax

City	Per Capita Property Taxes, FY 79	Property Tax Burdens, FY 79	Property Taxes/ Total Taxes		Sales Taxes/ Total Taxes		Income Taxes/ Total Taxes	
			FY 69	FY 79	FY 69	FY 79	FY 69	FY 79
Kansas City	$57	0.76%	37%	17%	0%	18%	25%	32%
New York[a]	446	6.13	59	52	16	16	17	23
St. Louis	70	1.19	37	18	0	18	36	29
Mean	63	0.98						

the 38 cities experienced real declines in retail sales between 1967 and 1977. The steepest declines occurred in New York, −18 percent; Detroit, −22 percent; Newark, −35 percent; Kansas City, −18 percent; Buffalo, −18 percent; Boston, −24 percent; Baltimore, −17 percent; and St. Louis, −15 percent. By contrast, sunbelt cities, such as Houston, Dallas, Oklahoma City, San Diego, San Antonio, Memphis, Phoenix, and Honolulu, experienced strong sales growth during the 1967–77 decade. Retail sales posted real increases of 26% in Memphis and San Diego and 25% in San Antonio and Honolulu.

Each city's income tax base was measured in terms of the level of per capita personal income. In 1979, per capita incomes ranged from a low of $4525 in Newark to a high of $9282 in Seattle. This represents a range of 205%, narrower than that for either property values or retail sales. Between 1969 and 1979, the nominal rate of increase ranged from a low of 81 percent in Newark to a high of 166 percent in Houston. In constant 1967 dollars, this was equivalent to an increase of 15% in Newark and 80% in Houston. Other sunbelt cities, including Denver, Dallas, Oklahoma City, New Orleans, and San Antonio, also experienced above-average income growth during the 1970s.

It is interesting to note that between 1967 and 1977, nominal increases in retail sales averaged 123% in the growing cities and only 60% in the declining cities. However, income growth held up reasonably well, even in the declining cities. Between 1969 and 1979, nominal growth of per capita income was 130% in the growing cities and 110% in the declining cities. These statistics help to explain why growing cities generally opted for a general sales tax and declining cities selected an income tax to supplement revenues from the property tax.

These findings are summarized in Figure 3.3 and Table 3.11.

Based on the foregoing results, it is possible to make some judgments concerning tax base strengths and weaknesses in given cities. Eleven northeastern or midwestern cities—Boston, Detroit, Pittsburgh, St. Louis, Baltimore, Milwaukee, Newark, Philadelphia, Buffalo, Cleveland, and Chicago—demonstrated some weakness in at least two of the three major tax bases. Detroit was characterized by weaknesses in all three tax bases: property, sales, and income. That is, Detroit was characterized by below-average property values, retail sales, and personal income, and by below-average growth of property values, sales, and income. Boston, Pittsburgh, St. Louis, Baltimore, and Milwaukee demonstrated weaknesses in their property and sales tax bases. Newark, Philadelphia, Buffalo, Cleveland, and Chicago had relatively weak income and sales tax bases.

Those cities with a weakness in the tax base that generated a large share of their tax revenues would appear to be in the greatest actual or potential fiscal difficulty. For example, both Baltimore and Boston were characterized by below-average property values and by below-average growth of property values. Yet, as of fiscal 1979, the property tax accounted for 99% of Boston's tax revenues and for 66% of Baltimore's. St. Louis, Chicago, and Oakland were characterized by below-average retail sales and by below-average growth of retail sales. Yet, each relied on a general sales tax for some portion of their tax revenues: St. Louis, 18%; Chicago, 14%; and Oakland, 29%. Cleveland, Philadelphia, Detroit, and Louisville were characterized by below-average per capita personal income and income growth. Yet, each of these cities made extensive use of a local personal income tax. In fiscal 1979, the ratio of income taxes-to-total taxes was 60% in Cleveland, 65% in Philadelphia, 41% in Detroit, and 62% in Louisville.

A number of other cities demonstrated consistent strength in at least two of the three tax bases studied. Virtually all were growing, sunbelt cities. For example, Denver showed strength in all three tax bases. It was characterized by above-average property values, retail sales, and personal income, and by above-average growth of property values, retail sales, and personal income. Phoenix, Omaha, Houston, Dallas, and Oklahoma City had relativley strong sales and income tax bases. Other cities were characterized by strength in one tax base and relied extensively on that base for their tax revenues. For example, Minneapolis had a strong property tax base that generated 84% of its tax revenues. Los Angeles, Phoenix, Omaha, Denver, Ft. Worth, Houston, and Dallas had strong sales tax bases and each used a general sales tax to some extent. In fiscal 1979, the ratio of sales taxes-to-total taxes was 58% in Oklahoma City, 45% in Denver, and 44% in Phoenix. The findings suggest that those cities with at least one strong tax base utilized that tax base. However, cities with pervasive weaknesses in one or more of their tax bases had no option but to push hard on these deficient tax bases.

The Relationship Between User Charges and Tax Burdens

Cities with weak tax bases also have the option of supporting selected public services through user charges. This section analyzes the extent to which user charges have been implemented by large U.S. cities. It demonstrates the relationships between "fee-intensity," defined as the ratio of user fees-to-tax revenues, and tax burdens. For purposes of analysis, the sample cities were designated as "low," "medium," and "high" fee-intensity cities. The ratio of user charges to taxes exceeded 45% in the high-fee-intensity cities, ranged between 25% and 45% in the medium-fee-intensity cities, and was below 25% in the low-fee-intensity cities.

In fiscal 1979, per capita user fees ranged from a low of $7 in Pittsburgh to a high of $210 in San Francisco. Long Beach, Oakland, Atlanta, Cleveland, Indianapolis, Denver, San Francisco, Columbus, Memphis,

A. Relationship Between Per Capita Property Values and Growth of Property Values

Percent Change 1966–76	Per Capita Market Value of Property, 1976	
	Above Average	Below Average
Above Average	Denver Honolulu Minneapolis New York San Diego	Louisville Newark New Orleans

B. Relationship Between Per Capita Retail Sales and Growth of Retail Sales

Percent Change 1967–77	Per Capita Retail Sales, 1977	
	Above Average	Below Average
Above Average	Columbus Dallas Denver Ft. Worth Houston Indianapolis Los Angeles Memphis Oklahoma City Omaha Phoenix San Francisco Toledo	Honolulu New Orleans San Antonio San Diego

C. Relationship Between Per Capita Income and Growth of Income

Percent Change 1969–79	Per Capita Personal Income, 1979	
	Above Average	Below Average
Above Average	Dallas Denver Ft. Worth Honolulu Houston Indianapolis Kansas City Oklahoma City Omaha Phoenix Portland San Diego Seattle	Columbus Memphis Milwaukee New Orleans Pittsburgh San Antonio

Long Beach
Los Angeles
Oakland
San Francisco

Below
Average

Baltimore
Boston
Detroit
Milwaukee
Pittsburgh
St. Louis

Atlanta
Kansas City
Long Beach
Minneapolis
Portland
Seattle

Below
Average

Baltimore
Boston
Buffalo
Chicago
Cincinnati
Cleveland
Detroit
Louisville
Milwaukee
Newark
New York
Oakland
Philadelphia
Pittsburgh
St. Louis

Long Beach
Los Angeles
Minneapolis
New York
Oakland
San Francisco

Below
Average

Atlanta
Baltimore
Boston
Buffalo
Chicago
Cincinnati
Cleveland
Detroit
Louisville
Newark
Philadelphia
St. Louis
Toledo

FIGURE 3.3.

TABLE 3.11. The Value and Rate of Growth of the Property, Sales, and Income Tax Bases in Selected Large Cities

The Property Tax Base

City	Per Capita Market Value, 1976	Percent Change, 1966–76		Reliance on the Property Tax, FY 1979
		Nominal	Constant 1967 Dollars	
Pittsburgh	$6,584	+27%	−26	53%
St. Louis	6,909	+ 4	−39	18
Baltimore	6,945	+50	−16	66
Detroit	7,471	+ 8	−39	47
Boston	8,408	+39	−22	99
Milwaukee	9,176	+50	−12	96
Newark	9,360	+91	+ 6	71
Louisville	10,689	+73	+ 2	31
New Orleans	13,135	+89	+10	30
New York	15,909	+92	+ 6	52
Minneapolis	16,216	+80	+ 2	84
Oakland	17,165	+25	−28	28
San Diego	19,227	+147	+40	29
Honolulu	19,759	+169	+61	81
Long Beach	20,310	+57	− 9	23
Los Angeles	20,476	+71	− 1	32
Denver	23,200	+184	+64	37
San Francisco	29,498	+34	−22	46
Mean	14,469	+72	− 1	51

The Sales Tax Base

City	Per Capita Retail Sales, 1977	Percent Change, 1967–77		Reliance on the General Sales Tax, FY 1979
		Nominal	Constant 1967 Dollars	
Newark	$1985	+20	−35	0%
Detroit	2302	+41	−22	0
New York	2360	+53	−18	16
Philadelphia	2433	+60	−13	0
Buffalo	2436	+48	−18	0
Baltimore	2597	+55	−17	0
Honolulu	2654	+113	+25	0
Cleveland	2693	+59	−12	18
St. Louis	2723	+50	−15	14
Chicago	2925	+56	−11	0
Milwaukee	3001	+71	− 4	0
Boston	3051	+40	−24	0
New Orleans	3178	+86	+ 4	47

(continued on next page)

TABLE 3.11 *(cont'd)*

The Sales Tax Base

City	Per Capita Retail Sales, 1977	Percent Change, 1967–77		Reliance on the General Sales Tax, FY 1979
		Nominal	Constant 1967 Dollars	
San Antonio	3292	+125	+25	34
Oakland	3364	+61	−11	29
Cincinnati	3415	+69	− 7	0
Louisville	3428	+73	− 5	0
Pittsburgh	3428	+57	−12	0
San Diego	3506	+129	+26	45
Toledo	3531	+88	+ 4	0
Memphis	3561	+123	+26	0
Long Beach	3570	+81	+ 1	31
Minneapolis	3646	+65	−10	0
Los Angeles	3726	+91	+ 6	27
Phoenix	3738	+110	+15	44
Omaha	3782	+104	+14	33
Kansas City	3890	+47	−18	18
Denver	4020	+99	+ 8	45
Ft. Worth	4239	+97	+ 9	28
Columbus	4268	+121	+22	0
San Francisco	4350	+89	+ 5	16
Atlanta	4483	+64	− 9	0
Portland	4532	+75	− 3	0
Seattle	4598	+82	+ 3	17
Houston	4598	+141	+26	28
Indianapolis	4644	+163	+49	0
Dallas	4697	+116	+20	24
Oklahoma City	4895	+137	+33	58
Mean	3514	+83	+ 2	30

The Income Tax Base

City	Per Capita Income, 1979	Percent Change, 1969–79		Reliance on Income Taxes, FY 1979
		Nominal	Constant 1967 Dollars	
Newark	$4,525	+ 81	+15	0
San Antonio	5,672	+134	+60	0
Cleveland	5,770	+104	+38	60
Baltimore	5,877	+104	+30	19
St. Louis	5,880	+116	+46	29
Buffalo	5,929	+106	+38	0
Philadelphia	6,053	+101	+30	65
Detroit	6,215	+94	+26	41
Louisville	6,281	+112	+34	62
Memphis	6,476	+133	+59	0

(continued on next page)

TABLE 3.11 *(cont'd)*

The Income Tax Base

City	Per Capita Income, 1979	Percent Change, 1969–79		Reliance on Income Taxes, FY 1979
		Nominal	Constant 1967 Dollars	
New Orleans	6,547	+142	+68	0
Atlanta	6,550	+107	+38	0
Boston	6,555	+112	+47	0
Columbus	6,783	+124	+53	84
Pittsburgh	6,845	+123	+50	21
Cincinnati	6,875	+119	+46	71
Chicago	6,939	+104	+40	0
Toledo	7,050	+117	+46	77
Milwaukee	7,104	+123	+53	0
New York	7,273	+97	+35	23
Ft. Worth	7,336	+127	+57	0
Kansas City	7,480	+124	+52	32
Minneapolis	7,490	+115	+40	0
Omaha	7,529	+130	+58	0
Phoenix	7,552	+130	+56	0
Indianapolis	7,585	+120	+50	0
Oakland	7,701	+113	+44	0
Honolulu	7,914	+127	+63	0
Oklahoma City	7,991	+147	+73	0
San Diego	8,027	+132	+60	0
Portland	8,100	+129	+54	0
Long Beach	8,343	+111	+41	0
Los Angeles	8,422	+114	+47	0
Denver	8,556	+142	+59	0
Dallas	8,614	+134	+63	0
Houston	8,796	+166	+80	0
San Francisco	9,267	+119	+49	0
Seattle	9,282	+129	+56	0
Mean	7,189	+120	+50	49

Note: No adjustment has been made for boundary changes between 1969 and 1979.
Source: Computations based on Census Bureau data.

Toledo, and New Orleans were high-fee-intensity cities. The ratio of user fees-to-taxes was 75% in Oakland, 64% in Atlanta, and 62% in Cleveland; user fees exceeded tax revenues in Long Beach. Louisville, Seattle, Detroit, San Antonio, Ft. Worth, Los Angeles, Cincinnati, Portland, Houston, Oklahoma City, Dallas, San Diego, Phoenix, Minneapolis, and Kansas City were medium-fee-intensity cities. In fiscal 1979, the ratio of fees-to-taxes was 44% in Louisville, 43% in Seattle, 40% in San Antonio, and 32% in

Houston. It is clear that the high- and medium-fee-intensity cities were generally located in the south and west; none were located in the northeast. All of the northeastern cities and a significant proportion of the midwestern cities were low-fee-intensity cities. Buffalo, Baltimore, St. Louis, New York, Boston, Philadelphia, and Newark were low-fee-intensity cities. In fiscal 1979, the ratio of fees-to-taxes was 19% in Boston, 16% in Philadelphia, 14% in Chicago, and 4% in Newark and Pittsburgh.

Reliance on user fees by large U.S. cities increased considerably during the fiscal 1969–79 decade. The ratio of user fees-to-taxes increased from 55% to 109% in Long Beach, from 33% to 75% in Oakland, from 24% to 62% in Cleveland, from 13% to 55% in Indianapolis, and from 28% to 52% in San Francisco. Only in 11 cities—Cincinnati, Kansas City, Louisville, Memphis, Minneapolis, Oklahoma City, Philadelphia, Portland, San Diego, Seattle, and St. Louis—did the ratio of user fees-to-taxes decline between fiscal 1969 and 1979.

Fees for sewage-disposal services, hospitals, and airports accounted for a significant proportion of user fees in large U.S. cities. In fiscal 1979, fees for sewage-disposal services accounted for 72% of user fees in Louisville, 60% in Cincinnati, 69% in Omaha, 65% in Cleveland, 70% in Columbus, and 58% in Honolulu. Airport-use fees generated 58% of user fees in Atlanta, 32% in Denver, 37% in San Francisco, 37% in Los Angeles, 57% in Kansas City, and 71% in Chicago. Hospital charges accounted for 38% of user fees in Indianapolis, 26% in Denver, 25% in Detroit, 37% in St. Louis, 23% in New York, and 62% in Boston.

The degree of fee-intensity was related to the level of tax burdens in given cities. Mean tax burdens in the high- and medium-fee-intensity cities were 2.80% and 2.73% respectively; mean tax burdens in the low-fee-intensity cities were more than twice as high, 5.85%. In fiscal 1979, mean per capita taxes in the low-fee-intensity cities were almost double those of the high-fee-intensity cities, $372 versus $208. The average ratio of taxes-to-general revenues was 31% in the high-fee-intensity cities as compared with 42% in the low-fee-intensity cities.

Greater utilization of current charges by northeastern cities is a promising vehicle for easing tax burdens in those cities. However, it would be a mistake to attribute their relatively high tax burdens solely to their failure to employ user fees to a greater extent. It has already been demonstrated that the extensive functional responsibilities borne by northeastern cities are a major cause of high municipal taxes and tax burdens in those cities.

These findings are summarized in Table 3.12.

Changes in Revenue Growth

The growth of general revenues in large cities slowed dramatically after fiscal 1975. Between fiscal 1969 and 1975, virtually all cities experienced

TABLE 3.12. The Utilization of Current Charges in Large Cities, Fiscal Years 1969 and 1979

High-Fee-Intensity Cities	Per Capita User Charges FY 79	Fee-Intensity (%) FY 79	Fee-Intensity (%) FY 69	Tax Burdens, 1979 (%)	Per Capita Taxes, FY 79	Tax Reliance, FY 79 (%)	Primary Source Of User Charges, FY 79
Long Beach	$155	109	55	1.70	$142	25	Water Transpt; Terminals
Oakland	130	75	33	2.25	173	30	Water Transpt; Terminals
Atlanta	146	64	62	3.52	230	33	Airports; Sewage
Cleveland	117	62	24	3.26	188	32	Sewage; Airports
Indianapolis	89	55	13	2.12	161	31	Hospitals; Sewage
Denver	180	53	39	3.95	338	37	Airports; Hospitals
San Francisco	210	52	28	4.34	402	27	Airports; Sewage
Columbus	76	52	43	2.17	147	36	Sewage
Memphis	74	49	59	2.33	151	23	Sewage; Sanitation
Toledo	75	49	32	2.15	152	37	Sewage
New Orleans	92	46	40	3.06	200	34	Sewage
Mean	122	61	39	2.80	208	31	
Medium-Fee-Intensity Cities							
Louisville	97	44	65	3.45	217	33	Sewage
Seattle	95	43	54	2.37	220	39	Sewage; Sanitation
Detroit	117	42	21	4.54	282	33	Sewage; Hospitals
San Antonio	36	40	24	1.59	90	32	Sewage
Ft. Worth	58	36	33	2.16	158	43	Sewage
Los Angeles	67	35	19	2.24	188	39	Airports; Water Transpt.
Cincinnati	94	33	91	4.11	282	39	Sewage

Portland	67	33	36	2.50	202	39	Sewage; Parks & Rec.
Houston	65	32	14	2.35	207	55	Sewage; Airports
Oklahoma City	63	30	43	2.60	207	42	Airports; Sewage
Dallas	65	29	13	2.59	223	57	Sewage; Sanitation
San Diego	33	29	34	1.40	112	31	Sewage; Parks & Rec.
Phoenix	39	28	22	1.83	138	34	Airports
Minneapolis	57	28	31	2.74	206	34	Sewage
Kansas City	91	27	34	4.48	335	51	Airports; Sewage
Mean	70	34	36	2.73	204	40	
Low-Fee-Intensity Cities							
Buffalo	59	24	16	4.01	238	22	Sewage; Housing & U.R.
Omaha	45	23	18	2.63	198	44	Sewage
Baltimore	87	23	21	6.54	384	32	Hospitals; Sewage
St. Louis	87	22	25	6.72	395	52	Airports; Hospitals
New York	173	20	14	11.88	864	43	Housing & U.R.; Hospitals
Boston	143	19	16	11.72	768	47	Hospitals; Sewage
Milwaukee	27	18	16	2.22	158	33	Housing & U.R.
Philadelphia	68	16	17	7.10	430	53	Sewage; Airports
Chicago	34	14	13	3.44	239	51	Airports
Honolulu	27	12	7	2.80	222	52	Sewage
Newark	14	4	3	8.12	367	32	Sewage
Pittsburgh	7	4	2	3.03	207	49	Parking; Parks & Rec.
Mean	64	17	14	5.85	372	42	

Source: Computations based on Census Bureau data.

real growth in per capita general revenues. Between fiscal 1975 and 1979, general revenue declined in real terms in New York, Baltimore, Newark, Cincinnati, Oakland, and Milwaukee; revenue growth slowed in real terms in 16 of the remaining 32 cities. This, in turn, reflected much slower growth of intergovernmental aid after fiscal 1975. Between fiscal 1969 and 1975, intergovernmental aid grew in real terms in each sample city except for Seattle and San Francisco. Average annual growth rates exceeded 50% in St. Louis, Kansas City, Cleveland, Dallas, Houston, Ft. Worth, and San Diego; they ranged from 25% to 50% in Newark, Atlanta, Oakland, Honolulu, New Orleans, and Omaha. Between fiscal 1975 and 1979, by contrast, intergovernmental aid declined in real terms in New York, Baltimore, Newark, Cincinnati, Oakland, and Milwaukee; it increased at a slower pace in 25 of the 32 remaining cities.

Own-source revenues grew even more slowly than outside aid after fiscal 1975. This reflected the slow growth of tax revenues in most large cities. Tax revenues declined in real terms in 17 of the sample cities between fiscal 1975 and 1979. These findings are summarized in Figure 3.4 and Table 3.13.

AN INDEX OF FISCAL STRESS: REVENUES

Based on the foregoing analysis, an index of revenue stress was developed for each of the sample cities. It incorporates fifteen indicators grouped under four broad categories: indicators of general revenue, indicators of tax position, indicators of aid dependence, and indicators of tax efficiency. The measures of general revenue include per capita general revenue in fiscal 1979 and percent change in per capita general revenue between fiscal 1969 and 1979. The measures of tax position include per capita taxes in fiscal 1979, tax burdens in fiscal 1979, the percent change in tax burdens between fiscal 1969 and 1979, and the degree of reliance on property taxes in fiscal 1979. Measures of aid dependence include the degree of reliance on intergovernmental aid in fiscal 1979, the ratio of own-source revenue-to-intergovernmental aid in fiscal 1979, the ratio of increase in own-source revenues relative-to-intergovernmental aid between fiscal 1969 and 1979, the ratio of intergovernmental aid-to-general expenditures in fiscal 1979, and the ratio of aid-to-expenditure increases between fiscal 1969 and 1979. Measures of tax efficiency include the coefficients of tax efficiency for police and fire protection, sanitation, and parks and recreation as of fiscal 1979. These indicators are summarized in Figure 3.5.

The raw scores for each variable were first converted to standard (z) scores. Composite z scores were then computed for general revenue, tax position, aid dependence, and tax efficiency. These composite z scores

TABLE 3.13. Changes in Revenue Levels, Fiscal 1969–75 versus Fiscal 1975–79 (Per Capita Constant 1972 Dollars)

City	General Revenue			Intergovernmental Revenue			Own-Source Revenue		
	FY 1969	FY 1975	FY 1979	FY 1969	FY 1975	FY 1979	FY 1969	FY 1975	FY 1979
Atlanta	214	354	414	36	107	136	178	246	277
Baltimore	647	931	706	321	597	408	327	334	298
Boston	684	821	949	215	279	395	469	543	554
Buffalo	420	585	626	209	349	428	211	236	198
Chicago	212	271	271	53	85	101	159	186	170
Cincinnati	592	717	421	259	271	170	333	446	251
Cleveland	204	273	339	21	96	145	183	178	194
Columbus	148	204	236	31	57	84	118	147	151
Dallas	145	202	228	3	29	39	142	173	189
Denver	329	490	533	96	153	168	232	338	365
Detroit	308	403	503	86	172	247	223	232	256
Ft. Worth	128	159	213	5	25	64	122	134	149
Honolulu	229	246	250	24	63	94	206	183	156
Houston	119	176	220	5	28	36	114	148	184
Indianapolis	98	265	302	13	114	143	85	151	159
Kansas City	220	338	383	16	82	104	204	256	279
Long Beach	287	287	337	33	57	113	253	231	224
Los Angeles	234	257	284	38	64	104	196	193	180
Louisville	313	336	385	76	111	155	236	225	230
Memphis	298	362	388	147	213	235	151	149	153
Milwaukee	260	292	278	107	146	139	152	146	140
Minneapolis	223	257	357	66	97	181	157	160	176
Newark	487	749	675	123	466	431	364	284	244
New Orleans	219	296	348	32	110	158	188	186	190
New York	1017	1360	1175	473	714	530	544	646	646
Oakland	281	359	341	56	140	138	225	219	203
Oklahoma City	153	195	291	26	59	92	127	136	199
Omaha	122	215	263	21	73	109	101	143	154
Philadelphia	309	392	474	64	127	148	245	265	326
Phoenix	159	209	238	49	87	115	110	121	123
Pittsburgh	203	207	245	44	76	101	159	131	144
Portland	216	254	305	39	94	110	177	160	195
San Antonio	80	133	163	6	39	62	74	94	101
San Diego	161	185	212	27	64	89	135	120	123
San Francisco	737	743	859	272	256	441	465	486	418
Seattle	261	289	327	96	81	101	165	208	226
St. Louis	286	377	443	24	109	139	262	268	304
Toledo	163	206	242	33	64	99	130	142	143

Source: Computations based on Census Bureau data.

Intergovernmental Revenue

	Above-Average Growth FY 1975–79	Below-Average Growth FY 1975–79	Real Decline FY 1975–79
Above-Average Growth FY 1969–75	Cleveland Dallas Ft. Worth New Orleans Omaha San Antonio	Atlanta Houston Indianapolis Kansas City St. Louis	Newark
Below-Average Growth FY 1969–75	Boston Columbus Detroit Honolulu Long Beach	Buffalo Chicago Denver Memphis Philadelphia	Baltimore Cincinnati Milwaukee New York Oakland

Own-Source Revenue

	Real Increase FY 1975–79	Real Decline FY 1975–79
Real Increase FY 1969–75	Atlanta Boston Columbus Dallas Denver Detroit Ft. Worth Houston Indianapolis Kansas City Minneapolis New York* Oklahoma City	Baltimore Buffalo Chicago Cincinnati San Francisco

Taxes

	Real Increase FY 1975–79	Real Decline FY 1975–79
Real Increase FY 1969–75	Atlanta Boston Denver Ft. Worth Houston Kansas City Memphis* Minneapolis Oklahoma City Omaha Philadelphia Phoenix Seattle St. Louis	Buffalo Chicago Cincinnati Columbus Dallas Detroit Indianapolis Long Beach New York San Antonio San Diego

	Real Growth FY 1969–75		Real Decline FY 1969–75
Real Growth FY 1975–79	Los Angeles Lousiville Minneapolis Oklahoma City San Diego Toledo	Phoenix Pittsburgh Portland	Omaha Philadelphia Phoenix San Antonio Seattle St. Louis Toledo
	Honolulu Long Beach Los Angeles Milwaukee Newark Oakland		Baltimore Honolulu Milwaukee Newark Oakland San Francisco
Real Decline FY 1969–75	San Francisco Seattle	Cleveland Louisville Memphis New Orleans Pittsburgh Portland San Diego	Cleveland Los Angeles Louisville New Orleans Pittsburgh Portland Toledo

*There was no change in these cities between fiscal 1975 and 1979.

FIGURE 3.4. Changes in Revenue Growth, Fiscal 1969–75 versus Fiscal 1975–79 (Average Annual Growth in Constant 1972 Dollars)

119

General Revenue	Tax Position	Aid Dependence	Tax Efficiency
1. Per Capita General Revenue, FY 1979	3. Per Capita Taxes, FY 1979	7. Reliance on Intergovernmental Aid, FY 1979	12. Police Protection, 1979
2. Percent Change in Per Capita General Revenue, FYs 1969–79	4. Total Tax Burdens, 1979	8. Ratio of Own Source Revenue to Intergovernmental Aid, FY 1979	13. Fire Protection, 1979
	5. Percent Change in Tax Burdens, 1969–79	9. Ratio of Increase, Own Source Revenue/Intergovernmental Aid, FYs 1969–79	14. Sanitation, 1979
	6. Reliance on Property Taxes, FY 1979	10. Ratio of Intergovernmental Aid to General Expenditures, FY 1979	15. Parks & Recreation, 1979
		11. Ratio of Aid-to Expenditure Increases, FYs 1969–79	

FIGURE 3.5. Revenue Measures Used to Denote Fiscal Stress

represent a simple average of the z scores for variables within each major category. The composite z scores were then averaged to develop an overall measure of revenue stress for each city. This measure was interpreted as follows: a z score of $-.675$ or less indicated stress; a z score of $+.675$ or more indicated the relative absence of stress; z scores between $-.675$ and $+.675$ indicated a moderate amount of stress. Scores of $-.675$ or less include the lower quarter of the distribution; scores of $+.675$ or more include the upper quarter; scores between $-.675$ and $+.675$ include the middle 50% of the distribution. The methodology is designed to measure relative stress. If all of the sample cities were distressed in absolute terms, this methodology could fail to detect it.

The findings indicate that five cities—New York, Boston, Newark, Buffalo, and Indianapolis—were distressed in terms of their revenue profiles. A sixth city, Baltimore, also fell close to the preselected cutoff point for revenue distress. Indianapolis' poor ranking undoubtedly reflects the 1970 consolidation of the City of Indianapolis with most of its surrounding suburbs inside Marion County. This move greatly boosted the City's general revenues and caused a highly unfavorable z score for general revenues. The revenue stress manifested by each of the other cities is real and does not reflect such statistical anomalies. For example, New York City was characterized by an unfavorable general revenue position, by disproportionately high taxes and tax burdens, and by extremely low coefficients of tax efficiency. Its z score for tax position was -2.11; its tax efficiency z score was -1.42, the lowest of any city studied. Boston was in a similar revenue position; its tax position z score was -2.34 and its tax efficiency z score was only -1.18. By contrast, Newark and Buffalo ranked as distressed, largely because of their disproportionate dependence on intergovernmental aid. Their z scores for aid dependence were -1.27 and -1.99 respectively. Newark was also handicapped by a relatively low z score for tax efficiency; only -1.06.

Two cities, Dallas and Long Beach, ranked as non-distressed in terms of revenues. Long Beach was characterized by a highly favorable tax position and by unusually high coefficients of tax efficiency. Its tax positon z score was $+1.16$; its z score for tax efficiency was $+2.93$. Dallas ranked favorably by virtue of its extensive dependence on locally-generated revenues. Its z score for aid dependence was $+2.32$.

Most of the sample cities ranked as moderately distressed. Of this group, Omaha, Philadelphia, Detroit, San Francisco, Atlanta, and Minneapolis were among the more-distressed cities, and Oakland, San Diego, Columbus, Toledo, Phoenix, and Los Angeles were among the less-distressed cities. Philadelphia was characterized by an unfavorable tax position and by relatively low tax efficiency. Its z scores for tax position and tax efficiency were -1.14 and -0.88 respectively. However, Philadelphia

TABLE 3.14. An Index of Revenue Stress for Large Cities

Rank	City	An Index of Revenue Stress	Composite z scores for			
			General Revenue	Tax Position	Aid Dependence	Tax Efficiency
1	New York	−1.19	−1.35	−2.11	+0.12	−1.42
2	Boston	−1.08	−1.12	−2.34	+0.32	−1.18
3	Newark	−0.76	−0.50	−0.19	−1.27	−1.06
4	Buffalo	−0.75	−0.52	−0.05	−1.99	−0.45
5	Indianapolis	−0.74	−1.78	−0.68	−0.30	−0.21
6	Baltimore	−0.64	−0.19	−0.36	−1.15	−0.86
7	Omaha	−0.46	−0.54	−0.55	−0.23	−0.51
8	Philadelphia	−0.35	−0.22	−1.14	+0.83	−0.88
9	Detroit	−0.33	−0.40	−0.16	−0.76	−0.01
10	San Francisco	−0.32	−0.64	+0.45	−0.66	−0.42
11	Atlanta	−0.28	−0.58	−0.81	+0.75	−0.46
12	Minneapolis	−0.26	−0.03	−0.38	−0.93	+0.28
13	Kansas City	−0.20	−0.28	−0.70	+0.83	−0.66
14	St. Louis	−0.19	−0.17	−0.43	+0.90	−1.07
15	New Orleans	−0.10	0.00	+0.76	−0.68	−0.48
16	Oklahoma City	−0.08	−0.26	−0.24	+0.63	−0.44
17	Memphis	0.00	+0.28	+0.32	−1.59	+1.00
18	Denver	+0.04	−0.47	−0.32	+1.26	−0.33
19	Honolulu	+0.06	+0.86	+0.45	−0.52	−0.56
20	Louisville	+0.12	+0.38	+0.14	−0.03	−0.01
21	Cleveland	+0.13	−0.07	+0.70	−0.24	+0.12
22	Chicago	+0.15	+0.58	−0.01	+0.05	−0.03
23	Ft. Worth	+0.18	+0.21	+0.05	+0.63	−0.16
24	Milwaukee	+0.19	+0.82	+0.32	−0.91	+0.52
25	San Antonio	+0.19	−0.14	+0.43	+0.14	+0.34
26	Cincinnati	+0.22	+0.96	−0.03	+0.25	−0.28
27	Portland	+0.27	+0.33	+0.12	+0.14	+0.47
28	Pittsburgh	+0.38	+0.74	+0.58	−0.08	+0.27
29	Los Angeles	+0.39	+0.63	+1.06	−0.38	+0.24
30	Phoenix	+0.39	+0.37	+0.64	−0.51	+1.06
31	Toledo	+0.41	+0.38	+0.81	−0.04	+0.48
32	Columbus	+0.46	+0.26	+0.32	+0.54	+0.72
33	San Diego	+0.49	+0.67	+1.16	−0.93	+1.06
34	Oakland	+0.54	+0.48	+1.24	−0.34	+0.79
35	Seattle	+0.59	+0.48	−0.24	+0.97	+1.14
36	Houston	+0.60	−0.04	+0.07	+2.57	−0.18
37	Dallas	+0.72	+0.30	−0.02	+2.32	+0.26
38	Long Beach	+1.24	+0.56	+1.16	+0.32	+2.93

Source: Computations based on Census Bureau data.

relied primarily on locally-generated revenue. It was characterized by a highly favorable z score for aid dependence, $+0.83$. Kansas City, St. Louis, and Denver were also characterized by favorable z scores for aid dependence but by less favorable z scores for tax position. Conversely, Oakland, San Diego, Toledo, and Los Angeles had favorable z scores for tax position but generally unfavorable z scores for aid dependence. Throughout the analysis, there has been a clearcut tradeoff between reliance on taxes and reliance on outside aid. That is, extensive reliance on outside aid has been coupled with a favorable or improving tax positon and vice versa.

Table 3.14 summarizes the findings concerning relative levels of revenue stress in large U.S. cities as of fiscal 1979.

NOTES

1. See, for example, Harvey Brazer, *City Expenditures in the United States* (New York: National Bureau of Economic Research, 1959); Roy W. Bahl, *Metropolitan City Expenditures, A Comparative Analysis* (Lexington, Ky: University of Kentucky Press, 1969.)

2. Susan A. MacManus, *Revenue Patterns In U.S. Cities and Suburbs, A Comparative Analysis* (New York: Praeger, 1978), p. 3.

3. George F. Break, *Financing Government in a Federal System* (Washington: The Brookings Institution, 1980), pp. 76–7.

4. Ibid., p. 77.

5. Robert L. Bish and Hugh O. Nourse, *Urban Economics and Policy Analysis* (New York: McGraw-Hill, 1975), Table 6.3, p. 161, by permission.

6. Break, p. 223.

7. Break, p. 95.

8. See Advisory Commission on Intergovernmental Relations, *Categorical Grants: Their Role and Design* (Washington: U.S. Government Printing Office, May 1977.)

9. See Paul N. Courant, Edward M. Gramlich, and Daniel L. Rubinfeld, "The Stimulative Effects of Intergovernmental Grants: Or Why Money Sticks Where it Hits," in *Fiscal Federalism and Grants-in-Aid*, eds. Peter Mieszkowski and William H. Oakland (Washington: The Urban Institute, 1979), pp. 5–21.

10. See Patrick D. Larkey, *Evaluating Public Programs, The Impact of General Revenue Sharing On Municipal Government* (Princeton: Princeton University Press, 1979.) pp. 10–15.

11. See Will Myers and John Shannon, "Revenue Sharing for States: An Endangered Species," *Intergovernmental Perspective* 5 (Summer, 1979):10–18.

12. Advisory Commission on Intergovernmental Relations, *The Comprehensive Employment and Training Act: Early Readings From a Hybrid Block Grant* (Washington: U.S. Government Printing Office, June 1977.)

13. Advisory Commission on Intergovernmental Relations, *Community Development: The Workings of a Federal Local Block Grant* (Washington: U.S. Government Printing Office, March 1977.)

14. See Ann R. Markusen, Annalee Saxenian, and Marc A. Weiss, "Who Benefits From Intergovernmental Transfers," in *Cities Under Stress, The Fiscal Crisis of Urban America*, eds. Robert W. Burchell and David Listokin (Piscataway, N.J.; Rutgers University Center for Urban Policy Research, 1981), pp. 617–64.

15. George F. Break, *Agenda for Local Tax Reform* (Berkeley: Institute of Government Studies, University of California, 1970), pp. 7–35.

16. Glenn W. Fisher, "What is the Ideal Revenue Balance - A Political View" in *Cities Under Stress*, pp. 439–57.

17. Henry J. Aaron, *Who Pays the Property Tax? A New View* (Washington: The Brookings Institution, 1975), p. 93.

18. See Robert D. Ebel, "Research and Policy Developments: Major Types of State and Local Taxes," in *Essays in Public Finance and Financial Management, State and Local Perspectives,* eds. John E. Peterson and Catherine Lavigne Spain (Chatham, N.J.: Chatham House Publishers, 1978), pp. 1–21.

19. Congress of the United States, Congressional Budget Office, *Proposition 13: Its Impact on the Nation's Economy, Federal Revenues, and Federal Expenditures* (Washington: U.S. Government Printing Office, July, 1978.) p. 4.

20. MacManus, pp. 8–11.

21. Charles M. Tiebout, "A Pure Theory of Local Expenditures," *Journal of Political Economy* 64(October, 1956):416–24.

22. Steven David Gold, *Property Tax Relief* (Lexington, Mass: Lexington Books, 1979), p. 189.

23. Larkey, pp. 217–18.

24. See William Oakland, *Financial Relief for Troubled Cities* (Columbus, Ohio: Academy for Contemporary Problems, January, 1978), p. 7.

25. See. U.S. Bureau of the Census, "Taxable Property Values and Assessment/Sales Price Ratios," *1977 Census of Governments* Vol. 2, GC 77(2), (Washington: U.S. Government Printing Office, November, 1978), pp. 16–78.

4

Fiscal Stress in Large Cities: Expenditures

Revenue patterns constitute one side of the municipal fiscal equation. The fiscal difficulties currently being experienced by large cities are often a product of the interaction of revenues and expenditures. Extensive and growing expenditure requirements can cause fiscal problems which are as severe as those created by difficulties in generating public revenues.

This chapter analyzes municipal expenditures, employment, and wages in each of the sample cities. It reviews the theory of public goods and selectively reviews the literature concerning the determinants of municipal expenditures. This is followed by an analysis of expenditure patterns for broad groupings of cities and for the individual cities. The various expenditure measures are then incorporated into an index of expenditure stress by which the individual cities are ranked. The goal is to distinguish between cities that appear unable to sustain their present level and/or rate of expenditure growth and those that appear to be maintaining a more viable balance between expenditures and resources.

THE THEORY OF PUBLIC GOODS

Before analyzing the configuration of expenditures, employment, and wages in large cities, it is useful to review the rationale for publicly provided goods and services. The theory of public goods has been used to justify intervention by the public sector.[1] It suggests that pure public goods, goods with spillovers, merit goods, and goods involving extraordinary technical risks should be provided by the public sector; government intervention is also needed to regulate "common-pool" resources.

Public goods include national defense, mosquito control, and street lighting, among others. Such goods are jointly consumed by the public at large; consumption by one person does not affect consumption by others; it is not readily possible to stop non-payers from consuming these goods. For example, the nation's defense umbrella covers everyone; nobody can be denied its protection regardless of whether he or she pays for it. Unless individuals are compelled to pay for public goods through taxation, many would undoubtedly refuse to do so. The existence of such "free riders" would cause an under-allocation of resources to the good or service in question. Thus, in the case of pure public goods, government must step in because the private market is unable to function effectively.

The private market also fails to allocate resources efficiently for those goods characterized by spillovers or externalities. Such externalities affect individuals not directly involved in the transaction. For example, the motorist who pollutes the air around major highways pays only for the private costs of driving; costs associated with the purchase, maintenance, and operation of a vehicle. He is not charged for the "social" costs he imposes on others by polluting the air. The market's failure to price the externality leads to economic inefficiency. That is, the motorist drives more than he otherwise would if he were required to pay the full costs of driving. Government intervention is needed to motivate drivers to select the correct level of mobility and thereby correct the inefficient allocation of resources.

Public sector action is also needed in supplying merit goods. These goods are considered so useful to society that any under-allocation of resources must be corrected by public sector intervention. Services associated with human resource development, such as education and training, are merit goods. If education were left solely to private providers, people might underspend for education because as individuals they might not value education as highly as society does. Sub-optimal educational expenditures might also result if education were left solely to local government. This is because people are mobile and local governments cannot fully internalize the benefits of their educational expenditures. This helps to explain the relatively high level of state support for public education.

Public sector intervention is needed in the case of common-pool resources, such as air sheds or water bodies. Like public goods, common-pool resources are jointly consumed and non-payers cannot be readily excluded. Unlike public goods, one person's consumption can reduce the value of the resource for others. Government intervention is needed to ration use.

Natural monopolies or situations involving extraordinary technical risks also lend themselves to government intervention. Natural monopolies include telephone services, cable television, water supply, and electric power. The market for these services is such that one firm can generally serve it most economically. Government has the option of providing these services directly or regulating private providers so as to limit monopoly profits. Public sector action is also sometimes needed in situations involving extraordinary technical risks, such as the development of nuclear energy.

In most of these situations, government intervention is needed to help achieve "Pareto Optimality." Pareto Optimality exists when resources are allocated in such a manner than nobody's position can be improved without a loss to someone else.

Government intervention is not costless. It interferes with individual freedom because individuals are compelled to pay for goods and services that they may not value. The political process by which public funds are appropriated is subject to manipulation by pressure groups and may not accurately reflect individual choices. The most serious criticism leveled against public sector action is that there is no market test for public goods and services. Since there is no profit motive, as in the private sector, and since it is technically difficult, if not impossible, to accurately measure the costs and benefits of given public services, there is no guarantee that public funds will be wisely spent. The current tax revolt was largely a response to the widely-held perception that government had abused the public trust in its spending decisions.

THE DETERMINANTS OF MUNICIPAL SPENDING

There is a large body of literature that seeks to explain intercity or interstate differences in public expenditures. The typical expenditure determination study uses multiple-regression analysis to relate levels of spending for all functions or for selected public functions to local demographic and socio-economic conditions. Solomon Fabricant and Harvey Brazer performed some of the earlier expenditure determination studies.[2] Fabricant used income, population density, and degree of urbanization to statistically explain interstate differences in state and local spending. These variables accounted for about 70% of interstate differences in per capita spending. Roy Bahl studied intercity variations in per capita spending using 198 cities.[3] His dependent variables were per capita general expenditures net education, per capita operating expenditures net education, and per capita current expenditures for selected common functions. His seventeen independent variables included population, income, wealth, and capacity-to-finance measures. The population variables included population size, density and rate of growth, and the ratio of city-to-fringe area population. The income and wealth variables included median family income, per capita retail sales, and median value of owner-occupied housing. The capacity-to-finance variables included per capita intergovernmental revenue, the ratio of intergovernmental revenue-to-total general revenue, and the ratio of property taxes-to-total general revenues. Bahl incorporated both 1950 and 1960 data in his 1969 study. His seventeen variables explained 40% of intercity variations in total spending, 45% of intercity variations in current spending, and 48% of intercity differences in common function spending. He concluded that " . . . the level of per capita central city expenditures is closely related to the size of the central city population relative to that of the entire SMSA . . . [and that] . . . spending for certain functions, notably police, fire, and highways, shows a close association with population density."[4] Bahl attributed the relatively low explanatory power of his model to differences in spending "within" the city and spending by municipal government itself. This, in turn, reflects intercity differences in the arrangements for performing given functions. For example, a given function may be performed by the city itself, by independent special districts, by a higher level of government, or by a private firm. The latter types of arrangements involve spending in the city, but not by city government.

The traditional expenditure determination studies have several inherent limitations. They generally ignore the role of grants-in-aid in determining expenditures, possibly because such grants were not significant until the 1970s. Richard Gustely suggests that the traditional expenditure determination studies also hide interactions among variables, thereby making it difficult to isolate the demand influences on expenditures from the supply influences. He also contends that the use of reduced form equations does not lend itself to policy prescriptions and is not particularly useful in forecasting expenditures.[5]

Gustely attempted to overcome these limitations by developing a model capable of revealing the behavioral relationships that underlie the process of expenditure determination. His sample included 39 city governments ranging in size from Lancaster, Pennsylvania to New York City. His model used cross-sectional data for the years 1966 and 1971. His dependent variables included payroll and non-payroll costs, with payroll costs further subdivided into wages and employment. Gustely theorized that public sector wages were a function of the opportunity wage of public employees, which he defined as the average earnings of private-sector service workers, the fiscal capacity of the population, the degree of unionization, and the mobility of public employees into the private sector, among others. He attributed public employment levels to the service needs of the population, the degree of population centralization within the metropolitan area, and the fiscal capacity of the population, among others. Gustely found that " . . . the most important single determinant of public-sector wages is the level of living of the community."[6]

These and other expenditure determination studies provided a guide to the expenditure variables to be analyzed in this study and provided the necessary framework for interpreting the results.

EXPENDITURES: GROUPS OF CITIES

This section contrasts differences in municipal expenditures, employment, and wages for broad groups of cities. It attempts to answer questions such as these: Are public expenditures in declining, northern cities substantially higher than those in growing, southern and western cities? If so, where do the expenditure pressures in northern cities originate? Are higher personnel costs a factor? Are diverse functional responsibilities a factor? To what extent do population densities influence the level of expenditures for selected municipal functions? How have municipal expenditures and personnel costs changed over time? How have they changed since fiscal year 1975, when New York City's fiscal crisis erupted?

The findings show clearly discernible intergroup differences in the level and composition of municipal spending, in the level of municipal employment, and in municipal wage costs. The declining, high-density, and northeastern cities were characterized by consistently higher expenditures, employment levels, and wage costs than the other groups of cities. Their disproportionately high expenditures and employment levels were largely a function of their extensive responsibilities for non-common functions.

It was anticipated that New York City's well-publicized fiscal crisis would trigger a wave of belt-tightening by northern cities. This has, in fact, occurred. However, the sunbelt cities have also started to retrench, thereby dashing hopes of any substantial narrowing of north–south municipal employment or expenditure differentials.

Expenditure Patterns, Fiscal Year 1979

In fiscal 1979, general spending in the declining cities was double that of the growing cities; $727 versus $371 per capita. Their operating expenditures were also twice as high; $554 versus $267 per capita. Per capita general spending by the northeastern cities, $955, was much higher than comparable spending by the western cities, $493 per capita, the midwestern cities, $542 per capita, and the southern cities, $544 per capita. Per capita operating expenditures in the northeastern cities were more than double those of the western cities; $734 versus $359. Per capita general spending by the high-density cities was almost double that of the low-density cities; $817 versus $447. Their per capita operating expenditures were also more than double those of the low-density cities; $636 versus $305. The clearest differences emerged when cities were grouped by differences in functional responsibility. Cities responsible for two of the least-common functions spent almost 2.5 times as much as cities that performed none of them; $1058 versus $432 per capita. Their operating expenditures were also 2.6 times as high; $805 versus $305 per capita. New York City, which performed all three least common functions—education, public welfare, and hospitals—had general expenditures of $1684 per capita. This was approximately double the level of general spending in the declining cities, the high-density cities, and the northeastern cities. New York's operating expenditures, $1185 per capita, were also substantially above those of the declining cities, $554, the northeastern cities, $734, and the high-density cities, $636.

For purposes of analysis, operating expenditures have been disaggregated into "common function" spending and "all other" operating expenditures. Common function spending describes expenditures for that core of functions commonly performed by most cities. In this study, common function spending is defined as current expenditures for highways, police and fire protection, sanitation, parks and recreation, financial administration, and general control. Financial administration and general control are the overhead functions of government. The general control function includes the courts, the governing body, the office of the chief executive, and a variety of central staff services. All other operating expenditures include spending for the optional or least-common functions.

In fiscal 1979, the declining cities spent 55% more than the growing cities for the designated common functions; $250 versus $161 per capita. Within the common functions, the declining cities spent 66% more for police protection, 43% more for fire protection, and more than twice as much for general control as the growing cities. The relatively high overhead costs of the declining cities reflect their extensive responsibilities for the non-common functions. For example, all other operating expenditures in the declining cities were almost triple those of the growing cities; $305 versus $106 per capita. This expenditure category includes the least-common functions.

The same pattern of expenditures emerged when cities were grouped by region, by population density, and by differences in functional responsibility. That is, northern, high-density cities with extensive functional responsibilities spent more than their low-density, sunbelt counterparts for both the common and all other functions; intergroup spending differences were most pronounced for the all other category. For example, the northeastern cities spent 2.8 times as much as the western cities in the all other category; $451 versus $161 per capita. They also spent 44% more than the western cities for the common functions; 50% more for police protection, 40% more for fire protection, and more than twice as much for general control. The high-density cities spent almost three times as much as the low-density cities in the all other spending category; $370 versus $141 per capita. They also spent 62% more than the low-density cities for the common functions, including twice as much for police protection, and twice as much for general control. Cities responsible for two of the least common functions spent four times as much in the all other category as cities responsible for none of them; $541 versus $130 per capita. They also spent 50% more for the common functions; 53% more for police protection, 48% more for fire protection, and more than twice as much for financial administration and general control. New York City, which performed all three least-common functions, spent more than three times as much as the declining cities in the all other category; $938 versus $305 per capita. The City's common function spending was virtually identical to that of the declining cities; $247 versus $250 per capita.

The distribution of expenditures by type underscores the fact that extensive functional responsibilities place a severe strain on municipal finances. For example, all other operating expenditures accounted for 42% of general spending in the declining cities, 47% in the northeastern cities, 45% in the high-density cities, 51% in cities performing two least-common functions, and 55% in New York City. By contrast, all other operating expenditures accounted for only 29% of general spending in the growing cities, 33% in the western cities, 31% in the low-density cities and 30% in cities that performed no least-common functions.

It seems clear that extensive functional responsibilities consume disproportionate amounts of revenue and cause higher spending for some common functions, particularly the overhead functions. There is also evidence that such responsibilities divert resources from capital spending. In fiscal 1979, the ratio of capital-to-general spending was only 14% in the declining cities and in those performing two least common functions; it was only 13% in the northeastern and high-density cities, and 5% in New York City. By contrast, this ratio was 21% in the growing and southern cities, and 22% in the low-density cities and in cities performing no least common functions.

These findings are summarized in Tables 4.1 and 4.2.

Personnel Costs

Disproportionately high personnel costs were largely responsible for disproportionately high general expenditures in declining, northern cities. Personnel costs reflect the level of municipal employment, the mix of occupations within the municipal workforce, and the wages paid to municipal workers. In October, 1979, full-time equivalent employment per 10,000 residents was 82% higher in the declining than in the growing cities, 227 versus 125 employees; it was 76% higher in the northeastern than in the western cities, 262 versus 149 employees; it was 67% higher in the high-density than in the low-density cities, 252 versus 151 employees. Levels of

TABLE 4.1. Expenditure Patterns for Major City Groupings, Fiscal Year 1979 ($ Per Capita)

Type of Expenditure	By Population Change			By Region			
	Growing	Mixed	Declining	Northeast	No. Central	South	West
Total General Expenditures	371	583	727	955	542	544	493
Capital Expenditures	77	118	103	127	75	116	91
Operating Expenditures	267	407	554	734	412	385	359
Common Function	161	199	250	283	222	173	197
All Other Operating	106	208	305	451	190	212	161
Other Expenditures[a]	27	58	70	94	55	43	43
Common Function Spending	161	199	250	283	222	173	197
Highways	15	25	21	19	25	15	18
Police Protection	61	59	101	107	94	57	71
Fire Protection	30	39	43	52	37	34	37
Sanitation	15	19	26	32	24	20	14
Parks & Recreation	21	29	26	24	21	24	29
Financial Administration	9	12	11	14	8	10	12
General Control	10	16	22	35	13	13	16

| | By Population Density | | | By Differences in Functional Responsibilities | | | | |
Type of Expenditure	Low	Medium	High	Three[b] Functions	Two Functions	One Function	Minimal Amounts	None
Total General Expenditures	447	487	817	1,684	1,058	798	452	432
Capital Expenditures	100	82	110	83	144	121	69	93
Operating Expenditures	305	358	636	1,185	805	609	337	305
Common Function	164	201	266	247	264	279	197	175
All Other Operating	141	157	370	938	541	330	140	130
Other Expenditures[a]	42	47	71	416	109	68	46	34
Common Function Spending	164	201	266	247	264	279	197	175
Highways	17	21	20	20	22	22	18	19
Police Protection	54	72	114	95	87	110	89	57
Fire Protection	31	38	44	43	52	40	34	35
Sanitation	17	18	28	40	18	30	21	18
Parks & Recreation	23	26	24	17	34	32	17	24
Financial Administration	10	11	11	14	18	14	7	9
General Control	12	15	25	18	33	31	11	13

[a] Includes intergovernmental expenditures, assistance and subsidies and interest on the general debt.
[b] Denotes New York City
Source: Computations based on Census Bureau data.

TABLE 4.2. Distribution of Expenditures, by Type, for Major City Groupings, Fiscal Year 1979 (Percents)

Type of Expenditure	By Population Change			By Region			
	Growing	Mixed	Declining	Northeast	No. Central	South	West
Total General Expenditures	100	100	100	100	100	100	100
Capital Expenditures	21	20	14	13	14	21	18
Operating Expenditures	72	70	76	77	76	71	73
Common Function	43	34	34	30	41	32	40
All Other Operating	29	36	42	47	35	39	33
Other Expenditures[a]	7	10	10	10	10	8	9
Common Function Spending	100	100	100	100	100	100	100
Highways	9	13	9	7	11	9	9
Police Protection	38	30	40	38	42	33	36
Fire Protection	19	19	17	18	17	20	19
Sanitation	9	10	10	11	11	11	7
Parks & Recreation	13	14	10	9	9	14	15
Financial Administration	6	6	5	5	4	6	6
General Control	6	8	9	12	6	7	8

Type of Expenditure	By Population Density			By Differences in Functional Responsibilities				
	Low	Medium	High	Three[b] Functions	Two Functions	One Function	Minimal Amounts	None
Total General Expenditures	100	100	100	100	100	100	100	100
Capital Expenditures	22	17	13	5	14	15	15	22
Operating Expenditures	68	73	78	70	76	76	75	71
Common Function	37	41	33	15	25	35	44	41
All Other Operating	31	32	45	55	51	41	31	30
Other Expenditures[a]	10	10	9	25	10	9	10	7
Common Function Spending	100	100	100	100	100	100	100	100
Highways	10	10	8	8	8	8	9	11
Police Protection	33	36	43	39	33	39	45	33
Fire Protection	19	19	17	17	20	14	17	20
Sanitation	10	9	10	16	7	11	11	10
Parks & Recreation	14	13	9	7	13	12	8	14
Financial Administration	6	5	4	6	7	5	4	5
General Control	8	8	9	7	12	11	6	7

[a]Includes intergovernmental expenditures, assistance and subsidies and interest on the general debt.
[b]Denotes New York City

Source: Computations based on Census Bureau data.

municipal employment also increased consistently with the number of least-common functions performed. For example, the ratio of employment-to-population was 132 in cities that performed no least-common functions, 147 in cities that performed minimal amounts, 247 in cities that performed one least-common function, 349 in cities that performed two of them, and 459 in New York City, which performed all three least-common functions.

The declining, northern cities employed more municipal workers in both the common functions and in all other functions. However, staffing differences were most pronounced in the all other category, which includes the least-common functions. Common function employment per 10,000 residents was 55% higher in the declining than in the growing cities, 116 versus 75 employees; all other employment was more than twice as high, 111 versus 50 workers. Common function employment per 10,000 residents was 59% higher in the northeastern than in the western cities, 130 versus 82 workers; all other employment was about twice as high, 132 versus 67 workers. Common function employment per 10,000 residents was 41% higher in the high-density cities than in the low-density cities, 120 versus 85 workers; all other employment was twice as high, 132 versus 66 workers. The ratio of common function employment-to-population was 45% higher in cities performing two least-common functions than in cities performing none, 122 versus 84 workers; all other employment was almost five times as high: 227 versus 48 workers. In New York City, which performed all three least common functions, all other employment was seven times as high as in cities with no such responsibilities; 352 versus 48 workers. These findings help to explain why all other operating expenditures were so high in declining, northern cities.

There was considerable diversity in staffing levels even within the common functions. For example, the declining cities employed 1.8 times as many full-time workers as the growing cities in sanitation, financial administration, and general control, and 1.7 times as many in highways and police protection. The northeastern cities employed 1.6 times as many workers as their southern or western counterparts for police protection; they employed twice as many as the southern or western cities in financial administration and general control. These figures suggest the presence of a large administrative bureaucracy in northeastern cities, a phenomenon that is undoubtedly linked to their diverse functional responsibilities. The fact that cities responsible for two least-common functions employed almost twice as many workers in financial administration and general control as cities that performed none of them seems to support this hypothesis. In effect, as a city's functional responsibilities expand, so does its administrative bureaucracy. Although the evidence is fragmentary, it also appears that declining, northern cities sacrificed "quality-of-life" functions to pay for basic protective services. For example, the high-density cities employed 1.9 times as many workers relative to population as the low-density cities in police protection; they employed only 64% as many in parks and recreation.

It is more difficult to document intergroup differences in wage costs because Census Bureau information is confined to average October earnings for "municipal employees other than teachers." These statistics are more a reflection of intercity differences in functional responsibilities and in the occupational mix of the municipal workforce than of intercity differences in actual wage costs. Moreover, the presence of CETA workers also distorts wage comparisons because CETA employees are generally among the lowest-paid workers. The Census Bureau information also fails to reflect intercity differences in municipal benefit packages.

A better source of comparative wage data is the municipal wage survey conducted annually by the U.S. Bureau of Labor Statistics. The B.L.S. has constructed index numbers that depict relative municipal pay in large U.S. cities using average salaries in 26 large cities as a base of 100. Index numbers above 100 indicate above-average pay and vice versa. Information for the October 1978 to September 1979 period is available for the following occupations: clerical workers, skilled maintenance workers, public safety workers, sanitation workers, and janitorial workers.[7] By removing the effect of intercity differences in employment composition within each occupation, the statistics make it possible to compare pay levels for generally equivalent job functions.

Information from the municipal wage survey indicates that the declining cities were generally characterized by above-average wages and that the growing and mixed cities generally paid below-average wages; wage costs were consistently lowest in the mixed cities. For example, the index of wage costs for sanitation workers was 115 in the declining cities, 94 in the growing cities, and 86 in the mixed cities. The index for skilled maintenance workers was 107 in the declining cities, 91 in the growing cities, and 83 in the mixed cities. The index for janitorial workers was 112 in the declining cities, 93 in the growing cities, and 89 in the mixed cities. However, wage costs for public-safety workers were roughly comparable in the growing and declining cities.

The northeastern cities were also characterized by above-average wages for most municipal occupations, but their wage costs were surpassed by those of the western cities. The high-density cities exhibited above-average wage costs for all five occupations studied; the low-density cities demonstrated below-average wage costs for each of these occupations. For example, the index of wage costs for sanitation workers was 123 in the high-density cities and 86 in the low-density cities. The index for janitorial workers was 117 in the high-density cities and 89 in the low-density cities.

No clearcut wage differences emerged when cities were differentiated by scope of functional responsibilities. However, New York City, which performed all three least common functions, generally paid above-average wages. The wage index for skilled maintenance workers was 131 in New York City, 107 in the declining cities, 88 in the northeastern cities, and 106 in the high-density cities. New York's wages for public-safety and sanitation workers were also well above the average for the 26 cities.

The findings clearly demonstrate that the declining, high-density, and northern cities were handicapped, not only by disproportionately high staffing levels, but also by above-average wage costs. These findings are consonant with those of Tom Muller who noted: "The major factor contributing to higher operating outlays in declining cities is personnel: more workers and higher wages. . . . A second factor is that some declining cities, particularly New York City, provide more services, such as health care, than their growing city counterparts."[8]

These findings are summarized in Tables 4.3 and 4.4.

Changing Expenditure Patterns, Fiscal Years 1969-79.

For purposes of analysis, per capita expenditures for fiscal years 1969, 1975 and 1979 were converted to constant 1972 dollars by applying the implicit GNP deflator for state and local purchases for each of these years. The results show that the growth of municipal spending in large U.S. cities slowed perceptibly after fiscal 1975. The slowdown was especially pronounced in the declining and high-density cities. It affected both capital and operating expenditures. For example, in the declining cities, operating expenditures grew at an average annual rate of 4.9% between fiscal 1969 and 1975, but slowed to an average annual rate of only 1.8% during the fiscal 1975-79 period. Capital spending in the declining cities fell in real terms throughout the fiscal 1969-79 period, but the rate of decline accelerated after fiscal 1975. Between fiscal 1969 and 1975, capital spending in these cities fell at an average annual rate of 0.5%; between fiscal 1975 and 1979, the average annual rate of decline increased to 3.2%.

The growing, sunbelt cities also started to retrench after fiscal 1975. In the western cities, the average annual rate of increase in operating expenditures declined from 5.1% during the fiscal 1969-75 period to only 0.1% between fiscal 1975 and 1979; in the growing cities, the average annual rate of growth in operating expenditures slowed from 5.8% to 2.6%.

Common function spending bore the brunt of attempts to hold the line on spending. Between fiscal 1975 and 1979, common function spending declined in real terms in the northeastern and western cities, in cities performing two least-common functions, and in New York City. Common function spending failed to grow or increased at an average annual rate of less than 2% in the growing, mixed, and declining cities, in the southern cities, and in the medium- and high-density cities. Spending for general control was one of the few common functions to be spared the budget ax. It grew in real terms in most groups of cities, even after fiscal 1975. The growth of such spending was especially rapid in the southern and western cities. However, real spending for general control declined sharply in the northeastern cities and in New York City during the fiscal 1975–79 period. New York's general control expenditures had increased at an average annual rate of 6.1% in real terms between fiscal 1969 and 1975; it declined at an average annual rate of 12.7% during the fiscal 1975–79 period as the City attempted to slash its overhead costs.

All other operating expenditures continued to expand at a relatively rapid pace after fiscal 1975 in most groups of cities. This would appear to indicate that expenditure pressures originated in the non-common or optional municipal functions.

Municipal employees bore the brunt of attempts to hold the line on operating expenditures after fiscal 1975. Between October 1975 and October 1979, full-time municipal employment per 10,000 residents declined from 133 to 125 in the growing cities, from 274 to 262 in the northeastern cities, from 162 to 149 in the western cities, from 169 to 154 in the medium-density cities, and from 467 to 459 in New York City. In those groups in which municipal employment continued to grow after October 1975, the rate of growth was much slower than in prior years.

The lack of sufficient data makes it more difficult to evaluate changing municipal wage costs. Some analysts have suggested that the combination of growth pressures and the increased unionization of municipal workers would elevate municipal wages in southern cities. At the same time, forced belt-tightening in the north was expected to depress municipal wage costs in northern cities. The result would be some convergence in wage costs between northern and southern cities. Available data indicate that southern cities were characterized by lower wage costs than their northern counterparts in both 1975–76 and 1978–79. Equally significant, the southern cities appeared to increase their relative wage advantages vis-à-vis the northeastern cities in several of the occupations studied. For example, between 1975–76 and 1978–79, the wage index for clerical workers declined from 93 to 88 in the southern cities but increased from 106 to 107 in the northeastern cities. The wage index for sanitation workers declined from 84 to 80 in the southern cities but increased from 112 to 114 in the northeastern cities.

Available evidence regarding expenditure retrenchment in large U.S. cities, by major grouping, is summarized in Tables 4.5 and 4.6. It appears that expenditure retrenchment was underway in both growing and declining, northern and southern cities after fiscal 1975. The fact that sunbelt cities also

TABLE 4.3. Full-Time Equivalent Employment Per 10,000 Residents, October, 1979 Major City Groupings

Type of Employment	By Population Change			By Region			
	Growing	Mixed	Declining	Northeast	No. Central	South	West
Total Employment	125	184	227	262	164	212	149
Common Function	75	92	116	130	100	96	82
All Other	50	92	111	132	64	116	67
Common Function Employment	75	92	116	130	100	96	82
Highways	6	9	10	9	10	9	6
Police Protection	27	27	46	49	43	30	29
Fire Protection	14	18	20	24	17	19	14
Sanitation	6	9	11	14	9	11	4
Parks & Recreation	12	16	11	10	9	15	15
Financial Administration & General Control	10	13	18	24	12	12	14

	By Population Density			By Differences in Functional Responsibilities				
Type of Employment	Low	Medium	High	Three[a] Functions	Two Functions	One Function	Minimal Amounts	None
Total Employment	151	154	252	459	349	247	147	132
Common Function	85	89	120	107	122	128	88	84
All Other	66	65	132	352	227	119	59	48
Common Function Employment	85	89	120	107	122	128	88	84
Highways	7	9	10	10	10	7	8	9
Police Protection	27	31	51	41	40	49	39	27
Fire Protection	16	16	20	18	24	20	14	17
Sanitation	8	7	12	17	8	16	7	7
Parks & Recreation	14		9	8	16	16	10	7
Financial Administration & General Control	13	13	18	13	24	20	10	11
	13	13	18	13	24	20	10	13

[a]Denotes New York City

Source: Computations based on Census Bureau data.

141

TABLE 4.4. Indexes of Municipal Pay in Large Cities, by Occupation, October 1978 to September 1979 Major City Groupings (City Average = 100)

Occupation	By Population Change			By Region			
	Growing	Mixed	Declining	Northeast	No. Central	South	West
Clerical	97	90	107	107	105	88	105
Skilled Maintenance	91	83	107	88	110	78	108
Public Safety	103	90	101	99	99	92	110
Sanitation	94	86	115	114	103	80	119
Janitorial	93	89	112	104	109	83	108

Occupation	By Population Density			By Differences in Functional Responsibilities				
	Low	Medium	High	Three[a] Functions	Two Functions	One Function	Minimal Amounts	None
Clerical	92	102	111	N.A.	95	116	98	98
Skilled Maintenance	83	106	106	131	88	103	113	90
Public Safety	94	101	106	114	98	99	102	99
Sanitation	86	102	123	120	113	94	102	97
Janitorial	89	102	117	103	102	109	98	99

N.A.—Not Available
[a]Denotes New York City
Source: Computations based on data from the U.S. Bureau of Labor Statistics

started to retrench precluded any substantial narrowing of north–south municipal expenditure or employment differentials.

Conclusions

It is now possible to answer some of the questions posed at the beginning of this section. Are public expenditures in declining, northern cities substantially higher than those in growing, southern and western cities? Yes, in fiscal 1979, general spending in the declining cities was double that of the growing cities; general spending in the northeastern cities was almost double that of the western cities. If so, where do the expenditure pressures in northern cities originate? Higher personnel costs are one factor. The northern cities were generally characterized by higher municipal employment levels and higher municipal wage costs. Diverse functional responsibilities are also a factor. The declining, northern cities, many of which performed one or more of the least-common functions, were characterized by disproportionately high expenditures and employment levels for all other operating functions, a category that includes the non-common or optional functions. To what extent do population densities influence the level of expenditures for selected municipal functions? In fiscal 1979, general spending by the high-density cities was 1.8 times that of the low-density cities; common function spending was 1.6 times as high; all other operating expenditures were almost three times as high. Clearly population densities were associated with differences in municipal spending. How have municipal expenditures and personnel costs changed over time, particularly since fiscal 1975? The growth of municipal spending in large cities slowed measurably after fiscal 1975. Both capital and operating expenditures were affected. Common function spending and municipal employment were hardest hit by attempts to control expenditures during the latter part of the 1970s.

EXPENDITURES: INDIVIDUAL CITIES

This section analyzes the unique configuration of expenditures in each of the sample cities. It compares the level and rate of expenditure growth with the revenue potential of each city. It analyzes the separate components of operating expenditures and underscores the unique mix of common function spending and other operating expenditures in each city. It evaluates the balance between capital and operating expenditures and assesses the extent to which capital spending has been sacrificed to satisfy current operating needs in fiscally hard-pressed cities. It demonstrates how personnel costs have influenced overall operating expenditures in each city. The analysis

TABLE 4.5. Changing Municipal Expenditures for Major City Groupings, Fiscal 1969–79 (Per Capita Spending in Constant 1972 Dollars)

	By Population Change			By Region			
	Growing	Mixed	Declining	Northeast	No. Central	South	West
General Expenditures							
Fiscal 1969	166	223	344	416	239	255	256
Fiscal 1975	206	311	410	510	297	310	294
Fiscal 1979	217	341	425	558	317	318	288
Capital Expenditures							
Fiscal 1969	50	64	71	76	61	63	62
Fiscal 1975	50	74	69	75	55	80	56
Fiscal 1979	45	69	60	74	44	68	53
Operating Expenditures							
Fiscal 1969	105	141	234	294	162	165	160
Fiscal 1975	141	205	302	393	219	197	209
Fiscal 1979	156	238	324	429	241	225	210
Common Function Spending							
Fiscal 1969	76	82	115	131	96	78	102
Fiscal 1975	94	108	138	167	116	97	118
Fiscal 1979	94	116	146	166	130	101	115
All Other Operating Expenditures							
Fiscal 1969	29	59	118	163	66	87	58
Fiscal 1975	47	96	164	226	103	101	91
Fiscal 1979	62	122	178	263	111	124	94

	By Population Density			By Differences in Functional Responsibilities				
	Low	Medium	High	Three[a] Functions	Two Functions	One Function	Minimal Amounts	None
General Expenditures								
Fiscal 1969	179	232	386	941	535	313	222	196
Fiscal 1975	239	280	458	1,240	647	401	254	242
Fiscal 1979	261	285	478	984	619	466	264	253
Capital Expenditures								
Fiscal 1969	51	65	72	89	86	58	63	59
Fiscal 1975	62	58	72	156	105	67	49	60
Fiscal 1979	59	48	64	48	84	71	41	54
Operating Expenditures								
Fiscal 1969	112	152	264	674	343	234	147	121
Fiscal 1975	155	200	342	882	452	309	185	163
Fiscal 1979	178	209	372	693	471	356	197	178
Common Function Spending								
Fiscal 1969	71	95	124	159	127	117	96	81
Fiscal 1975	89	113	152	130	161	145	118	92
Fiscal 1979	96	117	155	144	154	163	115	102
All Other Operating Expenditures								
Fiscal 1969	41	57	140	515	216	117	51	41
Fiscal 1975	66	87	190	752	291	164	67	71
Fiscal 1979	82	92	216	548	317	193	82	76

[a]Denotes New York City

Source: Computations based on Census Bureau data.

TABLE 4.6. Changing Municipal Employment Levels and Wage Costs for Major City Groupings

Full-Time Equivalent Employment Per 10,000 Residents

October Employment	By Population Change			By Region			
	Growing	Mixed	Declining	Northeast	No. Central	South	West
1969	113	144	196	228	139	183	146
1975	133	179	225	274	166	201	162
1979	125	184	227	262	164	212	149

October Employment	By Population Density			By Differences in Functional Responsibilities				
	Low	Medium	High	Three[a] Functions	Two Functions	One Function	Minimal Amounts	None
1969	122	148	212	457	282	209	135	119
1975	146	169	244	467	348	224	155	141
1979	151	154	252	459	349	247	147	132

Indexes of Municipal Pay, by Occupation

Occupation	By Population Change			By Region			
	Growing	Mixed	Declining	Northeast	No. Central	South	West
Clerical Workers							
1975–76	98	88	110	106	103	93	105
1978–79	97	90	107	107	105	88	105
Skilled Maintenance Workers							
1975–76	90	85	110	87	110	80	107
1978–79	91	83	107	88	110	78	108

Public-Safety Workers								
1975–76	102	90	104	95	101	90	111
1978–79	103	90	101	99	99	92	110
Sanitation Workers							
1975–76	101	88	112	112	103	84	118
1978–79	94	86	115	114	103	80	119
Janitorial Workers							
1975–76	95	86	111	103	112	82	107
1978–79	93	89	112	104	109	83	108

	By Population Density			By Differences in Functional Responsibilities				
Occupation	Low	Medium	High	Three[a] Functions	Two Functions	One Function	Minimal Amounts	None
Clerical Workers								
1975–76	91	101	114	105	96	116	99	100
1978–79	92	102	111	N.A.	95	116	98	98
Skilled Maintenance Workers								
1975–76	87	104	106	116	89	101	115	92
1978–79	83	106	106	131	88	103	113	90
Public-Safety Workers								
1975–76	92	102	108	125	99	98	105	99
1978–89	94	101	106	114	98	99	102	99
Sanitation Workers								
1975–76	88	106	118	125	108	95	104	103
1978–79	86	102	123	120	113	94	102	97
Janitorial Workers								
1975–76	90	98	120	110	104	108	100	99
1978–79	89	102	117	103	102	109	98	99

[a]Denotes New York City

N.A.—Not Available

Source: Computations based on Census Bureau and BLS data.

concludes with evidence of expenditure retrenchment in large U.S. cities during the fiscal 1969–79 decade.

Expenditures versus Revenue Potential

High and rising expenditures coupled with a weak revenue base, high tax burdens, and/or extensive reliance on outside aid suggest that a city is in actual or impending fiscal difficulty. This section demonstrates the relationships between expenditure levels and selected measures of revenue potential in each city.

In fiscal 1979, per capita general spending for the sample cities ranged from a low of $280 in San Diego to a high of $1684 in New York City; the mean spending level was $648 per capita. New York, Boston, San Francisco, Baltimore, Newark, Buffalo, Denver, Atlanta, Philadelphia, Detroit, St. Louis, and Cincinnati exceeded this spending mean. However, only four of them—Atlanta, Philadelphia, Detroit, and St. Louis—were also characterized by above-average expenditure growth during the fiscal 1969–79 decade. As a general rule, the high-spending cities experienced below-average expenditure growth between fiscal 1969 and 1979 and vice versa. For example, general spending in high-spending cities such as Baltimore, Cincinnati, and New York grew at 55%, 32%, and 62% respectively of the 38-city mean growth rate. By contrast, expenditures by low-spending cities such as San Antonio, Ft. Worth, Houston, and Phoenix grew at rates considerably in excess of this mean. The rate of spending growth in these cities exceeded the 38-city mean by 26% to 35%. There was, however, a third group of cities in which below-average spending was accompanied by below-average spending growth. This group included San Diego, Honolulu, Los Angeles, Milwaukee, and Chicago. San Diego's fiscal 1979 general expenditures were only $280 per capita; they grew at only 62% of the mean rate for the sample cities between fiscal 1969 and 1979. Honolulu's fiscal 1979 general expenditures were $361 per capita; they grew at only 46% of the mean rate for the sample cities.

The significance of intercity differences in spending levels and rates of spending growth becomes clearer when the revenue potential of each city is factored into the analysis. For purposes of analysis, per capita income has been used to measure the strength of the local tax base. It is a direct measure of revenue potential in cities that use a local income tax; it is an indirect measure of the value of the local property tax base.

Cities with above-average expenditures and below-average incomes would appear to be most vulnerable to fiscal difficulties. In fiscal 1979, nine of the sample cities were characterized by above-average general spending and by below-average per capita personal incomes. They included Atlanta, Baltimore, Boston, Buffalo, Cincinnati, Detroit, Newark, Philadelphia, and

St. Louis. All except Atlanta were characterized by above-average fiscal 1979 tax burdens. Baltimore, Buffalo, and Newark were also highly dependent on outside aid. These cities appear least able to sustain fiscal 1979 spending levels in the long run.

Other large cities appeared better able to sustain fiscal 1979 spending levels. Kansas City, Oakland, Portland, Seattle, Los Angeles, Honolulu, and San Diego were characterized by below-average general spending and by below-average spending growth. Each was characterized by above-average personal income. All except Kansas City had below-average tax burdens. All except San Diego exhibited below-average dependence on outside aid.

These results are summarized in Figure 4.1 and Table 4.7.

The Mix of Operating Expenditures

Total general expenditures include capital and operating expenditures. In most cities, operating expenditures are the largest and most-rapidly growing component of general spending. In fiscal 1979, the ratio of operating-to-general expenditures ranged from a low of 45% in Atlanta to a high of 87% in Newark. Operating expenditures accounted for at least 80% of general spending in Baltimore, Newark, Buffalo, Memphis, Toledo, Chicago, and Los Angeles.

In absolute terms, per capita operating expenditures ranged from a low of $198 in San Diego to a high of $1238 in Boston; mean operating expenditures for the sample cities was $472 per capita. Eleven cities, Boston, New York, Baltimore, Newark, Buffalo, San Francisco, Detroit, Philadelphia, Denver, St. Louis, and Memphis, exceeded this mean. However, only three of them—Philadelphia, Detroit, and Denver—were also characterized by above-average growth of operating expenditures during the fiscal 1969–79 decade.

There was a close correlation between the overall level of operating expenditures in given cities and their unique mix of operating expenditures. For purposes of analysis, operating expenditures have been disaggregated into common function spending and all other current operating expenditures. Ratios of common function-to-other operating expenditures were computed for each city. In fiscal 1979, they ranged from a low of 26% in New York City to a high of 214% in San Diego. A low ratio implies extensive responsibilities for the non-common functions and is associated with relatively high overall operating expenditures. A high ratio implies few responsibilities outside of the traditional common functions, which is, in turn, reflected in a relatively low level of operating expenditures. Baltimore, Boston, New York, Newark, and Buffalo were characterized by low ratios of common function-to-other operating expenditures; each was characterized by disproportionately high operating expenditures. By contrast, San Diego,

A. Relationship Between Expenditures and Income

Index of Change, FY 1969–79	Per Capita General Expenditures, FY 1979	
	Above Average	Below Average
Above Average	Atlanta Detroit Philadelphia St. Louis	Cleveland Columbus Dallas Ft. Worth Houston Indianapolis Long Beach Minneapolis New Orleans Oklahoma City Omaha Phoenix San Antonio
Below Average	Baltimore Boston Buffalo Cincinnati Denver Louisville Newark New York San Francisco	Chicago Honolulu Kansas City Los Angeles Memphis Milwaukee Oakland Pittsburgh Portland San Diego Seattle Toledo

B. Relationship Between Expenditures, Tax Burdens, and Outside Aid

Tax Burdens, FY 1979	Per Capita General Expenditures, FY 1979	
	Above Average	Below Average
Above Average	Baltimore Boston Buffalo Cincinnati Denver Detroit Newark New York Philadelphia San Francisco St. Louis	Kansas City
Below Average	Atlanta Louisville	Chicago Cleveland Columbus Dallas Ft. Worth Honolulu Houston Indianapolis Long Beach Los Angeles Memphis Milwaukee Minneapolis New Orleans Oakland Oklahoma City Omaha Phoenix Pittsburgh Portland San Antonio San Diego Seattle Toledo

Per Capita General Expenditures, FY 1979

Per Capita Personal Income, 1979	Above Average	Below Average
Above Average	Denver, New York, San Francisco	Dallas, Ft. Worth, Honolulu, Houston, Indianapolis, Kansas City, Long Beach, Los Angeles, Minneapolis, Oakland, Oklahoma City, Omaha, Phoenix, Portland, San Diego, Seattle
Below Average	Atlanta, Baltimore, Boston, Buffalo, Cincinnati, Detroit, Louisville, Newark, Philadelphia, St. Louis	Chicago, Cleveland, Columbus, Memphis, Milwaukee, New Orleans, Pittsburgh, San Antonio, Toledo

Per Capita General Expenditures, FY 1979

Aid Reliance, FY 1979	Above Average	Below Average
Above Average	Baltimore, Boston, Buffalo, Detroit, Newark, New York, San Francisco	Cleveland, Indianapolis, Memphis, Milwaukee, Minneapolis, New Orleans, Omaha, Phoenix, Pittsburgh, San Diego, Toledo
Below Average	Atlanta, Cincinnati, Denver, Louisville, Philadelphia, St. Louis	Chicago, Columbus, Dallas, Ft. Worth, Honolulu, Houston, Kansas City, Long Beach, Los Angeles, Oakland, Oklahoma City, Portland, San Antonio, Seattle

FIGURE 4.1

TABLE 4.7. Relationship Between Expenditures and Selected Measures of Revenue Potential

		Per Capita General Expenditures	Index of Change	Measures of Revenue Potential		
				Per Capita Income,	Tax Burdens,	Aid Reliance, Fiscal Year
Rank	City	Fiscal Year 1979	FY 1969–79	1979	1979	1979
1	New York	$1684	62	$7273	11.88%	45%
2	Boston	1573	82	6555	11.72	42
3	San Francisco	1185	63	9267	4.34	51
4	Baltimore	1182	55	5877	6.54	58
5	Newark	1105	73	4525	8.12	64
6	Buffalo	1048	92	5929	4.01	68
7	Denver	841	95	8556	3.95	32
8	Atlanta	828	164	6550	3.52	33
9	Philadelphia	825	109	6053	7.10	31
10	Detroit	808	138	6215	4.54	49
11	St. Louis	693	106	5880	6.72	31
12	Cincinnati	652	32	6875	4.11	40
13	Louisville	648	75	6281	3.45	40
14	Memphis	639	80	6476	2.33	61
15	Cleveland	633	120	5770	3.26	43
16	Kansas City	592	99	7480	4.48	27
17	Long Beach	581	105	8343	1.70	34
18	Minneapolis	552	120	7490	2.74	51
19	New Orleans	549	102	6547	3.06	45
20	Oakland	526	74	7701	2.25	40
21	Portland	506	81	8100	2.50	36
22	Indianapolis	505	247	7585	2.12	47
23	Columbus	497	132	6783	2.17	36
24	Seattle	493	96	9282	2.37	31
25	Oklahoma City	469	147	7991	2.60	32
26	Pittsburgh	457	93	6845	3.03	41
27	Toledo	455	94	7050	2.15	41
28	Chicago	433	67	6939	3.44	37
29	Milwaukee	432	50	7104	2.22	50
30	Omaha	422	137	7529	2.63	41
31	Phoenix	421	131	7552	1.83	48
32	Dallas	386	104	8614	2.59	17
33	Los Angeles	372	68	8422	2.24	37
34	Honolulu	361	46	7914	2.80	38
35	Houston	355	135	8796	2.35	16

(continued on next page)

TABLE 4.7 *(cont'd)*

Rank	City	Per Capita General Expenditures Fiscal Year 1979	Index of Change FY 1969–79	Measures of Revenue Potential		
				Per Capita Income, 1979	Tax Burdens, 1979	Aid Reliance, Fiscal Year 1979
36	Ft. Worth	347	126	7336	2.16	30
37	San Antonio	305	130	5672	1.59	38
38	San Diego	280	62	8027	1.40	42
	Mean	648	100	7189	3.74	41

Source: Computations based on Census Bureau data.

San Antonio, Houston, Ft. Worth, and Oklahoma City were characterized by unusually high ratios of common function-to-other operating expenditures. Their functional responsibilities were largely confined to the traditional common functions, and their overall operating expenditures were correspondingly low.

In absolute terms, common function spending ranged from a low of $122 per capita in San Antonio to a high of $365 per capita in Boston; the 38-city mean was $212 per capita. The mix of common function spending indicates the unique public-service packages available in given cities. For the 38 cities as a group, mean per capita fiscal 1979 expenditures for each function were as follows: police protection, $73; fire protection, $41; parks and recreation, $28; financial administration and general control, $30; highways, $21; and sanitation, $21. Thus, approximately half of all common function spending was earmarked for police and fire protection. Individual cities deviated widely from these means. For example, highway spending in Toledo was five times that of Houston; $35 versus $7 per capita. Detroit spent 2.6 times as much as Minneapolis for police protection; $145 versus $55 per capita. Per capita spending for parks and recreation was $49 in San Francisco and $5 in Milwaukee. Per capita spending for financial administration was $27 in Denver and only $4 in Omaha. Per capita expenditures for general control were $50 in Boston and $5 in Chicago.

In absolute terms, other operating expenditures, a category which includes the least-common functions, ranged from a low of $63 per capita in San Diego to a high of $938 per capita in New York City; the 38-city mean was $260 per capita. Eleven cities, Boston, New York, Baltimore, Newark, Buffalo, San Francisco, Detroit, Philadelphia, Denver, St. Louis, and

Memphis, exceeded this mean. Each experienced below-average growth in other operating expenditures during the fiscal 1969–79 decade. However, other operating expenditures in these cities were already so high that even a small relative increase could strain their budgets. The findings confirm that increases in other operating expenditures were responsible for much of the increase in total operating expenditures in these cities during the fiscal 1969–79 decade. In Boston, New York, Baltimore, Newark, and Buffalo, the increase in other operating expenditures was responsible for more than 70% of the increase in total operating expenditures between fiscal 1969 and 1979.

The need to finance other operating expenditures appeared to be a source of stress even in those cities that were not responsible for any of the least-common functions. Increases in other operating expenditures accounted for at least 50% of the rise in total operating expenditures in Omaha, Indianapolis, Toledo, Ft. Worth, Columbus, Atlanta, Oakland, New Orleans, and Kansas City. It may well be that the proliferation of Federal grant programs, many of which are targeted to optional municipal functions, helped to stimulate additional local spending for these functions, thereby indirectly contributing to fiscal stress in large cities during the 1970s.

Expenditure increases for the common municipal functions did not appear to be a major cause of expenditure stress in large cities during the 1970s. Between fiscal 1969 and 1979, common function spending grew slowly or declined in real terms in several cities. Declines were recorded in New York City and Buffalo; common function spending remained unchanged in constant dollars in Philadelphia; common function spending grew by less than 10% in constant dollars in Baltimore, Newark, Oakland, Milwaukee, Los Angeles, Honolulu, and San Diego. Nevertheless, increases in common function spending accounted for at least half the increase in total operating expenditures between fiscal 1969 and 1979 in each of the following cities: San Diego, San Antonio, Houston, Oklahoma City, Honolulu, Phoenix, Dallas, Los Angeles, Milwaukee, Pittsburgh, Chicago, Seattle, Portland, Minneapolis, Cleveland, Long Beach, Louisville, Cincinnati, and Detroit. Most were sunbelt cities and were characterized by relatively low operating expenditures in fiscal 1979.

The mix between common function and other operating expenditures in each of the sample cities and its relationship to overall operating expenditures is summarized in Figure 4.2 and Table 4.8.

Operating Versus Capital Expenditures

There are strong indications that escalating operating expenditures siphoned resources from capital spending in large cities during the 1970s.

Index of Change FY 1969–79	Per Capita Operating Expenditures, Fiscal Year 1979			
	Above Average		Below Average	
Above Average	Denver Detroit Philadelphia		Atlanta Columbus Dallas Ft. Worth Houston Indianapolis	Kansas City Minneapolis New Orleans Oklahoma City Omaha San Antonio Phoenix Toledo
Below Average	Baltimore San Francisco Boston St. Louis Buffalo Cincinnati Memphis Newark New York		Chicago Cleveland Honolulu Long Beach Los Angeles Louisville Milwaukee	Oakland Pittsburgh Portland Seattle San Diego

Common Function/ Other Operating Expenditures, FY 1979	Per Capita Operating Expenditures, Fiscal Year 1979		
	Above Average		Below Average
Less Than Unity	Baltimore Memphis Boston Newark Buffalo New York Denver Philadelphia San Francisco St. Louis		Indianapolis Louisville New Orleans Omaha Toledo
Greater Than Unity	Detroit		Atlanta Los Angeles Chicago Milwaukee Cincinnati Minneapolis Cleveland Oakland Columbus Oklahoma City Dallas Phoenix Ft. Worth Pittsburgh Honolulu Seattle Houston San Antonio Kansas City San Diego Long Beach

FIGURE 4.2. Relationship Between Level, Growth and Mix of Operating Expenditures

TABLE 4.8. Relationship Between Level, Growth, and Mix of Operating Expenditures

Rank	City	Per Capita Expenditures, FY 79			Index of Change, FY 69–79			Common Function/Other Operating, FY 79	Net Change, Other Operating/Total Operating Expenditures, FY 69–79
		Operating	Common Function	Other Operating	Operating	Common Function	Other Operating		
1	Boston	$1238	$365	$873	90	105	58	42%	71%
2	New York	1185	247	938	52	52	34	26	81
3	Baltimore	995	273	721	71	70	49	38	75
4	Newark	956	268	688	76	71	54	39	75
5	Buffalo	854	209	645	78	58	59	32	81
6	San Francisco	764	275	489	71	63	55	56	69
7	Detroit	628	327	300	124	140	90	109	49
8	Philadelphia	597	293	304	106	106	86	96	54
9	Denver	585	257	327	112	132	75	79	57
10	St. Louis	549	256	293	83	84	64	87	57
11	Memphis	510	205	305	66	134	31	67	53
12	Cincinnati	449	237	211	34	105	7	112	21
13	Kansas City	433	229	204	127	117	125	112	52
14	Louisville	426	206	220	80	154	36	94	45
15	Long Beach	423	269	154	89	103	67	175	38
16	New Orleans	413	181	232	100	81	95	78	63
17	Cleveland	408	237	171	94	144	47	139	39

#	City							
18	Oakland	387	217	170	82	73	87	128	51
19	Minneapolis	385	214	171	111	109	100	125	49
20	Portland	385	227	158	92	83	108	144	48
21	Toledo	375	182	192	121	85	168	95	60
22	Seattle	374	246	128	94	101	87	192	38
23	Atlanta	370	191	179	126	92	181	107	57
24	Columbus	364	193	171	135	130	123	113	51
25	Chicago	361	209	152	78	86	60	138	45
26	Indianapolis	360	162	198	264	184	377	82	60
27	Pittsburgh	338	210	127	82	75	98	165	45
28	Milwaukee	315	192	123	70	70	65	156	45
29	Los Angeles	299	180	120	78	70	87	150	48
30	Dallas	283	174	109	132	121	168	160	44
31	Phoenix	278	178	100	109	128	81	178	38
32	Omaha	275	129	146	144	93	229	88	62
33	Honolulu	274	157	117	74	69	73	134	49
34	Oklahoma City	247	147	100	105	101	109	147	46
35	Ft. Worth	247	133	114	126	87	238	116	55
36	Houston	226	136	90	127	121	136	151	44
37	San Antonio	201	122	79	141	140	142	154	44
38	San Diego	198	135	63	59	69	45	214	35
	Mean	472	212	260	100	100	100		

(continued on next page)

157

TABLE 4.8 *(cont'd)*

Per Capita Common Function Spending, by Function, FY 1979

Rank	City	Total	Highways	Police	Fire	Sanitation	Parks & Recreation	Financial Administration	General Control
1	Boston	365	18	131	90	28	29	19	50
2	Detroit	327	28	145	38	26	45	19	26
3	Philadelphia	293	22	116	36	39	24	12	44
4	San Francisco	275	12	83	55	8	49	22	46
5	Baltimore	273	25	94	47	25	38	16	28
6	Long Beach	269	20	85	59	21	49	17	18
7	Newark	268	8	111	73	22	16	22	16
8	Denver	257	25	76	42	18	42	27	27
9	St. Louis	256	23	107	33	15	35	16	27
10	New York	247	20	95	43	40	17	14	18
11	Seattle	246	21	65	48	25	46	13	28
12	Cleveland	237	24	100	44	28	12	11	18
13	Cincinnati	237	27	76	58	16	39	9	12
14	Kansas City	229	34	80	45	16	26	15	13
15	Portland	227	25	72	49	6	44	12	19
16	Oakland	217	20	75	54	3	44	12	9
17	Minneapolis	214	34	55	34	25	39	8	19
18	Pittsburgh	210	18	72	46	29	24	10	11
19	Chicago	209	19	109	34	29	8	5	5

158

	City	209	17	69	53	21	20	14	15
20	Buffalo								
21	Louisville	206	10	72	37	30	33	14	10
22	Memphis	205	14	55	47	31	32	8	18
23	Columbus	193	22	60	38	21	30	9	13
24	Milwaukee	192	24	74	35	27	5	13	14
25	Atlanta	191	23	61	30	22	28	15	12
26	Toledo	182	35	54	43	23	11	6	10
27	New Orleans	181	16	52	27	17	26	14	29
28	Los Angeles	180	17	82	32	12	16	9	12
29	Phoenix	178	15	70	30	23	20	7	13
30	Dallas	174	13	59	32	27	26	9	8
31	Indianapolis	162	34	47	22	10	24	8	17
32	Honolulu	157	24	51	24	12	24	9	13
33	Oklahoma City	147	24	39	33	12	22	7	10
34	Houston	136	7	53	36	12	13	9	6
35	San Diego	135	8	42	23	13	31	7	11
36	Ft. Worth	133	14	43	29	14	16	10	7
37	Omaha	129	28	10	35	21	20	4	11
38	San Antonio	122	16	37	20	14	23	6	6
	Mean	212	21	73	41	21	28	12	18

Source: Computations based on Census Bureau data.

George Peterson notes:

> "Disinvestment in capital facilities represents a means by which a community may, for a time, borrow against the future . . . [but] . . . for each dollar saved in maintenance spending, a much larger burden of capital repair or replacement eventually must be shouldered. However, these costs may be shifted to a different group of taxpayers at a future date that is difficult to pinpoint."[9]

The process of capital disinvestment is a relatively invisible way of generating additional operating funds in fiscally hard-pressed cities. As such, it has become an attractive option for some northern cities.

There are relatively few studies that detail the capital requirements of large U.S. cities.[10] This study infers "capital need" in given cities from the financial statistics themselves. For example, a low average ratio of capital-to-general expenditures for the fiscal 1969–79 period is presumed *a priori* to indicate inadequate capital spending. This is probably a safe assumption in most older cities, but could be a questionable premise in the newer, sunbelt cities where a low or declining ratio may simply indicate that the desired capital stock has been achieved.

The average ratio of capital-to-general spending for the fiscal 1969–79 period ranged from a low of 5.5% in Newark to a high of 35.0% in Atlanta; the mean ratio for the distribution was 21.0%. There was generally an inverse relationship between the ratio of capital-to-general spending and the overall level of operating expenditures in the sample cities. That is, the higher the ratio of capital-to-general spending, the lower the level of operating expenditures and vice versa. This is entirely consistent with the hypothesis that the need to finance a high and rising level of operating expenditures depressed capital spending in fiscally hard-pressed cities during the 1970s.

Most sunbelt cities were characterized by above-average capital spending ratios during the fiscal 1969–79 decade. Many needed to build an urban infrastructure, sometimes from scratch, to accommodate their growing populations. Capital spending accounted for more than 30% of general spending in Atlanta, Omaha, Ft. Worth, Oklahoma City, and Louisville during this period. Dallas and Oakland were also characterized by above-average ratios of capital-to-general spending; 28% in Dallas and 25% in Oakland.

Researchers have recently evaluated the condition of public capital facilities in both Dallas and Oakland as part of a broader analysis of the public infrastructure of large U.S. cities. As regards Oakland, Mary Miller and her colleagues noted that capital improvements claimed a diminishing share of local revenues.

> "While the present condition of Oakland's physical plant compares favorably on many counts with that of other fiscally strained cities,

Oakland is now struggling to continue locally-financed maintenance and capital investment."[11]

As regards Dallas, Peter Wilson concluded:

"The city's strong fiscal condition places it in a good position to meet its capital needs. . . . The bright future for Dallas's capital plant provides a sharp contrast to the uncertain outlook for the older, more fiscally-distressed cities."[12]

The study also noted that Dallas was fortunate in that local developers help to finance public streets, sewers, and water mains as part of their obligations under the city's subdivision requirements.

A number of large cities were distinguished by their disproportionately low average ratios of capital-to-general spending for the fiscal 1969–79 period. For example, capital spending accounted for less than 15% of total general spending in Chicago, San Francisco, Boston, St. Louis, New York, and Newark. Researchers have evaluated the condition of public capital facilities in both Boston and New York. New York's average ratio of capital-to-general spending for the study period was 8.5%; Boston's was 12.8%. In evaluating New York's capital plant, David Grossman noted:

"Because of the serious financial troubles it has experienced, New York provides an extreme example of the cutbacks in capital investment and maintenance than can result from budgetary pressure on city governments. . . . The current condition of the basic systems in the city's physical plant . . . warrant concern, although the systems by and large are managing to perform their designated functions. . . ."[13]

Grossman found that many of the city's water mains were more than 75 years old and nearing the end of their planned life, and that about one-quarter of the city's waterway bridges were in poor condition.

In evaluating Boston's capital plant, Mary Miller and her colleagues noted that spending for basic infrastructure was at historically low levels, and that the city's ability to finance its capital needs was limited, particularly as a result of Proposition 2½. The study found that Boston was rebuilding its major thoroughfares on a 75-year cycle as compared with the norm of 25 years, that more than half of Boston's 200 bridges needed major rehabilitation, that 48 of them needed to be replaced, and that public transit in the Boston metropolitan area was characterized by " . . . poor vehicle performance and high operating costs."[14]

The fiscal 1979 mix between capital and operating expenditures in each of the sample cities is summarized in Table 4.9.

TABLE 4.9. The Mix of Capital and Operating Expenditures

Rank	City	Capital Spending/ Total General Spending Fiscal 1969–79 Average	Per Capita Expenditures Fiscal Year 1979	
			Capital	Operating
1	Atlanta	35.0%	$343	$370
2	Omaha	34.3	119	275
3	Ft. Worth	31.9	79	247
4	Oklahoma City	31.5	184	247
5	Louisville	30.3	146	426
6	Kansas City	28.3	74	433
7	Dallas	28.0	82	283
8	Phoenix	27.9	120	278
9	Honolulu	26.0	60	274
10	Houston	25.2	90	226
11	Oakland	24.9	111	387
12	Minneapolis	23.1	76	385
13	San Antonio	22.9	74	201
14	Long Beach	22.0	125	423
15	Seattle	21.5	61	374
16	San Diego	20.8	57	198
17	Toledo	20.6	60	375
18	Baltimore	20.3	138	995
19	Milwaukee	20.1	79	315
20	Cincinnati	19.6	143	449
21	Indianapolis	19.6	75	360
22	Los Angeles	19.4	50	299
23	Columbus	19.3	102	364
24	New Orleans	19.3	98	413
25	Denver	18.3	154	585
26	Cleveland	18.2	65	408
27	Pittsburgh	18.1	99	338
28	Portland	18.0	98	385
29	Philadelphia	17.8	136	597
30	Detroit	17.8	135	628
31	Buffalo	16.7	153	854
32	Memphis	16.6	79	510
33	Chicago	14.5	38	361
34	San Francisco	14.2	260	764
35	Boston	12.8	161	1238
36	St. Louis	10.4	66	549
37	New York	8.5	83	1185
38	Newark	5.5	26	956
	Mean	21.0	108	472

Source: Computations based on Census Bureau data.

Personnel Costs and Operating Expenditures

In fiscal 1979, wage and salary expenditures accounted for at least half of total operating expenditures in all cities except Kansas City.* The ratio of wage and salary spending-to-operating expenditures was 80% or more in Memphis, Seattle, Los Angeles, and San Antonio. Since non-wage benefits, such as employer pension contributions, are not reflected in these figures, the total price tag for the municipal workforce is even higher. Elizabeth Dickson, Harold Hovey, and George Peterson compared total compensation packages for workers in twelve large cities. Their work covered seven specific job categories. They found that as of January 1979, non-wage benefits were a substantial proportion of annual compensation; such benefits accounted for 24% of the annual compensation of Boston police officers, 19% of the compensation of Detroit firefighters, and 16% of the compensation of general stenographers in New York City.[15] Clearly, personnel costs are the largest single component of operating expenditures in large cities, and even minor changes in the size of the municipal workforce or in the level of municipal wages can have a major impact on municipal budgets.

In October 1979, the ratio of full-time equivalent municipal employment-to-population varied from a low of 81 per 10,000 residents in San Diego to a high of 527 per 10,000 in Baltimore; the mean for the sample cities was 198 workers per 10,000 residents.† Cities with extensive functional responsibilities generally exceeded this mean and vice versa.

For purposes of analysis, municipal employment has been disaggregated into common function employment and all other municipal employment. The latter category includes employees who provide non-common functions. Those cities with disproportionately high municipal employment levels generally provided one or more of these functions. Hence, the relatively large number of workers in the all other category. For example, Baltimore employed 372 municipal workers for every 10,000 residents in the all other category, and only 155 per 10,000 in the common functions. New York City employed 352 workers per 10,000 residents in the all other category, but only 107 per 10,000 in the common functions. Buffalo employed 206 workers per 10,000 residents in the all other category, but only 97 per 10,000 in the common functions.

Those cities with disproportionately low municipal employment levels generally failed to provide the non-common functions and were characterized by fewer workers in the all other category. For example, Phoenix employed 73 workers per 10,000 residents in the common functions, and only 39 per

---

*Wage and salary expenditures are defined as gross amounts expended for employee compensation prior to deduction of income taxes, social security or pension contributions.

† Part-time employment has been converted to a full-time equivalent basis and added to full-time employment to derive full-time equivalent employment.

10,000 in all other functions. Oklahoma City employed 71 workers per 10,000 in the common functions, and only 36 per 10,000 in all other functions. Ft. Worth employed 82 workers per 10,000 residents in the common functions, and only 39 per 10,000 in all other functions.

These figures suggest that extensive functional responsibilities are associated with higher municipal employment in both common and non-common functions. For example, Boston employed almost twice as many workers as Phoenix in the common functions, and almost eight times as many in all other functions; Baltimore employed more than twice as many workers as Houston in the common functions, and almost eleven times as many in the all other category; New York employed twice as many workers as San Diego in the common functions, and almost thirteen times as many in all other functions. Once again, the explanation seems to be that the responsibility for a diverse array of municipal services generates a large municipal bureaucracy.

In October 1979, there were substantial intercity employment differences even within the basic common functions. For example, police protection accounted for 54% of common function employment in Chicago, but for only 21% of the total in Memphis. Financial administration and general control accounted for 29% of common function employment in Indianapolis, but for only 5% of the total in Memphis.

The findings regarding wage and salary spending and levels of municipal employment in each of the sample cities are summarized in Figure 4.3 and Table 4.10.

Wage and salary expenditures reflect both employment levels and relative wages. For purposes of analysis, Bureau of Labor Statistics' wage indexes for each of five occupations—clerical workers, skilled maintenance workers, public safety workers, sanitation workers, and janitorial workers—were averaged to develop a composite wage index for each city. This information was available for 25 of the sample cities. The findings indicated that 10 cities—Boston, Baltimore, St. Louis, Memphis, Kansas City, New Orleans, Atlanta, Indianapolis, Dallas, and San Antonio—paid below-average wages in 1978–79. Four cities—Columbus, Phoenix, Houston, and San Diego—paid average wages. The remaining 11 cities—New York, San Francisco, Detroit, Philadelphia, Denver, Cleveland, Seattle, Chicago, Pittsburgh, Milwaukee, and Los Angeles—paid above-average wages.

Although the wage data pertain to selected municipal occupations in a limited number of cities, it is nevertheless possible to draw some tentative conclusions regarding the factors responsible for high wage and salary expenditures in certain cities. For example, it appears that high wage and salary expenditures in Boston, Baltimore, St. Louis, and Memphis were more a product of high employment levels than of high wage costs; each of these cities paid below-average wages for most of the occupations studied. High wage and salary expenditures in New York, San Francisco, Detroit, and

Philadelphia were attributable to above-average employment levels and above-average wage levels. Below-average wage and salary expenditures in Kansas City, Indianapolis, Dallas, and San Antonio reflected the combination of below-average employment levels and below-average wage levels. And, although Cleveland, Seattle, Chicago, Milwaukee, and Los Angeles paid above-average wages for most of the occupations studied, each was characterized by below-average municipal employment levels. (See Table 4.11.)

Evidence of Retrenchment

There is convincing evidence of expenditure retrenchment in the individual cities after fiscal 1975. For purposes of analysis, per capita expenditures for fiscal years 1969, 1975, and 1979 were expressed in constant 1972 dollars by applying the implicit price deflator for state and local government purchases. Average annual rates of change for the fiscal 1969–75 and fiscal 1975–79 periods were then computed.

Operating expenditures in the sample cities increased at an average annual rate of 6.2% between fiscal 1969 and 1975; expenditures increases slowed to an average annual rate of 3.4% during the fiscal 1975–79 period. Slower growth of operating expenditures was evident in virtually all of the sample cities. During the fiscal 1975–79 period, operating expenditures actually declined in real terms in New York, Newark, San Francisco, Cincinnati, and San Diego. Only ten cities experienced faster real growth of operating expenditures between fiscal 1975 and 1979 than between fiscal 1969 and 1975. They were: Detroit, Memphis, Louisville, Minneapolis, Toledo, Columbus, Pittsburgh, Dallas, Ft. Worth, and Houston.

Municipal employees were seriously affected by retrenchment efforts. Real wage and salary spending in the sample cities increased at an average annual rate of 5.8% between fiscal 1969 and 1975, but at a rate of only 2.1% annually between fiscal 1975 and 1979. Whereas, only Buffalo, Cleveland, and Pittsburgh experienced real declines in wage and salary spending between fiscal 1969 and 1975, 29 cities experienced real declines during the fiscal 1975–79 period. Such declines were, in turn, a function of the contraction of the municipal workforce in some cities. Between October 1969 and October 1975, the ratio of municipal employment-to-population declined in five cities: Detroit, Memphis, Louisville, Seattle, and Pittsburgh. Between October 1975 and October 1979, this ratio declined in 15 cities: New York, Newark, Buffalo, Philadelphia, Cincinnati, Long Beach, Oakland, Minneapolis, Portland, Toledo, Milwaukee, Los Angeles, Omaha, Honolulu, and San Diego. Even where the municipal workforce continued to expand after 1975, the rate of increase was much smaller than in previous years.

Per Capita
Wage & Salary
Expenditures,
FY 1979

Municipal Employment Per 10,000 Residents

	Above Average	Below Average
Above Average	Baltimore, Boston, Buffalo, Denver — Detroit, Memphis, Newark, New York — Philadelphia, San Francisco, St. Louis	Seattle
Below Average	Atlanta, Louisville, New Orleans	Chicago, Cincinnati, Cleveland, Columbus, Dallas, Ft. Worth, Honolulu, Houston — Indianapolis, Kansas City, Long Beach, Los Angeles, Milwaukee, Minneapolis, Oakland, Oklahoma City — Omaha, Phoenix, Pittsburgh, Portland, San Antonio, San Diego, Toledo

Common Function/ All Other Employment October 1979	Municipal Employment Per 10,000 Residents	
	Above Average	**Below Average**
Less Than One	Baltimore Boston Buffalo Denver Memphis Newark New York San Francisco St. Louis	Indianapolis San Antonio Seattle Toledo
One or More	Atlanta Detroit Louisville New Orleans Philadelphia	Chicago Cincinnati Cleveland Columbus Dallas Ft. Worth Honolulu Houston Kansas City Long Beach Los Angeles Milwaukee Minneapolis Oakland Oklahoma City Omaha Phoenix Pittsburgh Portland San Diego

FIGURE 4.3. Relationship Between Employment, Wages, and the Functional Mix of Employment

167

TABLE 4.10. Wage and Salary Expenditures versus Level of Municipal Employment

Rank	City	Per Capita Expenditures, FY 79			Full-Time Equivalent Employment/10,000 Residents, Oct. 1979			
		Operating	Wage and Salary	Wage & Salary/Operating	Total	Common Function	All Other	Common Function/Other Employees
1	Boston	$1238	$855	69%	431	134	297	0.45
2	New York	1185	851	72	459	107	352	0.30
3	Baltimore	995	631	63	527	155	372	0.42
4	Newark	956	582	61	389	128	261	0.49
5	Buffalo	854	478	56	303	97	206	0.47
6	San Francisco	764	586	77	314	125	189	0.66
7	Detroit	628	412	66	204	114	90	1.27
8	Philadelphia	597	356	60	205	141	64	2.20
9	Denver	585	409	70	253	109	144	0.76
10	St. Louis	549	379	69	297	147	150	0.98
11	Memphis	510	409	80	371	123	248	0.50
12	Cincinnati	449	294	65	162	93	69	1.35
13	Kansas City	433	211	49	150	98	52	1.88
14	Louisville	426	237	56	201	115	86	1.34
15	Long Beach	423	224	53	124	68	56	1.21
16	New Orleans	413	245	59	224	112	112	1.00
17	Cleveland	408	276	68	193	126	67	1.88

18	Oakland	387	212	55	116	71	45	1.58
19	Minneapolis	385	251	65	134	97	37	2.62
20	Portland	385	231	60	110	76	34	2.24
21	Toledo	375	191	51	102	71	31	2.29
22	Seattle	374	322	86	177	107	70	1.53
23	Atlanta	370	249	67	201	121	80	1.51
24	Columbus	364	210	58	123	81	42	1.93
25	Chicago	361	282	78	158	100	58	1.72
26	Indianapolis	360	201	56	161	76	85	0.89
27	Pittsburgh	338	190	56	132	108	24	4.50
28	Milwaukee	315	240	76	140	98	42	2.33
29	Los Angeles	299	268	90	138	75	63	1.19
30	Dallas	283	216	76	154	93	61	1.52
31	Phoenix	278	176	63	112	73	39	1.87
32	Omaha	275	174	63	94	69	25	2.76
33	Honolulu	274	183	67	120	89	31	2.87
34	Oklahoma City	247	164	66	107	71	36	1.97
35	Ft. Worth	247	182	74	121	82	39	2.10
36	Houston	226	157	69	103	68	35	1.94
37	San Antonio	201	169	84	152	68	84	0.81
38	San Diego	198	143	72	81	53	28	1.89
	Mean	472	312		198	98	100	

169

(continued on next page)

TABLE 4.10 *(cont'd)*

Common Function Employment/10,000 Residents, Oct. 1979

Rank	City	Total	Highways	Police	Fire	Sanitation	Parks & Recreation	Financial Administration & General Control
1	Boston	134	10	52	37	1	11	23
2	New York	107	10	41	18	17	8	13
3	Baltimore	155	18	54	26	19	19	19
4	Newark	128	9	41	31	11	9	27
5	Buffalo	97	6	33	29	14	6	9
6	San Francisco	125	4	37	23	5	21	35
7	Detroit	114	6	53	16	10	16	13
8	Philadelphia	141	8	55	18	19	10	31
9	Denver	109	9	34	19	8	23	16
10	St. Louis	147	10	60	21	9	17	30
11	Memphis	123	5	26	24	25	37	6
12	Cincinnati	93	8	28	22	6	14	15
13	Kansas City	98	9	39	23	2	12	13
14	Louisville	115	2	34	24	14	16	25
15	Long Beach	68	3	23	13	5	17	7
16	New Orleans	112	6	38	18	12	13	25
17	Cleveland	126	10	52	19	13	19	13
18	Oakland	71	8	25	14	1	15	8
19	Minneapolis	97	21	22	14	7	17	16

20	Portland	76	11	25	18	2	12	8
21	Toledo	71	6	22	16	9	5	13
22	Seattle	107	13	25	20	2	18	29
23	Atlanta	121	21	33	18	15	19	15
24	Columbus	81	7	24	16	10	11	13
25	Chicago	100	11	54	16	10	2	7
26	Indianapolis	76	6	23	12	4	9	22
27	Pittsburgh	108	12	37	25	12	12	10
28	Milwaukee	98	18	35	18	13	2	12
29	Los Angeles	75	4	32	11	4	14	10
30	Dallas	93	12	29	18	9	12	13
31	Phoenix	73	5	28	11	6	9	14
32	Omaha	69	11	23	18	1	8	8
33	Honolulu	89	8	25	13	7	22	14
34	Oklahoma City	71	7	22	19	3	11	9
35	Ft. Worth	82	8	24	15	8	15	12
36	Houston	68	4	26	18	6	8	6
37	San Antonio	68	10	18	14	7	10	9
38	San Diego	53	4	20	9	3	8	9
	Mean	98	9	33	19	9	13	15

Source: Computations based on Census Bureau data.

171

TABLE 4.11. Relationship Between Wage and Salary Expenditures, Employment Levels, and Wages

City	Per Capita Wage and Salary Expenditures, FY 79	Full-Time Equivalent Employment/10,000 Residents, Oct. 1979	1978–79 Composite Wage Index[a]
Boston	$855	431	91
New York	851	459	117
Baltimore	631	527	88
San Francisco	586	314	124
Detroit	412	204	134
Denver	409	253	105
Memphis	409	371	85
St. Louis	379	297	89
Philadelphia	356	205	109
Seattle	322	177	115
Chicago	282	158	123
Cleveland	276	193	115
Los Angeles	268	138	113
Atlanta	249	201	82
New Orleans	245	224	74
Milwaukee	240	140	114
Dallas	216	154	86
Kansas City	211	150	85
Columbus	210	123	100
Indianapolis	201	161	82
Pittsburgh	190	132	102
Phoenix	176	112	100
San Antonio	169	152	71
Houston	157	103	100
San Diego	143	81	100

[a] Represents a simple average of wage indexes for clerical, skilled maintenance, public safety, sanitation and janitorial workers.

Source: Computations based on data from the Census Bureau and the Bureau of Labor Statistics.

Evidence concerning changes in municipal wages during the late 1970s is more fragmentary and somewhat contradictory. Between 1975–76 and 1978–89, there were some wage declines in a number of "high-wage" cities. In New York City, the wage index for public-safety workers declined from 125 to 114, the index for sanitation workers fell from 125 to 120, and the index for janitorial workers declined from 110 to 103. In San Francisco, the wage index for clerical workers fell from 113 to 106, the index for skilled maintenance workers declined from 137 to 129, the index for public-safety workers fell from 116 to 108, and the index for janitorial workers declined from 125 to 114. However, a number of high-wage cities continued to sustain municipal wage increases and a number of low-wage cities appeared to experience wage declines. Detroit and Seattle were both high-wage cities. In

Detroit, the wage index for clerical workers rose from 149 to 153, and the index for skilled maintenance workers increased from 132 to 138. In Seattle, the wage index for sanitation workers increased from 115 to 119, and the index for janitorial workers rose from 113 to 119. Atlanta, Kansas City, and San Antonio were relatively low-wage cities. Atlanta's index of municipal wage costs declined for all five occupations: from 101 to 97 for clerical workers, from 82 to 78 for skilled maintenance workers, from 82 to 80 for public-safety workers, from 81 to 77 for sanitation workers, and from 80 to 77 for janitorial workers. Similar declines were evident in Kansas City and San Antonio.

The available evidence indicates that a process of expenditure retrenchment was under way in large U.S. cities by the mid-1970s. The growth of operating expenditures slowed in real terms after fiscal 1975. There were also widespread real declines in wage and salary spending. The latter reflected slower growth and in some cities, absolute declines, in the municipal workforce.

These findings are summarized in Figure 4.4 and in Tables 4.12 and 4.13.

	Operating Expenditures				
	Above-Average Growth FY 1975–79		Below-Average Growth FY 1975–79		Real Decline FY 1975–79
Above-Average Growth FY 1969–75	Atlanta Columbus Dallas Detroit Houston Indianapolis Kansas City	Omaha San Antonio	Denver Honolulu Long Beach Philadelphia Phoenix		Cincinnati Newark
Below-Average Growth FY 1969–75	Ft. Worth Minneapolis New Orleans Oklahoma City Pittsburgh Toledo		Baltimore Boston Buffalo Chicago Cleveland Los Angeles Memphis Milwaukee Oakland Portland	St. Louis Seattle	New York San Diego San Francisco
Real Decline FY 1969–75	Louisville				

FIGURE 4.4. Retrenchment in Large Cities: Expenditures (Average Annual Growth in Constant 1972 Dollars)

TABLE 4.12. Retrenchment in Large Cities: Expenditures
(Per Capita Constant 1972 Dollars)

City	Operating Expenditures (Per Capita Constant 1972 Dollars)			Full-Time Municipal Employment/ 10,000 Residents		
	FY 1969	FY 1975	FY 1979	Oct. 1969	Oct. 1975	Oct. 1979
Atlanta	118	177	216	139	195	201
Baltimore	473	569	581	427	480	527
Boston	503	645	723	354	414	431
Buffalo	381	475	499	258	323	303
Chicago	161	197	211	126	154	158
Cincinnati	316	536	262	275	415	162
Cleveland	160	214	239	183	191	193
Columbus	110	152	212	95	121	123
Dallas	87	124	166	119	152	154
Denver	203	321	342	179	244	253
Detroit	202	278	367	177	152	204
Ft. Worth	79	100	144	94	113	121
Honolulu	127	173	160	106	128	120
Houston	72	98	132	79	101	103
Indianapolis	63	169	211	60	161	161
Kansas City	137	213	253	108	137	150
Long Beach	172	243	247	128	143	124
Los Angeles	134	173	175	149	163	138
Louisville	186	172	249	172	170	201
Memphis	253	271	298	368	334	371
Milwaukee	151	176	184	133	143	140
Minneapolis	135	168	225	116	138	134
Newark	433	600	559	370	517	389
New Orleans	156	201	241	161	183	224
New York	674	882	693	457	467	459
Oakland	167	212	226	106	125	116
Oklahoma City	90	120	145	90	99	107
Omaha	79	131	161	61	109	94
Philadelphia	216	312	349	173	210	205
Phoenix	98	154	163	92	107	112
Pittsburgh	146	153	197	144	118	132
Portland	153	202	225	113	127	110
San Antonio	59	98	117	111	148	152
San Diego	104	127	116	75	88	81
San Francisco	360	452	446	278	310	314
Seattle	147	194	219	183	172	177
St. Louis	235	293	321	199	253	297
Toledo	123	165	219	97	105	102

Source: Computations based on Census Bureau data.

TABLE 4.13. Indexes of Municipal Pay for Selected Occupations in Selected Cities, 1975–76 versus 1978–79 (City Average = 100)

	Occupation									
	Clerical		Skilled Maintenance		Public-Safety		Sanitation		Janitorial	
City	75–76	78–79	75–76	78–79	75–76	78–79	75–76	78–79	75–76	78–79
Boston	97	95	75	72	95	101	N.A.	N.A.	102	97
New York	105	N.A.	116	131	125	114	125	120	110	103
Baltimore	105	94	70	72	93	87	83	89	94	100
San Francisco	113	106	137	129	116	108	154	163	125	114
Detroit	149	153	132	138	123	115	121	119	147	145
Philadelphia	125	126	89	91	99	104	101	103	120	121
Denver	93	94	94	98	108	108	117	120	94	104
St. Louis	101	100	79	85	87	91	86	87	94	84
Memphis	88	87	102	99	84	86	71	69	85	85
Kansas City	86	84	81	75	92	94	91	86	80	85
Cleveland	96	106	178	173	103	97	95	97	92	102
Seattle	111	116	100	107	115	119	N.A.	N.A.	91	119
Atlanta	101	97	82	78	82	80	81	77	113	77
Columbus	107	104	85	87	97	95	103	103	80	111
Chicago	96	93	136	135	122	119	133	142	105	126
Indianapolis	72	87	67	67	82	84	78	79	129	94
Pittsburgh	97	101	97	100	90	92	123	125	N.A.	94
Milwaukee	117	116	120	123	104	96	115	109	87	128
Los Angeles	115	110	124	123	127	123	120	110	132	101
Phoenix	98	103	95	94	98	99	95	97	107	108
Houston	95	101	88	98	100	113	95	102	100	108
San Antonio	75	72	60	57	89	88	88	67	84	84
San Diego	99	99	91	94	104	102	104	103	103	72

N.A.—Not available.
Source: U.S. Bureau of Labor Statistics.

AN INDEX OF FISCAL STRESS: EXPENDITURES

Based on the foregoing analysis, an index of expenditure stress was developed for each city. It incorporates twelve variables that are grouped under three broad categories: expenditures versus revenue capacity, operating expenditures, and personnel costs. The measures of expenditures versus revenue capacity include per capita general expenditures in fiscal 1979, percent change in general expenditures between fiscal 1969 and 1979, and level of per capita personal income in 1979. The latter is a proxy for revenue potential. Measures of operating expenditures include the ratio of operating-to-general expenditures in fiscal 1979, the ratio of increase in operating-to-general expenditures between fiscal 1969 and 1979, the ratio of other operating-to-total operating expenditures in fiscal 1979, and the ratio of increase in other operating-to-total operating expenditures between fiscal 1969 and 1979. The personnel variables include per capita wage and salary expenditures in fiscal 1979, the ratio of wage and salary expenditures-to-operating expenditures in fiscal 1979, the ratio of increase in wage and salary-to-operating expenditures between fiscal 1969 and 1979, the level of full-time equivalent municipal employment per 10,000 residents in October 1979, and the percent change in employment relative to population between October 1969 and October 1979. These measures are summarized in Figure 4.5.

The raw scores for each variable were first converted to standard (z) scores. Composite z scores were then computed for expenditures versus revenue capacity, operating expenditures, and personnel costs. These composite measures represent a simple average of the z scores for variables within each group. The three composite measures were then combined, by means of a simple average, to develop an overall measure of expenditure stress for each city. A z score of $-.675$ or less indicated stress; z scores of $+.675$ or more indicated the relative absence of stress; z scores falling between $-.675$ and $+.675$ indicated a moderate amount of stress. The distressed cities included those within the bottom 25% of the distribution; the non-distressed cities included those within the top 25%. Although the methodology is useful in determining relative stress levels, it is not necessarily valid in establishing absolute stress levels. That is, if all of the sample cities were fiscally distressed in terms of expenditures, the methodology could fail to detect it.

Five cities were fiscally distressed in terms of expenditures. They were: Boston, Baltimore, Newark, New York, and Buffalo. Long Beach was the only sample city to rank as non-distressed. The remaining 32 cities exhibited some signs of expenditure distress based on their standard (z) scores.

The City of Boston was characterized by the most troubled expenditure profile as of fiscal 1979. Its expenditure z score, -1.19, reflected highly

Expenditures versus Revenue Capacity	Operating Expenditures	Personnel Costs
1. Per Capita General Expenditures, FY 1979	4. Ratio of Operating Expenditures to General Expenditures, FY 1979	8. Per Capita Wage & Salary Expenditures, FY 1979
2. Percent Change in General Expenditures, FYs 1969–79	5. Ratio of Increase, Operating-to-General Expenditures, FYs 1969–79	9. Ratio of Wage & Salary Expenditures to Operating Expenditures, FY 1979
3. Per Capita Income, 1979	6. Ratio of Other Operating-to-Total Operating Expenditures, FY 1979	10. Ratio of Increase, Wage & Salary-to-Operating Expenditures, FYs 1969–79
	7. Ratio of Increase, Other Operating-to-Total Operating Expenditures, FYs 1969–79	11. Full-time Equivalent Municipal Employment Per 10,000 Residents, October, 1979
		12. Percent Change in Municipal Employment/ Population Ratio, October, 1969 to 1979.

FIGURE 4.5. Expenditure Measures Used to Denote Fiscal Stress

177

TABLE 4.14. An Index of Expenditure Stress for Large Cities

Rank	City	An Index of Expenditure Stress	Composite z Scores For		
			Expenditures versus Revenue Capacity	Operating Expenditures	Personnel Costs
1	Boston	−1.19	−0.99	−1.20	−1.37
2	Baltimore	−1.05	−0.57	−1.78	−0.79
3	Newark	−1.03	−1.06	−1.73	−0.29
4	New York	−0.96	−0.70	−0.94	−1.25
5	Buffalo	−0.68	−0.73	−1.46	+0.16
6	Indianapolis	−0.54	−0.98	−0.17	−0.47
7	Memphis	−0.48	−0.04	−0.51	−0.89
8	Detroit	−0.33	−0.79	−0.16	−0.05
9	St. Louis	−0.32	−0.50	+0.18	−0.65
10	Denver	−0.18	+0.26	−0.14	−0.65
11	Philadelphia	−0.16	−0.61	−0.04	+0.18
12	Chicago	−0.16	+0.42	−0.42	−0.49
13	New Orleans	−0.13	−0.12	−0.46	+0.20
14	Seattle	−0.01	+0.85	−0.43	−0.45
15	Ft. Worth	+0.02	+0.13	+0.10	−0.17
16	Omaha	+0.09	+0.02	+0.13	+0.11
17	San Antonio	+0.09	−0.38	+1.06	−0.42
18	Columbus	+0.11	−0.25	+0.07	+0.50
19	Los Angeles	+0.12	+0.93	−0.25	−0.31
20	Atlanta	+0.15	−0.93	+1.54	−0.17
21	Toledo	+0.15	+0.20	−0.84	+1.09
22	Milwaukee	+0.18	+0.62	+0.05	−0.12
23	San Francisco	+0.19	+0.41	+0.96	−0.80
24	Minneapolis	+0.22	+0.02	+0.37	+0.26
25	San Diego	+0.22	+0.95	−0.53	+0.24
26	Dallas	+0.24	+0.67	+0.26	−0.21
27	Cleveland	+0.25	−0.59	+0.97	+0.37
28	Honolulu	+0.27	+0.97	−0.42	+0.26
29	Kansas City	+0.28	+0.15	−0.08	+0.76
30	Louisville	+0.28	−0.07	+0.41	+0.49
31	Portland	+0.42	+0.58	−0.02	+0.69
32	Oakland	+0.45	+0.50	−0.01	+0.85
33	Phoenix	+0.45	+0.08	+0.98	+0.30
34	Houston	+0.48	+0.49	+0.85	+0.10
35	Pittsburgh	+0.49	+0.14	+0.36	+0.96
36	Cincinnati	+0.56	+0.48	+0.74	+0.47
37	Oklahoma City	+0.61	+0.03	+1.50	+0.30
38	Long Beach	+0.69	+0.38	+0.62	+1.06

Source: Computations based on Census Bureau data.

unfavorable composite z scores for expenditures versus revenue capacity, −0.99, operating expenditures, −1.20, and personnel costs, −1.37. Boston was characterized by disproportionately high general expenditures, $1573 per capita, and by below-average per capita personal income, $6555. During the 1970s, it experienced considerable expenditure pressure from the non-common functions, as indicated by its high ratio of change in other operating expenditures relative to total operating expenditures, 71%. Boston's fiscal 1979 wage and salary expenditures, $855 per capita, and employment levels, 431 full-time employees for every 10,000 residents, were also disproportionately high.

By contrast, Long Beach was characterized by a vastly different expenditure profile. Its expenditure z score was +0.69, reflecting favorable z scores for operating expenditures, +0.62, and personnel costs, +1.06. the city's general expenditures, $581 per capita, were slightly below the mean for the 38 cities. Its per capita personal income, $8343, was well above the mean. Long Beach had a relatively low ratio of other operating-to-total operating expenditures, only 36%, indicating relatively few responsibilities outside the traditional common functions. Long Beach was also characterized by relatively low wage and salary expenditures, $224 per capita, and by relatively low employment levels, only 124 full-time municipal workers for every 10,000 residents.

Most sample cities ranked as moderately distressed. Within this group, Indianapolis, Memphis, Detroit, and St. Louis were among the more-distressed cities, and Oklahoma City, Cincinnati, Pittsburgh, Houston, and Phoenix were among the less-distressed cities. Indianapolis is not as distressed as its z score, −0.54, would indicate. In large measure, this ranking reflects the unusually rapid growth of general spending between fiscal 1969 and 1979. This, in turn, was caused by the 1970 consolidation between the City of Indianapolis and most of its suburbs inside Marion County. No such statistical anomalies apply to Memphis, Detroit, or St. Louis.

The findings regarding relative levels of expenditure stress in large U.S. cities are summarized in Table 4.14.

NOTES

1. See, for example, Paul A. Samuelson, "A Pure Theory of Public Expenditures," *Review of Economics and Statistics* 36(November, 1954):387–89.
2. See Solomon Fabricant, *The Trend of Government Activity in the United States Since 1900* (New York: National Bureau of Economic Research, 1952); Harvey Brazer, *City Expenditures in the United States* (New York: National Bureau of Economic Research, 1959.)
3. Roy W. Bahl, *Metropolitan City Expenditures, A Comparative Analysis* (Lexington, Ky: University of Kentucky Press, 1969.)

4. Ibid., p. 129.

5. Richard D. Gustely, *Municipal Public Employment and Public Expenditures* (Lexington, Mass: Lexington Books, 1974.)

6. Ibid., p. 32.

7. U.S. Department of Labor, Bureau of Labor Statistics, *Wage Differences Among Large City Governments and Comparisons with Industry and Federal Pay, 1978–79*. Report 633, (Washington: U.S. Government Printing Office, March, 1981.)

8. Thomas Muller, *Growing and Declining Areas: A Fiscal Comparison*, Draft report (Washington: The Urban Institute, 1975), p. 75.

9. George E. Peterson, "Transmitting the Municipal Fiscal Squeeze to a New Generation of Taxpayers: Pension Obligations and Capital Investment Needs," in *Cities Under Stress, The Fiscal Crisis of Urban America*, eds. Robert W. Burchell and David Listokin (Piscataway, N.J.: Rutgers University Center for Urban Policy Research, 1981), pp. 260–61.

10. See, for example, Mary J. Miller, J. Chester Johnson, and George E. Peterson, *The Future of Boston's Capital Plant* (Washington: The Urban Institute Press, 1981); Mary J. Miller, Marcy Avrin, Bonnie Berk, and George E. Peterson, *The Future of Oakland's Capital Plant* (Washington: The Urban Institute Press, 1981); Nancy Humphrey, George E. Peterson, and Peter Wilson, *The Future of Cincinnati's Capital Plant* (Washington: The Urban Institute Press, 1979); Peter Wilson, *The Future of Dallas's Capital Plant* (Washington: The Urban Institute Press, 1980); David A. Grossman, *The Future of New York City's Capital Plant* (Washington: The Urban Institute Press, 1979.)

11. Miller, *et al., The Future of Oakland's Capital Plant*, p. xiii.

12. Wilson, *The Future of Dallas's Capital Plant*, pp. xiv–xv.

13. Grossman, *The Future of New York City's Capital Plant*, p. xv.

14. Miller, *et al., The Future of Boston's Capital Plant*, pp. xiii–xv.

15. Elizabeth Dickson, Harold A. Hovey, and George E. Peterson, *Public Employee Compensation, A Twelve City Comparison* (Washington: The Urban Institute, 1980), Table 12, p. 48.

5

Fiscal Stress in Large Cities: Debt and Liquidity

This chapter analyzes the debt and liquidity positions of large U.S. cities. In many states, the payment of interest and the repayment of principal on general obligation debt, which is backed by a city's full faith, credit, and taxing power, holds the highest claim on its fiscal resources.

A number of debt indicators are useful in revealing the presence of fiscal stress. They include per capita gross debt, long-term and short-term debt, the rate of growth of outstanding debt, debt burdens, and debt-service payments. Gross debt, as defined by the Census Bureau, includes " . . . all long-term credit obligations of the city and its agencies, whether backed by the city's full faith and credit or nonguaranteed, and all interest-bearing short-term credit obligations."[1] Long-term debt includes debt that is payable more than one year after the date of issue. Short-term debt includes " . . . interest-bearing debt payable within 1 year from date of issue, such as bond anticipation notes, bank loans, and tax anticipation notes and warrants. . . . [It also] includes obligations having no fixed maturity date if payable from a tax levied for collection in the year of their issuance."[2] Debt burdens are defined in this study as the relationship between outstanding debt and local personal income and/or taxable property values. Debt burdens indicate the ability of municipal residents to bear given debt levels. Debt-service payments include interest on both short- and long-term debt, repayment of the principal on short-term debt and repayment of a segment of the principal on long-term debt. Debt-service payments are often expressed as a fraction of total general spending to indicate the extent to which debt-service is a constraint on municipal spending.

Two liquidity measures—net-cash position and unrestricted net-cash position—are used to measure each city's current financial position as well as its vulnerability to unforseen fiscal shocks. A city's net-cash position is defined as the excess of cash and marketable securities over short-term debt. Its unrestricted net cash position is defined as the excess of cash and securities less debt offsets over short-term debt.* Each measure is expressed as a fraction of annual operating expenditures, because any unforseen revenue shortfalls or expenditure emergencies are likely to be proportionate to annual operating expenditures. A similar methodology was used by George Peterson and his colleagues at the Urban Institute.[3]

A number of data constraints affect the findings. As indicated in Chapter 1, census debt statistics are reported in such a way that it is impossible to distinguish between general obligation (tax-supported) debt and revenue-supported debt. Revenue-supported debt is not a legal obligation of the municipality. Intercity comparisons of gross debt may therefore be somewhat misleading, particularly for cities with large volumes of revenue-supported debt outstanding. For example, it might be unfair to compare fiscal 1979 debt levels in Atlanta, $2092 per capita, with New York City debt levels, $1623 per capita. Whereas Atlanta has a large volume of revenue-supported airport debt outstanding, virtually all of New York City's outstanding debt is general obligation, tax-supported debt. Many municipalities throughout the northeast do not have the legal authority to issue revenue-supported debt. For bond rating purposes, the debt position of each city is generally evaluated only in terms of its tax-supported liabilities. In this study, however, a more general economic definition encompassing all outstanding debt is used.[†] Even this measure is inadequate because it relates only to municipal corporations and their dependent agencies and fails to include the outstanding debt of other local governments which overlie city areas.** Therefore, the total debt supported by the municipal tax base is not measured. It is virtually impossible to obtain debt figures for overlapping governmental units. Nor have the debt repayment schedules of each city been examined so that it cannot be determined if given cities are in fiscal difficulty because of their need to redeem large sums of debt in the immediate future.

Another major data constraint is the failure of census statistics to distinguish between short-term operating loans and other forms of short-term

---

*Debt offsets are monies held in sinking funds or as security for debt repayment.

† There is some justification for including both tax-supported and revenue debt. Although cities are not legally obligated to redeem revenue debt from tax revenues, in practice they could be under strong pressure to do so.

**Omission of the debt obligations of overlapping governmental units can seriously distort the results because of intercity differences in functional arrangements for performing given functions.

debt, such as Bond Anticipation Notes (BANs.) This distinction becomes critical in evaluating municipal liquidity. Short-term operating loans, which generally reflect seasonal borrowing in anticipation of revenues, are generally not a problem unless there is evidence of consistent rollovers. Many would argue that BANs should not be included in short-term debt, because they are used for capital purposes and are generally renewed or converted into long-term bonds. The inclusion of BANs results in negative net-cash positions for cities like Toledo and Columbus, which have large volumes of BANs outstanding.* Nevertheless, it could be argued that the need to issue BANs and then "bond them out" when funds become available to meet principal payments is, itself, a sign of fiscal weakness. It all depends on what access the city issuing the BANs has to the long-term bond market.

Unfortunately, the data base for comparative debt analysis is extremely inadequate. These data constraints should be kept in mind in interpreting the findings presented in this chapter.

THE CHARACTERISTICS OF PUBLIC DEBT

Alan Steiss has analyzed how public capital facilities are financed.[4] He notes that they can be financed on a pay-as-you-go basis or by means of long-term borrowing. The pay-as-you-go method places a heavy burden on current taxpayers for facilities that will be used both by current and future generations. Under the "sinking-fund" approach, funds are set aside annually from general revenue and earmarked for specific capital projects; funds are expended when needed. However, the many complexities inherent in managing sinking funds makes this a relatively unattractive financing alternative.

Steiss notes that borrowing for capital improvements in the long-term bond market shifts the financial burden for such improvements to future generations. This is generally more equitable because the financial burden is spread over several generations of users and, depending on the retirement schedule, payments made coincide more closely with benefits received. The major disadvantage of this approach is that long-term borrowing, especially in the present inflationary climate, can entail high-interest costs which are passed on to future generations in the form of higher tax liabilities.

State constitutions and statutes delegate authority to incur debt to their local governments. Most states also impose borrowing limitations on their localities. For example, in some states, general obligation borrowing by local

---

*Ohio law allows BANs to be outstanding for a maximum period of ten years.

governments is limited to a given fraction of the assessed value of local property. Sometimes, general obligation borrowing must be approved by a local referendum. Some states set maximum maturities for local bond issues, generally not to exceed the life of the improvement, and specify the maximum permissible interest to be paid.

Public facilities that benefit the community at large are often financed through general obligation bonds. Capital requirements in areas such as law enforcement, fire protection, schools, and public-health facilities are amenable to this type of financing. Public facilities that benefit a readily-identifiable group of users can be financed by revenue bonds. The security for such bonds is the revenue to be earned by the facility.[5] The city is not obligated to use tax revenues to redeem revenue bonds if the revenues generated by the facility prove insufficient.

In recent years, revenue bonds have become an increasingly popular means of financing capital facilities which indicate that they can be self-supporting. Revenue bond issues are generally excluded from municipal debt ceilings and in most cases do not require voter approval. They are an equitable method of financing public facilities because only those who benefit from a given facility are required to pay for it. The recent proliferation of non-guaranteed debt was given impetus by increasingly stringent regulations covering the issuance of general obligation, tax-supported debt and by the broadened concept of "public purpose." John Petersen says that this broader definition of public purpose has led to a broader definition of government securities. For example, industrial revenue bonds are now being issued by local agencies on a tax exempt basis to finance private industrial development. Petersen suggests that the sale of such bonds has put additional pressure on the municipal bond market, thereby forcing traditional state and local borrowers to pay higher interest rates. Petersen also says that:

" . . . tax exemption represents an inefficient form of subsidy because part of the Federal tax revenues foregone must be shared with investors and are not captured in their entirety by state and local borrowers in the form of lower interest rates."[6]

DEBT AND LIQUIDITY: GROUPS OF CITIES

This section analyzes the debt and liquidity positions of the designated groups of cities. It attempts to answer the following types of questions: Are there differences between growing and declining cities in terms of the level of outstanding debt? What is the relative mix of short-term and long-term debt,

general and utility debt, guaranteed and non-guaranteed debt in each group?*
Are there perceptible differences in the liquidity positions of growing versus
declining cities, northern versus southern cities, high-density versus low-
density cities?

Outstanding Debt, Fiscal 1979

The findings indicate that there were relatively minor intergroup
differences in per capita gross debt as of fiscal 1979. For example, such debt
was $680 in the growing cities, $703 in the mixed cities, and $659 in the
declining cities. It was $653 in the low-density cities, $699 in the medium-
density cities, and $664 in the high-density cities. Although there were some
interregional variations, debt levels in the northeastern cities were not
significantly different from those in the southern cities. Per capita gross debt
was $841 in the northeastern cities and $848 in the southern cities, as
distinguished from $659 in the western cities and $495 in the midwestern
cities. Those cities that performed one or more least-common functions also
tended to have higher debt levels than those cities without such responsibilities. For example, per capita gross debt was $781 in cities that performed
two least-common functions and $808 in cities which performed one of them.
This compares with $595 in cities performing minimal amounts of the least-
common functions and $647 in cities with no such responsibilities. In New
York City, which performed all three least-common functions, per capita
gross debt was $1623, double that of cities that performed two of the least-
common functions.

Upwards of 95% of gross debt outstanding was long-term debt in most
groups of cities. However, there were major intergroup differences in the mix
of long-term debt. The declining, northern cities were characterized by a
higher proportion of general-to-utility debt than their growing, sunbelt
counterparts. This reflects the ability of southern and western cities to issue
non-tax supported revenue debt and their need to install and upgrade their
utility systems to accomodate population and job growth. In fiscal 1979, per
capita general debt was $310 in the growing cities as compared with $515 in
the declining cities. It was $312 in the western cities as compared with $701
in the northeastern cities. It was $660 in cities that performed two least-
common functions and $429 in cities that performed none of them. New

---

*General debt is not synonomous with general obligation debt, which refers to debt that is
backed by a city's full faith, credit, and taxing power. General debt refers to all debt other than
that identified as having been issued specifically for utility purposes. General debt may or may
not be guaranteed by the municipality that issues it.

York City's general debt, $1180 per capita, was almost double that of cities that performed two least-common functions.

The fact that general debt accounted for 82% of all long-term debt in the declining cities, but for only 47% of such debt in the growing cities, is significant because general debt is frequently guaranteed by the full faith and credit of the issuing municipality. During the fiscal 1969–79 decade, general debt accounted for 91% of all guaranteed long-term debt issued by the sample cities; only 9% of the guaranteed debt was utility debt. Of the non-guaranteed debt issued by the sample cities during this period, 55% was general debt and 45% was utility debt.

During the fiscal 1969–79 decade, declining, northern cities issued considerably more guaranteed tax-supported debt than their growing, sunbelt counterparts. This reflects the fact that many northern cities are prohibited from issuing revenue bonds. The declining cities issued almost twice as much guaranteed debt as the growing cities: $404 versus $230 per capita. The northeastern cities issued 2.5 times as much guaranteed debt as the western cities: $649 versus $255 per capita. Cities performing two least-common functions issued almost twice as much guaranteed debt as cities performing none of them: $681 versus $351 per capita. During the fiscal 1969–79 decade, New York City issued tax-supported debt amounting to $2156 per capita. This was more than five times the level of guaranteed debt issued by the declining cities, more than three times the amount issued by the northeastern cities, and almost five times that issued by the high-density cities.

Although only a negligible proportion of all outstanding debt in the sample cities was short-term debt, as defined by the Census Bureau, the level of short-term debt outstanding was nevertheless greatest in declining, northern cities. For example, in fiscal 1979, per capita short-term debt was $32 in the declining cities and $24 in the growing cities, $52 in the midwestern cities and $8 in the southern cities, $37 in the high-density cities and $6 in the low-density cities. New York City's short-term debt was $59 per capita.

These findings are summarized in Table 5.1.

Debt Burdens and Debt-Service

For purposes of analysis, debt burdens are defined in two ways: as the ratio of per capita long-term debt-to-per capita personal income and as the ratio of per capita long-term general debt-to-income. These yardsticks indicate that the declining cities, the northeastern cities, the high-density cities, and those performing one or more least-common functions generally had higher debt burdens and were characterized by consistently higher debt-service payments than the other groups of cities.

TABLE 5.1. Outstanding Debt for Major City Groupings, Fiscal Year 1979 ($ Per Capita)

Type of Debt	By Type of City			By Region			
	Growing	Mixed	Declining	Northeast	No. Central	South	West
Gross Debt Outstanding	680	703	659	841	495	848	695
Short-term Debt	24	19	32	29	52	8	15
Long-term Debt	656	684	627	812	443	840	644
General Debt	310	558	515	701	371	598	312
Utility Debt	346	126	112	111	72	242	332
Long-Term Debt Issued	717	634	585	809	406	814	688
Guaranteed	230	334	404	649	269	358	255
Non-Guaranteed	487	300	181	160	137	456	433

Type of Debt	By Population Density			By Differences in Functional Responsibilities				
	Low	Medium	High	Three[a] Functions	Two Functions	One Function	Minimal Amounts	None
Gross Debt Outstanding	653	699	664	1623	781	808	595	647
Short-term Debt	6	37	37	59	30	22	24	31
Long-term Debt	647	662	627	1564	751	786	571	616
General Debt	528	319	532	1180	660	639	301	429
Utility Debt	119	343	95	384	91	147	270	187
Long-Term Debt Issued	632	667	602	2312	721	686	591	619
Guaranteed	346	225	456	2156	681	445	123	351
Non-Guaranteed	286	442	146	156	40	241	468	268

[a] Denotes New York City.

Source: Computations based on Census Bureau data.

In fiscal 1979, the ratio of long-term debt-to-income was 8.2% in the growing cities, 7.7% in the declining cities, and 9.2% in the mixed cities. This ratio was higher in the northeastern and southern cities—13.4% and 11.6% respectively—than in the midwestern and western cities—6.5% and 7.7% respectively. It was higher in the high-density cities than in the low-density cities: 9.5% versus 8.3%. It was also higher in cities performing one or more of the least-common functions than in cities with no such responsibilities. For example, the ratio of long-term debt-to-income was 12.8% in cities performing one least-common function and 8.1% in cities performing none. New York City's ratio was 22%, well above comparable ratios for the declining, northeastern and high-density cities.

A somewhat different pattern emerges when debt burdens are expressed in terms of the ratio of long-term general debt-to-income. When this yardstick is used, the gap between the declining, high-density, northern cities and their growing, low-density, southern counterparts becomes even greater. In fiscal 1979, for example, this ratio was 7.7% in the declining cities and 3.9% in the growing cities, 11.5% in the northeastern cities and 3.7% in the western cities, 8.1% in the high-density cities and 6.8% in the low-density cities, 9.2% in cities performing two least-common functions and 5.6% in cities performing none. In New York City, the ratio of long-term general debt-to-income was a disproportionately high 16.2%. These differences reflect the concentration of general debt, much of it guaranteed, in declining, northern cities.

Declining, northern cities were also characterized by significantly higher debt-service payments than the other groups of cities. In fiscal 1979, debt-service in the declining cities was 1.5 times that of the growing cities: $74 versus $48 per capita. Debt-service in the northeastern cities was more than double that of the western cities: $108 versus $46 per capita. Debt-service in the high-density cities was 1.4 times that of the low-density cities: $81 versus $58 per capita. Debt-service in cities performing two least-common functions was almost 1.8 times that of cities performing none: $93 versus $53 per capita. In fiscal 1979, debt-service payments in New York City were $669 per capita, six times those of the northeastern cities and nine times those of the declining cities.

Both interest payments and payments to redeem principal were higher in the declining, northern cities than in other groups of cities. For example, interest payments by the declining cities were 1.8 times those of the growing cities: $31 versus $17 per capita; payments to redeem principal were 1.4 times as high: $43 versus $31 per capita. Interest payments by the northeastern cities were triple those of the western cities: $50 versus $17 per capita. Their payments to redeem principal were double those of the western cities: $58 versus $29 per capita. The high-density cities paid almost 1.4 times as much as the low-density cities for interest: $34 versus $25 per capita. They also paid 1.4 times as much to redeem principal: $47 versus $33 per capita. In New York City, payments to redeem principal accounted for 90% of total debt-service payments. In absolute terms, New York's debt-redemption payments were $602 per capita; fourteen times the level of debt redemption in the declining cities.

It is interesting to note, however, that debt-service was a greater constraint on general spending in the growing cities than in the declining cities. In fiscal 1979, the ratio of debt-service-to-general spending was 12.2% in the growing cities and 10.2% in the declining cities, 11.3% in the northeastern cities and 13.0% in the southern cities, 12.9% in the low-density cities and 9.9% in the high-density cities, 8.8% in cities performing two least-common functions and 12.3% in cities performing none of them. These findings reflect the fact that overall spending levels were so much higher in declining, northern cities than in their growing, southern and western counterparts. New York City was a notable exception to this pattern. In fiscal 1979, debt-service payments were equivalent to 40% of total general spending in New York City, signifying that they were a major budgetary constraint.

These findings are summarized in Table 5.2

Municipal Liquidity

In fiscal 1979, declining, northern cities had consistently lower net-cash reserves as defined in this study than other groups of cities. Net-cash reserves were equivalent to only 45% of annual operating expenditures in the declining cities as compared with 99% in the growing cities. Unrestricted net-cash reserves equalled 37% of annual operating expenditures in the declining cities and 82% in the growing cities. The ratio of net-cash reserves-to-annual operating expenditures was 31% in the northeastern cities and 37% in the midwestern cities as compared with 100% in the southern cities and 94% in the western cities. The ratio of unrestricted net-cash reserves-to-operating expenditures was 26% in the northeastern cities and 29% in the midwestern cities as compared with 80% in the southern cities and 79% in the western cities. The high-density cities were also considerably less liquid than their medium- and low-density counterparts. The fiscal 1979 ratio of net-cash reserves-to-annual operating expenditures was 34% in the high-density cities, 75% in the medium-density cities, and 110% in the low-density cities. The ratio of unrestricted net-cash reserves-to-annual operating expenditures was 30% in the high-density cities, 60% in the medium-density cities, and 89% in the low-density cities. Cities that performed one or more least-common functions were less liquid than cities that performed none. For example, the ratio of net-cash reserves-to-annual operating expenditures was

TABLE 5.2. Debt Burdens and Debt-Service for Major City Groupings, Fiscal 1979

Indicator	By Type of City			By Region			
	Growing	Mixed	Declining	Northeast	No. Central	South	West
Long-Term Debt/Income	8.2%	9.2%	7.7%	13.4%	6.5%	11.6%	7.7%
Long-Term General Debt/Income	3.9	7.5	7.7	11.5	5.4	8.2	3.7
Per Capita Debt-Service	$48	$64	$74	$108	$54	$71	$46
Interest Payments	17	29	31	50	20	29	17
Redemption of Principal	31	35	43	58	34	42	29
Debt-Service/General Expenditures	12.2%	10.9%	10.2%	11.3%	9.9%	13.0%	9.3%

Indicator	By Population Density			By Differences in Functional Responsibilities				
	Low	Medium	High	Three[a] Functions	Two Functions	One Function	Minimal Amounts	None
Long-Term Debt/Income	8.3%	8.9%	9.5%	21.5%	10.4%	12.8%	7.6%	8.1%
Long-Term General Debt/Income	6.8	4.3	8.1	16.2	9.2	10.4	4.0	5.6
Per Capita Debt-Service	$58	$50	$81	$669	$93	$90	$47	$53
Interest Payments	25	18	34	67	37	40	18	21
Redemption of Principal	33	32	47	602	56	50	29	32
Debt-Service/General Expenditures	12.9%	10.2%	9.9%	39.7%	8.8%	11.3%	10.4%	12.3%

[a] Denotes New York City.
Source: Computations based on Census Bureau data.

46% in cities performing two least-common functions and 97% in cities performing none. New York City's net-cash reserves were equivalent to 45% of annual operating expenditures. Its unrestricted net-cash reserves were equal to only 15% of annual operating expenditures. It is interesting to note that only the southern and low-density cities possessed net-cash reserves equivalent to at least one year's operating expenditures in fiscal 1979.

These findings are summarized in Table 5.3.

Changing Debt Patterns, Fiscal 1969–79

This section analyzes the changing pattern of outstanding debt for major city groupings during the fiscal 1969–79 decade. Per capita debt measures for fiscal years 1969, 1975, and 1979 have been expressed in constant 1972 dollars. The results indicate that during the 1970s, per capita gross debt declined in constant dollars in most groups of cities and that the rate of decline accelerated after fiscal 1975. Short-term debt was also sharply reduced after fiscal 1975 in the wake of New York City's well-publicized fiscal crisis. It seems clear that most groups of cities made a determined effort to liquidate their short-term obligations and to avoid any future build-up of short-term debt. Long-term debt also declined in constant dollars, but not as dramatically as short-term debt. However, since long-term debt accounted for the preponderance of gross debt outstanding, even relatively modest declines in long-term debt had a beneficial impact on overall debt levels.

The following statistics illustrate the dramatic real declines in gross debt which occurred during the 1970s. Between fiscal 1969 and 1979, per capita gross debt declined from $479 to $398 in the growing cities and from $499 to $385 in the declining cities. It fell from $545 to $491 in the northeastern cities and from $468 to $385 in the western cities. It declined from $471 to $381 in the low-density cities and from $510 to $388 in the high-density cities. It declined from $526 to $456 in cities performing two least-common functions and from $433 to $378 in cities performing none of them. In New York City, per capita gross debt declined from $1281 to $948 during the fiscal 1969–79 decade.

The steepest declines occurred during the fiscal 1975–79 period. For example, in the growing cities, the average annual rate of decline in gross debt outstanding increased from 0.9% between fiscal 1969 and 1975 to 3.0% between fiscal 1975 and 1979. The rate of decline increased from 1.6% to 3.6% in the declining cities, from 2.1% to 5.3% in the midwestern cities and from 1.4% to 4.2% in the high-density cities. New York City's gross debt grew at an average annual rate of 3.8% in real terms between fiscal 1969 and 1975 before declining at an average annual rate of 10% during the fiscal 1975–79 period. However, these figures are somewhat

TABLE 5.3. Liquidity Measures for Major City Groupings, Fiscal 1979 (Percents)

Indicator	By Type of City			By Region				
	Growing	Mixed	Declining	Northeast	No. Central	South	West	
Net-Cash Position/Operating Expenditures	99	88	45	31	37	100	94	
Unrestricted Net-Cash Position/ Operating Expenditures	82	71	37	26	29	80	79	

Indicator	By Population Density			By Differences in Functional Responsibilities				
	Low	Medium	High	Three[a] Functions	Two Functions	One Function	Minimal Amounts	None
Net-Cash Position/Operating Expenditures	110	75	34	45	46	38	68	97
Unrestricted Net-Cash Position/ Operating Expenditures	89	60	30	15	43	32	56	74

[a]Denotes New York City.
Source: Computations based on Census Bureau data.

misleading. New York City was locked-out of the bond market during the fiscal 1975–79 period because of its fiscal difficulties. However, long-term borrowing was conducted indirectly through the Municipal Assistance Corporation (Big MAC.) Such debt is not included in the census figures although New York City's sales tax revenues were pledged as security for Big MAC debt.

There were also dramatic real declines in per capita short-term debt during the fiscal 1969–79 decade: from $29 to $15 in the growing cities, from $70 to $19 in the declining cities, from $104 to $16 in the northeastern cities, from $33 to $9 in the western cities, and from $75 to $22 in the high-density cities. During the fiscal 1975–79 period, average annual declines in short-term debt exceeded 20% in the northeastern and southern cities and ranged between 15% and 20% in the declining cities, the western cities, the high- and low-density cities, and in cities performing one or more of the least-common functions. New York City's per capita short-term debt increased from $141 to $520 in real terms between fiscal 1969 and 1975, but declined to only $34 by fiscal 1979.

During the fiscal 1969–79 period, long-term debt also declined in constant dollars in all but the northeastern cities. Such debt declined from $450 to $383 per capita in the growing cities and from $429 to $366 in the declining cities, from $360 to $259 in the midwestern cities and from $435 to $376 in the western cities, from $466 to $378 in the low-density cities and from $435 to $366 in the high-density cities. New York City's long-term debt declined from $1140 to $914 per capita in constant dollars during the fiscal 1969–79 decade, excluding Big MAC debt.

Real declines in outstanding debt helped to stabilize debt-service payments in most groups of cities. Debt-service payments also became less of a constraint on general spending, except in New York City. Debt burdens also generally declined during this period.

These findings are summarized in Table 5.4.

Changing Municipal Liquidity, Fiscal 1969–79

There were small but significant improvements in the net-cash reserves of declining, northern cities during the fiscal 1975–79 period. This enabled them to repair some of the erosion in liquidity that occurred between fiscal 1969 and 1975. For example, the ratio of unrestricted net-cash reserves-to-annual operating expenditures increased from 29% to 37% in the declining cities, from 6% to 26% in the northeastern cities, and from 17% to 30% in the high-density cities between fiscal 1975 and 1979. New York City moved from a negative net-cash position in fiscal 1975 to a positive net-cash position in fiscal 1979. (See Table 5.5).

TABLE 5.4. Changing Debt Patterns for Major City Groupings, Fiscal 1969–79 (Per Capita Debt in Constant 1972 Dollars)

Debt Indicator	By Type of City			By Region			
	Growing	Mixed	Declining	Northeast	No. Central	South	West
Gross Debt							
Fiscal 1969	479	425	499	545	421	551	468
Fiscal 1975	453	457	450	527	367	511	470
Fiscal 1979	398	411	385	491	289	496	385
Short-Term Debt							
Fiscal 1969	29	21	70	104	61	16	33
Fiscal 1975	18	23	73	88	60	25	28
Fiscal 1979	15	11	19	16	30	5	9
Long-Term Debt							
Fiscal 1969	450	404	429	441	360	535	435
Fiscal 1975	435	434	377	439	307	486	442
Fiscal 1979	383	400	366	475	259	491	376
Debt-Service							
Fiscal 1969	32	29	43	50	34	42	32
Fiscal 1975	30	38	44	67	36	41	27
Fiscal 1979	28	37	43	63	31	41	27
Debt-Service/General Spending							
Fiscal 1969	19.5%	13.2%	12.4%	11.9%	14.2%	16.3%	12.7%
Fiscal 1979	12.2	10.9	10.2	11.3	9.9	13.0	9.3
Long-Term Debt/Income							
Fiscal 1969	10.2	9.7	10.7	11.8	8.8	13.9	4.2
Fiscal 1979	8.2	9.2	7.7	13.4	6.5	11.6	7.7
Long-Term General Debt/Income							
Fiscal 1969	5.9	7.0	8.4	10.5	7.0	10.6	4.2
Fiscal 1979	3.9	7.5	7.7	11.5	5.4	8.2	3.7

Debt Indicator	By Population Density			By Differences in Functional Responsibilities				
	Low	Medium	High	Three[a] Functions	Two Functions	One Function	Minimal Amounts	None
Gross Debt								
Fiscal 1969	471	461	510	1281	526	559	469	433
Fiscal 1975	424	461	466	1576	511	514	478	378
Fiscal 1979	381	409	388	948	456	472	348	378
Short-Term Debt								
Fiscal 1969	5	57	75	141	60	60	48	40
Fiscal 1975	9	48	78	520	69	64	48	28
Fiscal 1979	3	22	22	34	17	13	14	18
Long-Term Debt								
Fiscal 1969	466	404	435	1140	466	499	421	393
Fiscal 1975	415	413	388	1056	442	450	430	350
Fiscal 1979	378	387	366	914	439	459	334	360
Debt-Service								
Fiscal 1969	35	34	43	113	51	44	30	36
Fiscal 1975	37	30	50	167	49	56	32	33
Fiscal 1979	34	29	47	391	54	53	28	31
Debt-Service/General Spending								
Fiscal 1969	19.8%	14.5%	11.2%	12.0%	9.5%	14.0%	13.6%	18.3%
Fiscal 1979	12.9	10.3	9.9	39.7	8.8	11.3	10.4	12.3
Long-Term Debt/Income								
Fiscal 1969	11.3	9.5	10.7	24.5	11.2	13.2	9.5	9.6
Fiscal 1979	8.3	8.9	9.5	21.5	10.4	12.8	7.6	8.1
Long-Term General Debt/Income								
Fiscal 1969	8.9	5.3	8.5	15.6	8.2	10.3	5.9	7.1
Fiscal 1979	6.8	4.3	8.1	16.2	9.2	10.4	4.0	5.6

[a]Denotes New York City.

Source: Computations based on Census Bureau data.

TABLE 5.5. Changing Municipal Liquidity for Major City Groupings, Fiscal 1969–79 (Percents)

Unrestricted Net-Cash Reserves/ Annual Operating Expenditures	By Type of City			By Region			
	Growing	Mixed	Declining	Northeast	No. Central	South	West
Fiscal 1969	115	87	36	11	49	72	102
Fiscal 1975	85	76	29	6	33	79	75
Fiscal 1979	82	71	37	26	29	80	79

Unrestricted Net-Cash Reserves/ Annual Operating Expenditures	By Population Density			By Differences in Functional Responsibilities				
	Low	Medium	High	Three[a] Functions	Two Functions	One Function	Minimal Amounts	None
Fiscal 1969	113	87	18	3	28	31	74	91
Fiscal 1975	79	73	17	−28	37	15	58	73
Fiscal 1979	89	60	30	15	43	32	56	74

[a] Denotes New York City.
Source: Computations based on Census Bureau data.

196

DEBT AND LIQUIDITY: INDIVIDUAL CITIES

This section analyzes the debt and liquidity positions of each of the sample cities. It examines the level of outstanding debt in each city as of fiscal 1979 and traces changes in gross debt, short-term, and long-term debt during the fiscal 1969–79 decade. It relates the levels of capital spending in given cities to the volume of long-term debt issued. It demonstrates how debt-service payments in each city have changed over time and analyzes the mix of newly-issued tax-supported and revenue debt in each city. It evaluates changes in municipal debt burdens and liquidity over time. It presents evidence of debt retrenchment in each city.

The Level and Growth of Debt

In fiscal 1979, per capita gross debt outstanding ranged from a low of $147 in San Diego to a high of $2092 in Atlanta; the mean for the 38 cities was $715 per capita. Eight cities—Atlanta, New York, San Francisco, San Antonio, Seattle, Boston, Oklahoma City, and Philadelphia—were characterized by gross debt in excess of $1000 per capita. Debt levels in excess of this amount are widely regarded as burdensome. Seven cities were characterized by above-average debt levels in fiscal 1979 and by above-average debt growth during the fiscal 1969–79 decade. They were: Atlanta, San Francisco, San Antonio, Seattle, Boston, Philadelphia, and Minneapolis. An equal number of cities with above-average debt levels experienced relatively slow debt growth during the fiscal 1969–79 decade.

Long-term debt accounted for virtually all of the outstanding debt in each of the sample cities except for Columbus and Toledo, which were characterized by a significant volume of short-term debt in the form of bond anticipation notes. In fiscal 1979, long-term debt exceeded $1000 per capita in Atlanta, New York, San Francisco, San Antonio, Seattle, and Philadelphia. Between fiscal 1969 and 1979, long-term debt in Atlanta, Minneapolis, and San Antonio grew at 2.6 to 3.3 times the mean rate of growth for the sample cities.

Only a handful of cities had significant amounts of short-term debt outstanding at the conclusion of their respective fiscal years. In fiscal 1979, 12 of the sample cities had no short-term debt outstanding. They were: Atlanta, Philadelphia, Minneapolis, Houston, Baltimore, Dallas, Indianapolis, Ft. Worth, Newark, St. Louis, Long Beach, and San Diego. Philadelphia does issue temporary loan notes and Indianapolis issues tax anticipation notes during the fiscal year, but both cities liquidated these obligations by the end of their fiscal years. Short-term debt was $45 per capita or less in 18 cities: San Antonio, Seattle, Milwaukee, Memphis, Los Angeles, Denver, Kansas City, Phoenix, Oakland, Cincinnati, Portland,

Omaha, Pittsburgh, Honolulu, Detroit, Chicago, New Orleans, and Oklahoma City. Only eight cities had significant amounts of short-term debt outstanding in fiscal 1979. These cities and their respective per capita debt levels are as follows: Columbus, $276; Toledo, $207; Buffalo, $103; Boston, $93; San Francisco, $76; Cleveland, $68; New York, $59; and Louisville, $58. Many of these cities also had short-term debt outstanding at the end of their fiscal years during much of the fiscal 1969–79 decade. The average ratio of short-term-to-gross debt for this period ranged between 15 and 20% in Boston, New York, San Francisco, and Louisville. It exceeded 20% in Columbus, Cleveland, and Buffalo and was greater than 50% in Toledo.

These findings are summarized in Figure 5.1 and Table 5.6.

The Relationship between Capital Spending and Long-Term Debt Issued

A high and rapidly-increasing level of long-term debt, particularly tax-supported debt, is presumed to introduce some risk into municipal finances. A large and growing overhang of long-term debt can be a problem if the municipal tax base is not growing. It is generally not of concern if the tax base that supports the debt is, itself, growing rapidly. Moreover, the risk introduced by the existence of long-term debt can be offset by capital improvements. Timely investments in capital facilities can prevent the costly accumulation of capital needs at some future date.

It is virtually impossible to determine what constitutes an adequate level of capital spending in given cities without a detailed on-site study of the capital needs of those cities. The average ratio of capital spending-to-total general spending for the fiscal 1969–79 period is a proxy, albeit an imperfect one, for recent levels of capital spending in each of the sample cities. When compared with net increases in long-term debt during the fiscal 1969–79 period, it provides some indication of the closeness of the "match" between capital spending and long-term debt. It should be remembered that because of differences in the assignment of functional responsbilities, the absence of capital expenditures by cities and their dependent agencies does not necessarily mean that capital spending is not occurring. Capital expenditures can also be made by the respective states, by special districts, and by other overlying governmental units.

Cities that issued above-average amounts of long-term debt between fiscal 1969 and 1979 were also characterized by above-average ratios of capital-to-general spending during the fiscal 1969–79 decade and vice versa. Atlanta, San Antonio, Minneapolis, Seattle, Oklahoma City, Houston, Oakland, Louisville, and Phoenix issued above-average amounts of long-

A. The Level and Growth of Long-Term Debt

Index of Change, FY 69–79	Per Capita Long-Term Debt, Fiscal Year 1979			
	Above Average		Below Average	
Above Average	Atlanta Boston Minneapolis Philadelphia San Antonio	San Francisco	Indianapolis Long Beach Oakland Omaha Portland	Toledo
Below Average	Baltimore Cleveland Denver Houston Los Angeles Louisville Memphis New York Oklahoma City Seattle		Buffalo Chicago Cincinnati Columbus Dallas Detroit Ft. Worth Honolulu Kansas City Milwaukee Newark	New Orleans Phoenix Pittsburgh San Diego St. Louis

B. The Degree of Reliance on Short-Term Debt

Short-Term Debt/Gross Debt, FY 1969–79	Per Capita Short-Term Debt, Fiscal Year 1979			
	Above Average		Below Average	
Greater than or equal to 15%	Boston Buffalo Chicago Cleveland Columbus Louisville New York	San Francisco Toledo	Oakland Pittsburgh Portland	
Less than 15%	Detroit New Orleans		Atlanta Baltimore Cincinnati Dallas Denver Ft. Worth Honolulu Houston Indianapolis Kansas City Long Beach Los Angeles Memphis	Milwaukee Minneapolis Newark Oklahoma City Omaha Philadelphia Phoenix San Antonio San Diego Seattle St. Louis

FIGURE 5.1.

TABLE 5.6. The Level and Growth of Debt, by Type ($ Per Capita)

Rank	City	Gross Debt FY 1979	Index of Change FYs 1969–79	Total FY 1979	Long-Term Debt Index of Change FYs 1969–79	General Debt FY 1979	Utility Debt FY 1979	Short-Term Debt FY 1979	Short-Term/ Gross Debt FY 1969–79 Average
1	Atlanta	$2092	347	$2092	301	$1792	$300	$ 0	0%
2	New York	1623	62	1564	65	1180	384	59	18
3	San Francisco	1202	172	1126	171	1012	114	76	16
4	San Antonio	1088	287	1076	269	206	870	12	4
5	Seattle	1065	113	1052	98	388	664	13	4
6	Boston	1032	139	939	182	910	29	93	20
7	Oklahoma City	1019	43	991	34	769	222	28	4
8	Philadelphia	1003	101	1003	114	801	202	0	8
9	Louisville	940	65	882	93	539	343	58	16
10	Minneapolis	902	381	902	330	874	28	0	0
11	Memphis	867	59	866	51	654	212	1	1
12	Columbus	800	91	524	99	355	169	276	29
13	Los Angeles	795	79	782	76	149	633	13	3
14	Cleveland	774	74	706	75	491	215	68	21
15	Buffalo	727	72	624	76	594	30	103	23
16	Houston	709	113	709	98	515	194	0	0
17	Detroit	698	76	653	76	532	121	45	12
18	Denver	692	44	686	46	386	300	6	4
19	Baltimore	691	21	691	21	599	92	0	6

20	New Orleans	669	71	637	54	612	25	32	1
21	Kansas City	644	14	640	16	558	82	4	3
22	Oakland	607	162	595	223	595	0	12	16
23	Dallas	574	64	574	55	489	85	0	0
24	Phoenix	552	85	539	69	378	161	13	1
25	Cincinnati	497	*	489	*	422	67	8	14
26	Indianapolis	486	165	486	143	483	3	0	0
27	Ft. Worth	477	52	477	45	397	80	0	**
28	Newark	456	66	456	92	433	23	0	8
29	Toledo	453	161	246	142	200	46	207	51
30	Portland	452	147	441	190	277	164	11	16
31	Milwaukee	443	31	418	29	365	53	25	8
32	Omaha	393	206	387	183	387	0	6	2
33	St. Louis	365	45	365	39	339	26	0	0
34	Pittsburgh	347	30	332	83	332	0	15	20
35	Honolulu	344	*	335	4	261	74	9	9
36	Chicago	275	*	235	*	187	48	40	18
37	Long Beach	273	221	273	191	260	13	0	1
38	San Diego	147	*	147	*	142	5	0	**
	Mean	715		683		523	160	32	

*—Indicates an absolute decline.
**—Less than 0.5%.
Source: Computations based on Census Bureau data.

201

term debt and were characterized by above-average ratios of capital-to-general spending during the fiscal 1969–79 decade. For example, Atlanta's average ratio of capital-to-general spending was 35%; Oklahoma City's was 32%. Relatively large net additions to long-term debt in these cities appeared to reflect recently completed capital projects.

Other cities were characterized by below-average net additions to long-term debt and by below-average ratios of capital-to-general spending. They included: Memphis, Columbus, Cleveland, Newark, Denver, Indianapolis, Buffalo, Toledo, New Orleans, Detroit, Chicago, Pittsburgh, Baltimore, Milwaukee, St. Louis, and Cincinnati. Between fiscal 1969 and 1979, the net increase in per capita long-term debt was $217 in Newark, $98 in Chicago, and $14 in St. Louis. The average ratio of capital-to-general spending for the fiscal 1969–79 period was 5.5% in Newark, 14.5% in Chicago, and 10.4% in St. Louis. These are relatively low ratios given the age of these cities and their presumed need to repair or replace elements of their public infrastructures.

The functional distribution of long-term general debt indicates the types of recent capital investments made by each city. In fiscal 1979, 34 cities had some outstanding debt for sewage facilities. Such debt accounted for a significant proportion of long-term general debt in Columbus, 48%, in Toledo, 41%, and in Indianapolis, 36%. Thirty-one cities had long-term debt outstanding for parks and recreation. Park debt accounted for 29% of long-term general debt in Philadelphia, 25% in San Diego, and 20% in St. Louis. Twenty-eight cities had some highway debt outstanding in fiscal 1979. Highway debt accounted for 24% of long-term general debt in Columbus and for 22% of the total in Cincinnati. Twenty-eight cities also showed some long-term debt for housing and urban renewal. Such debt accounted for 44% of long-term general debt in New York, 38% in Minneapolis, and 29% in Cincinnati. Twenty-five cities had incurred debt for the construction of airport facilities. Airport debt accounted for 72% of long-term general debt in Atlanta, 54% in Los Angeles, 42% in San Francisco, 48% in St. Louis, and 41% in Denver. Long-term debt for education, hospitals, and water transportation and terminals was less common among the sample cities. Many have separate school districts and port authorities. However, in some cities, such debt represented a significant proportion of long-term general debt outstanding. For example, educational debt accounted for 46% of long-term general debt in Boston and for 30% of the total in Baltimore. Hospital debt accounted for 36% of long-term general debt in Portland. Debt for water transportation or terminal facilities accounted for 55% of long-term general debt in Long Beach.

The relationship between the growth of long-term debt and relative capital spending levels is shown in Figure 5.2 and Table 5.7.

Capital/Total General Spending, FYs 1969–79	Per Capita Net Long-Term Debt Issued, Fiscal 1969–79			
	Above Average		Below Average	
Above Average	Atlanta Houston Louisville Minneapolis Oakland Oklahoma City	Phoenix San Antonio Seattle	Dallas Ft. Worth Honolulu Kansas City	Long Beach Omaha San Diego
Below Average	Boston Los Angeles New York Philadelphia Portland San Francisco		Baltimore Buffalo Chicago Cincinnati Cleveland Columbus Denver Detroit Indianapolis Milwaukee Memphis	Newark New Orleans Pittsburgh St. Louis Toledo

FIGURE 5.2. Linkages Between Capital Spending and Net Long-Term Debt Issued

Debt-Service

In fiscal 1979, debt-service payments ranged from a low of $14 per capita in San Diego to a high of $669 per capita in New York City; the mean for the distribution was $93 per capita. Ten of the 15 cities with above-average levels of gross debt outstanding were also characterized by above-average debt-service payments. They were: Atlanta, New York, San Francisco, Boston, Oklahoma City, Philadelphia, Minneapolis, Memphis, Los Angeles, and Buffalo. All of the 23 cities with below-average levels of gross debt were also characterized by below-average debt-service payments in fiscal 1979. This group of cities included Chicago, Houston, Detroit, Denver, Baltimore, Dallas, Honolulu, Long Beach, and Phoenix.

Debt-service is composed of short- and long-term interest payments and payments to redeem principal. In fiscal 1979, payments to redeem principal generally exceeded interest payments in large U.S. cities. Per capita interest payments ranged from a low of $7 in San Diego to a high of $108 in Los Angeles; the mean for the distribution was $31 per capita. Payments to redeem principal ranged from a low of $7 per capita in San Diego to a high of

TABLE 5.7. Net Long-Term Debt Issued versus Capital Spending

Rank	City	Per Capita Net Long-Term Debt Issued, FYs 69–79			Capital Spending/General Spending, Fiscal 1969–79 Average	The Dominant Type of Long-Term General Debt Outstanding, Fiscal 1979
		Net Issued	Issued	Retired		
1	Atlanta	$1468	$1787	$319	35.0%	Airports
2	San Antonio	914	1106	192	22.9	Other, Not Specified
3	Minneapolis	688	1165	477	23.1	Housing & Urban Renewal, Highways
4	San Francisco	676	1160	484	14.2	Airports, Sewers, Housing & U.R.
5	New York	626	2312	1686	8.5	Housing & U.R., Education
6	Boston	569	1121	552	12.8	Education, Housing & U.R.
7	Seattle	551	813	262	21.5	Sewers
8	Philadelphia	474	901	427	17.8	Parks & Recreation, Airports
9	Los Angeles	448	870	422	19.4	Airports, Sewers
10	Oklahoma City	439	876	437	31.5	Other, Not Specified
11	Houston	426	698	272	25.2	Airports, Sewers
12	Oakland	375	486	111	24.9	Water Transport & Terminals
13	Portland	367	509	142	18.0	Housing & U.R., Hospitals
14	Louisville	359	1059	700	30.3	Sewers, Housing & U.R.
15	Phoenix	336	818	482	27.9	Airports, Highways, Sewers
16	Memphis	301	978	677	16.6	Education, Airports
17	Columbus	298	503	205	19.3	Sewers, Highways
18	Dallas	289	777	488	28.0	Other, Not Specified

#	City					
19	Cleveland	227	599	372	18.2	Airports, Sewers
20	Newark	217	497	280	5.5	Education
21	Denver	211	688	477	18.3	Airports
22	Indianapolis	186	364	178	19.6	Sewers, Airports, Highways
23	Long Beach	186	273	87	22.0	Water Transport & Terminals
24	Buffalo	162	790	628	16.7	Sewers, Housing & U.R.
25	Omaha	153	431	278	34.3	Sewers, Highways
26	Ft. Worth	148	470	322	31.9	Airports, Sewers
27	Toledo	136	231	95	20.6	Sewers, Highways
28	New Orleans	111	331	220	19.3	Housing & U.R., Sewers
29	Detroit	106	408	302	17.8	Sewers, Housing & U.R., Highways
30	Chicago	98	312	214	14.5	Airports, Sewers
31	Pittsburgh	89	310	221	18.1	Other, Not Specified
32	Honolulu	78	321	243	26.0	Other, Not Specified
33	Baltimore	72	490	418	20.3	Education, Housing & U.R.
34	Kansas City	55	350	295	28.3	Airports, Sewers
35	Milwaukee	47	414	367	20.1	Education, Housing & U.R., Highways
36	St. Louis	14	246	232	10.4	Airports, Parks & Recreation
37	San Diego	1	80	79	20.8	Sewers, Parks & Recreation
38	Cincinnati	−54	410	464	19.6	Housing & U.R., Highways
	Mean	312	683	371	21.0	

Source: Computations based on Census Bureau data.

206 / Crisis in Urban Public Finance

$602 in New York; the mean for the distribution was $62 per capita. New York, Los Angeles, Boston, Buffalo, San Francisco, Memphis, and Minneapolis were characterized by above-average payments to redeem debt. For example, in fiscal 1979, Los Angeles spent $359 per capita to redeem debt; Buffalo spent $106 per capita. New York, Los Angeles, Boston, Atlanta, Buffalo, San Francisco, Minneapolis, Philadelphia, Oklahoma City, New Orleans, and Cleveland were characterized by above-average interest payments. In fiscal 1979, per capita interest payments were $67 in New York and Boston, $60 in Philadelphia, $108 in Los Angeles, and $100 in Atlanta.

Large debt-service payments can constrain municipal spending in other functional areas. Therefore, it is useful to examine changes in ratios of debt-service-to-general expenditures over time. Between fiscal 1969 and 1979, this ratio declined in 27 of the 38 cities, indicating that debt-service had become less of an expenditure constraint. However, as of fiscal 1979, the ratio of debt-service-to-general spending still exceeded 15% in New York, Atlanta, Memphis, Minneapolis, Oklahoma City, and Dallas. Between fiscal 1969 and 1979, this ratio increased in New York, Boston, Atlanta, Minneapolis, Toledo, and Oakland. In New York City, it increased from 12% in fiscal 1969 to 40% in fiscal 1979.

These findings are summarized in Figure 5.3 and Table 5.8.

Guaranteed versus Non-Guaranteed Debt

During the fiscal 1969–79 period, there were major intercity differences in the proportion of newly-issued tax-supported (guaranteed) debt. For example, none of the long-term debt issued by Oakland or Long Beach was guaranteed by those cities. Less than half the debt issued by Atlanta, San Antonio, Louisville, Oklahoma City, Los Angeles, Seattle, and St. Louis was guaranteed debt. San Antonio, Louisville, and Los Angeles issued large quantities of non-guaranteed utility debt during the fiscal 1969–79 period.

By contrast, at least half the long-term debt issued by the remaining cities was guaranteed by the full faith, credit, and taxing power of those cities. All of the long-term debt issued by Boston and Newark was tax-supported debt. At least 90% of the long-term debt issued by New York, San Francisco, Baltimore, Cincinnati, Indianapolis, Honolulu, and Pittsburgh was also tax-supported debt. The largest volume of tax-supported debt was issued by New York City, $2156 per capita, Boston, $1121 per capita, and San Francisco, $1048 per capita. During the fiscal 1969–79 decade, New York City issued five times as much guaranteed debt as the average for the sample cities; San Francisco and Boston each issued about 2.5 times as much.

These findings are summarized in Table 5.9.

Per Capita Debt-Service, Fiscal 1979	Per Capita Gross Debt Outstanding, Fiscal Year 1979			
	Above Average		**Below Average**	
Above Average	Atlanta Boston Buffalo Los Angeles Memphis	Minneapolis New York Oklahoma City Philadelphia San Francisco		
Below Average	Cleveland Columbus Louisville San Antonio Seattle		Baltimore Chicago Cincinnati Dallas Denver Detroit Ft. Worth Honolulu	Houston Indianapolis Kansas City Long Beach Milwaukee Newark New Orleans Oakland	Omaha Phoenix Pittsburgh Portland San Diego St. Louis Toledo

Debt Service/ General Spending, Fiscal 1979	Per Capita Gross Debt Outstanding, Fiscal Year 1979			
	Above Average		**Below Average**	
Above Average	Atlanta Boston Buffalo Los Angeles Memphis Minneapolis New York	Oklahoma City Philadelphia San Antonio Seattle	Cincinnati Dallas Ft. Worth Houston Milwaukee New Orleans Omaha	
Below Average	Cleveland Columbus Louisville San Francisco		Baltimore Chicago Denver Detroit Honolulu Indianapolis Kansas City Long Beach Newark	Oakland Phoenix Pittsburgh Portland San Diego St. Louis Toledo

FIGURE 5.3. Relationship Between Debt, Debt-Service, and General Spending

TABLE 5.8. Debt-Service and its Relationship to General Spending

Rank	City	Per Capita Debt-Service, FY 79			Index of Change FYs 1969–79			Debt-Service/ General Expenditures	
		Total	Interest Payments	Debt Redemption	Total	Interest Payments	Debt Redemption	FY 69	FY 79
1	New York	$669	$67	$602	338	79	479	12%	40%
2	Los Angeles	467	108	359	972	789	1155	15	13
3	Boston	182	67	115	143	122	151	8	12
4	Atlanta	146	100	46	232	254	140	14	18
5	Buffalo	144	38	106	91	80	97	14	14
6	San Francisco	123	52	71	35	183	7	14	10
7	Memphis	106	24	82	84	54	105	17	17
8	Minneapolis	98	35	63	146	153	145	16	18
9	Philadelphia	98	60	38	91	115	49	14	12
10	Oklahoma City	93	36	57	58	68	51	37	20
11	Baltimore	82	31	51	50	46	52	8	7
12	Cincinnati	76	21	55	23	9	32	13	12
13	Newark	75	27	48	71	91	56	7	7
14	Detroit	74	30	44	69	89	61	15	9
15	New Orleans	72	35	37	99	65	113	14	13
16	Kansas City	65	31	34	29	18	41	21	11
17	Cleveland	65	35	30	40	111	4	20	10
18	Dallas	61	21	40	39	42	37	28	16

19	Milwaukee	60	18	42	24	38	19	19	14
20	Seattle	57	20	37	47	153	26	18	12
21	Houston	55	25	30	49	68	35	30	15
22	Ft. Worth	51	20	31	51	57	38	27	15
23	Omaha	50	21	29	94	123	75	16	12
24	Denver	48	23	25	81	88	77	6	6
25	Columbus	47	20	27	16	26	8	27	10
26	Toledo	45	16	29	163	84	134	7	10
27	Oakland	44	29	15	141	120	122	6	8
28	Pittsburgh	44	15	29	15	26	10	21	10
29	Indianapolis	43	20	23	98	153	66	18	8
30	St. Louis	41	16	25	61	38	77	9	6
31	Honolulu	41	17	24	27	27	25	14	11
32	San Antonio	40	11	29	79	46	100	19	13
33	Louisville	40	23	17	*	20	*	22	6
34	Chicago	39	11	28	55	27	81	10	9
35	Long Beach	28	16	12	158	166	85	4	5
36	Portland	28	16	12	39	125	0	8	6
37	Phoenix	20	12	8	*	38	*	19	5
38	San Diego	14	7	7	9	7	10	10	5
	Mean	93	31	62	100	100	100	16	12

*Represents an absolute decline.

Source: Computations based on Census Bureau data.

209

TABLE 5.9. The Mix Between Guaranteed and Non-Guaranteed Debt

Per Capita Long-Term Debt Issued, Fiscal Years 1969–79

Rank	City	Total	Guaranteed			Non-Guaranteed			Percent Guaranteed
			Total	General	Utility	Total	General	Utility	
1	New York	$2312	$2156	$1913	$243	$156	$156	0	93%
2	Atlanta	1787	245	245	0	1542	1364	178	14
3	Minneapolis	1165	958	923	35	207	207	0	82
4	San Francisco	1160	1048	998	50	112	112	0	90
5	Boston	1121	1121	1107	14	0	0	0	100
6	San Antonio	1106	164	164	0	942	29	913	15
7	Louisville	1059	39	39	0	1020	287	733	4
8	Memphis	978	606	594	12	372	0	372	62
9	Philadelphia	901	610	588	22	291	241	50	68
10	Oklahoma City	876	416	416	0	460	389	71	47
11	Los Angeles	870	30	30	0	840	136	704	3
12	Phoenix	818	528	422	106	290	175	115	65
13	Seattle	813	353	353	0	460	66	394	43
14	Buffalo	790	654	624	30	136	136	0	83
15	Dallas	777	478	478	0	299	263	36	62
16	Houston	698	346	346	0	352	225	127	50
17	Denver	688	567	463	104	121	121	0	82
18	Cleveland	599	341	303	38	258	134	124	57

19	Portland	509	273	228	45	236	135	101	54
20	Columbus	503	340	242	98	163	102	61	68
21	Newark	497	497	473	24	0	0	0	100
22	Baltimore	490	484	458	26	6	2	4	99
23	Oakland	486	0	0	0	486	486	0	0
24	Ft. Worth	470	350	342	8	120	51	69	74
25	Omaha	431	375	375	0	56	56	0	87
26	Milwaukee	414	336	336	0	78	64	14	81
27	Cincinnati	410	367	352	15	43	43	0	90
28	Detroit	408	227	221	6	181	148	33	56
29	Indianapolis	364	355	351	4	9	9	0	98
30	Kansas City	350	181	181	0	169	122	47	52
31	New Orleans	331	235	235	0	96	79	17	71
32	Honolulu	321	300	236	64	21	21	0	93
33	Chicago	312	173	173	0	139	117	22	55
34	Pittsburgh	310	309	309	0	1	1	0	99
35	Long Beach	273	0	0	0	273	261	12	0
36	St. Louis	246	96	96	0	150	141	9	39
37	Toledo	231	139	134	5	92	52	40	60
38	San Diego	80	57	57	0	23	23	0	71
	Mean	683	415			268			

Source: Computations based on Census Bureau data.

Debt Burdens

Individual cities also differed in terms of their ability to bear given levels of debt. This study incorporates three measures of debt burdens: the ratio of per capita long-term debt-to-per capita personal income, the ratio of per capita long-term general debt-to-per capita personal income, and the ratio of per capita long-term general debt-to-taxable property values.

In fiscal 1979, the ratio of long-term debt-to-income ranged from a low of 1.8% in San Diego to a high of 31.9% in Atlanta; the mean ratio for the distribution was 9.7%. Long-term debt was equivalent to more than 15% of personal income in Atlanta, New York, San Antonio, and Philadelphia. By contrast, outstanding long-term debt was equivalent to less than 5% of personal income in San Diego, Long Beach, Chicago, Toledo, Honolulu, and Pittsburgh. Between fiscal 1969 and 1979, the ratio of long-term debt-to-income declined in 25 of the 38 cities. It fell from 22.2% to 12.4% in Oklahoma City, from 14.6% to 9.7% in New Orleans, from 16.2% to 8.6% in Kansas City, and from 12.8% to 8.0% in Denver. By contrast, this ratio increased from 15.2% to 31.9% in Atlanta, from 14.6% to 16.6% in Philadelphia, and from 10.0% to 14.3% in Boston.

A similar pattern of debt burdens was evident when the ratio of long-term general debt-to-income was used. However, the omission of utility debt resulted in substantially lower debt burdens in Denver, San Antonio, Seattle, and Los Angeles. It should be remembered that not all long-term debt or long-term general debt was tax-supported debt.

It was possible to compute taxable property values for 21 of the 38 cities based on information from the *1977 Census of Governments.*[7] In 1977, the ratio of long-term general debt-to-taxable property values was at least 20% in New Orleans, Oklahoma City, Philadelphia, Boston, and New York.* Each of these cities was also characterized by above-average debt burdens as measured by the ratio of long-term general debt-to-income. By contrast, the ratio of long-term general debt-to-taxable property values was less than 6% in Louisville, Los Angeles, Milwaukee, Honolulu, and San Diego. Except for Louisville, each of these cities was also characterized by below-average debt burdens as measured by the ratio of long-term general debt-to-income.

It is apparent that those cities with above-average per capita long-term general debt outstanding in fiscal 1979 were also characterized by above-average debt burdens as measured by the ratio of long-term general debt-to-income. Conversely, virtually all of the cities with below-average levels of long-term general debt were also characterized by below-average debt burdens.

These findings are summarized in Figure 5.4 and Table 5.10.

---

*Comparable information will become available when the results of the *1982 Census of Governments* are released.

Long-Term General Debt/ Income, FY 1979	Per Capita Long-Term General Debt Outstanding, Fiscal 1979		
	Above Average		Below Average
Above Average	Atlanta Baltimore Boston Buffalo Detroit Kansas City Louisville Memphis Minneapolis New Orleans New York Oakland Oklahoma City	Philadelphia San Francisco	Cleveland Newark
Below Average			Chicago Cincinnati Columbus Dallas Denver Ft. Worth Honolulu Houston Indianapolis Long Beach Los Angeles Milwaukee Omaha Phoenix Pittsburgh Portland San Antonio San Diego Seattle St. Louis Toledo

FIGURE 5.4. Relationship Between Debt Burdens and Outstanding Debt

TABLE 5.10. Debt Burdens (Percents)

Rank	City	Long Term Debt/Income		Long-Term General Debt/Income		Long-Term General Debt/Taxable Property Values
		FY 1979	FY 1969	FY 1979	FY 1969	FY 1977
1	Atlanta	31.9	15.2	27.4	12.7	N.A.
2	New York	21.5	24.5	16.2	15.6	25.8
3	San Antonio	19.0	11.0	3.6	4.9	N.A.
4	Philadelphia	16.6	14.6	13.2	12.6	21.2
5	Boston	14.3	10.0	13.9	10.0	26.4
6	Louisville	14.0	14.6	8.6	12.5	5.2
7	Memphis	13.4	19.8	10.1	11.4	N.A.
8	Oklahoma City	12.4	22.2	9.6	14.2	35.0
9	Cleveland	12.2	13.5	8.5	9.1	N.A.
10	San Francisco	12.2	9.1	10.9	4.8	15.5
11	Minneapolis	12.0	5.5	11.7	5.2	13.4
12	Baltimore	11.8	19.4	10.2	15.6	11.8
13	Seattle	11.3	12.3	4.2	2.9	N.A.
14	Detroit	10.5	11.0	8.6	7.7	8.8
15	Buffalo	10.5	11.7	10.0	10.7	19.2
16	Newark	10.1	9.0	9.6	7.9	7.1
17	New Orleans	9.7	14.6	9.3	14.1	20.0
18	Los Angeles	9.3	10.7	1.8	3.5	5.9
19	Kansas City	8.6	16.2	7.5	14.0	N.A.

20	Houston	8.1	10.2	5.9	7.9	N.A.
21	Denver	8.0	12.8	4.5	5.1	12.2
22	Columbus	7.7	8.2	5.2	5.7	N.A.
23	Oakland	7.7	4.7	7.7	4.7	12.8
24	Cincinnati	7.1	15.9	6.1	13.8	N.A.
25	Phoenix	7.1	9.2	5.0	5.7	N.A.
26	Dallas	6.7	9.6	5.7	9.2	N.A.
27	Ft. Worth	6.5	9.8	5.4	7.5	N.A.
28	Indianapolis	6.4	5.4	6.4	5.4	N.A.
29	St. Louis	6.2	9.3	5.8	8.7	10.9
30	Milwaukee	5.9	9.9	5.1	7.8	4.0
31	Portland	5.4	4.0	3.4	3.2	N.A.
32	Omaha	5.1	3.9	5.1	3.9	N.A.
33	Pittsburgh	4.8	5.6	4.8	5.2	8.4
34	Honolulu	4.2	9.2	3.3	7.5	2.5
35	Toledo	3.5	2.9	2.8	2.5	N.A.
36	Chicago	3.4	7.1	2.7	5.7	N.A.
37	Long Beach	3.3	2.2	3.1	1.8	9.3
38	San Diego	1.8	5.4	1.8	4.6	4.3
	Mean	9.7	10.8	7.5	8.0	

N.A.—Not Available.
Source: Computations based on Census Bureau data.

Municipal Liquidity

In fiscal 1979, the ratio of net-cash reserves-to-annual operating expenditures ranged from a low of 11% in Boston to a high of 296% in Atlanta. In effect, Boston's net-cash reserves were equivalent to only 11% of annual operating expenditures and Atlanta's were almost triple its annual operating expenditures. As a group, the 38 cities maintained net-cash reserves equivalent to 80% of annual operating expenditures. Toledo was characterized by a negative net-cash position, reflecting its large volume of bond anticipation notes outstanding. As indicated earlier, some analysts claim that BANs should not be included in calculating net-cash reserves because they are not meant to be repaid from operating expenditures. However, census data fail to distinguish between short-term operating debt and BANs.

The sample cities were considerably less liquid when unrestricted net-cash reserves was the yardstick used. In fiscal 1979, such reserves ranged from a low of 9% of annual operating expenditures in Boston to a high of 225% in Atlanta; the mean for the distribution was 63%. Unrestricted net-cash reserves equalled or exceeded annual operating expenditures in Atlanta, Oklahoma City, Houston, Seattle, Long Beach, San Francisco, and San Diego. They were equivalent to 20% or less of annual operating expenditures in Boston, Chicago, Columbus, and New York. Toledo was characterized by a negative ratio.

A majority of the sample cities experienced some erosion in net-cash reserves during the fiscal 1969–79 decade. This occurred even in those cities that continued to maintain relatively adequate net-cash balances. For example, the ratio of unrestricted net-cash reserves-to-annual operating expenditures declined from 178% to 104% in Seattle, from 139% to 94% in Dallas, and from 141% to 100% in San Diego. Cities with more meager net-cash reserves were similarly affected. In Detroit, the ratio of unrestricted net-cash reserves-to-annual operating expenditures declined from 50% to 21% between fiscal 1969 and 1979. In Cleveland, this ratio declined from 82% to 24%.

These findings are summarized in Table 5.11.

Evidence of Retrenchment

The bottom line in any analysis of municipal debt and liquidity patterns is the extent to which individual cities were able to improve their positions over time. In order to assess how debt and liquidity patterns changed during the fiscal 1969–79 decade, the various debt and liquidity indicators for fiscal years 1969, 1975, and 1979 were converted into constant 1972 dollars and average annual rates of change were computed for the fiscal 1969–75 and fiscal 1975–79 periods.

TABLE 5.11. Municipal Liquidity Position (Percents)

Rank	City	Net-Cash Reserves/ Annual Operating Expenditures		Unrestricted Net-Cash Reserves/Annual Operating Expenditures	
		FY 1979	FY 1969	FY 1979	FY 1969
1	Toledo	−20	− 3	−26	−13
2	Boston	11	10	9	− 2
3	Chicago	16	13	11	4
4	Newark	22	6	22	6
5	Columbus	22	−37	20	−44
6	Buffalo	27	17	22	14
7	Detroit	27	56	21	50
8	Baltimore	32	14	31	11
9	Cleveland	39	102	24	82
10	Omaha	41	55	32	44
11	Philadelphia	44	19	35	0
12	New York	45	26	15	3
13	Honolulu	46	80	36	45
14	St. Louis	48	71	42	63
15	Memphis	50	67	46	61
16	Indianapolis	59	73	51	60
17	Pittsburgh	63	16	62	13
18	New Orleans	63	124	46	103
19	Milwaukee	65	102	42	81
20	Denver	72	76	67	71
21	Phoenix	73	103	55	50
22	Los Angeles	75	123	69	120
23	Kansas City	86	276	67	236
24	Louisville	82	79	55	59
25	Ft. Worth	88	132	64	98
26	Minneapolis	88	86	78	76
27	Cincinnati	93	111	84	107
28	San Antonio	97	238	66	189
29	San Diego	105	146	100	141
30	San Francisco	110	87	105	86
31	Portland	114	65	90	52
32	Dallas	115	186	94	139
33	Oakland	126	96	79	82
34	Long Beach	132	156	105	156
35	Seattle	163	200	104	178
36	Houston	200	205	162	163
37	Oklahoma City	223	332	171	278
38	Atlanta	296	111	225	87
	Mean	80	95	63	78

Source: Computations based on Census Bureau data.

The group analysis had suggested that significant debt retrenchment occurred in large U.S. cities during the 1970s. This is confirmed by the analysis of debt patterns within individual cities. Seventeen of the sample cities experienced real declines in gross debt outstanding between fiscal 1969 and 1975 and between fiscal 1975 and 1979. They were: Oklahoma City, Memphis, Cleveland, Detroit, Denver, Baltimore, Kansas City, Dallas, Phoenix, Cincinnati, Ft. Worth, Newark, Milwaukee, Pittsburgh, Honolulu, Chicago, and San Diego. In thirteen of these cities, the average annual rate of decline accelerated after fiscal 1975. In Oklahoma City, for example, per capita gross debt expressed in constant dollars declined from $904 in fiscal 1969 to $779 in fiscal 1975 to $596 in fiscal 1979. This is equivalent to an average annual rate of decline of 2.3% between fiscal 1969 and 1975 and a rate of 5.9% between fiscal 1975 and 1979.

There were also a number of cities in which gross debt grew in real terms between fiscal 1969 and 1975 but declined in real terms during the fiscal 1975–79 period. Boston, Buffalo, Indianapolis, Long Beach, Los Angeles, Louisville, New York, and Omaha were in this category. In Boston, for example, per capita gross debt increased from $553 to $691 in constant dollars between fiscal 1969 and 1975 but declined to $603 in fiscal 1979. This is equivalent to an average annual increase of 4.2% between fiscal 1969 and 1975 and an average annual decline of 3.2% between fiscal 1975 and 1979. Of the remaining cities, Atlanta, Minneapolis, Oakland, San Antonio, San Francisco, and Toledo experienced real growth of outstanding debt during both the fiscal 1969–75 and fiscal 1975–79 periods. Columbus, New Orleans, and Philadelphia were characterized by real declines in gross debt between fiscal 1969 and 1975 and by real increases between fiscal 1975 and 1979.

There were widespread real declines in both short-term and long-term debt during the fiscal 1969–79 period. Between fiscal 1975 and 1979, long-term debt declined in real terms in 25 of the 38 cities. The average annual rate of decline exceeded 5% in Los Angeles, Denver, Kansas City, Dallas, Cincinnati, Ft. Worth, Chicago, Long Beach, and San Diego. New York City's fiscal crisis apparently jolted many large cities into reducing their reliance on short-term debt. Atlanta, Minneapolis, Houston, Dallas, Indianapolis, and St. Louis had no short-term debt outstanding during either the fiscal 1969–75 or fiscal 1975–79 periods. Twenty-eight of the remaining 32 cities reduced their average ratios of short-term-to-gross debt between the fiscal 1969–75 and fiscal 1975–79 periods. This ratio declined from 24% to 13% in New York, from 22% to 11% in San Francisco, from 25% to 15% in Boston, from 22% to 11% in Louisville, from 26% to 20% in Buffalo, and from 26% to 12% in Pittsburgh.

Between fiscal 1975 and 1979, debt-service payments declined in constant dollars in 21 of the 38 cities. Only a handful of cities including

	Per Capita Gross Debt	
	Real Increase, FY 1975–79	Real Decline, FY 1975–79
Real Increase FY 1969–75	Atlanta Minneapolis Oakland San Antonio San Francisco Toledo	Boston Buffalo Indianapolis Long Beach Los Angeles Louisville New York Omaha Seattle
Real Decline FY 1969–75	Columbus Houston New Orleans Philadelphia Portland	Baltimore Chicago Cincinnati Cleveland Dallas Denver Detroit Ft. Worth Honolulu Kansas City Memphis Milwaukee Newark Oklahoma City Phoenix Pittsburgh San Diego St. Louis

FIGURE 5.5. Retrenchment in Large Cities: Debt (Average Annual Change in Constant Dollars)

Atlanta, New York, Boston, Minneapolis, Newark, Buffalo, and Memphis experienced real increases in debt-service payments during both the fiscal 1969–75 and 1975–79 periods. In Atlanta, debt-service payments grew at an average annual rate of 15% between fiscal 1969 and 1975 and at a rate of 8% annually between fiscal 1975 and 1979. In New York City, debt-service payments grew at an average annual rate of 8% between fiscal 1969 and 1975 and at a rate of 34% annually between fiscal 1975 and 1979.

The findings also suggest that debt retrenchment may have occurred at the expense of capital investment. To test this hypothesis, the average ratio of capital-to-general spending was computed for each city for the fiscal 1969–75 and fiscal 1975–79 periods. In 31 of the 38 cities, this ratio

TABLE 5.12. Retrenchment in Large Cities: Debt and Liquidity (Per Capita Constant 1972 Dollars)

City	Gross Debt			Long-Term Debt			Debt-Service		
	FY 1969	FY 1975	FY 1979	FY 1969	FY 1975	FY 1979	FY 1969	FY 1975	FY 1979
Atlanta	603	967	1223	603	967	1223	34	64	85
Baltimore	727	531	404	703	471	404	53	50	48
Boston	553	691	603	389	531	549	62	83	106
Buffalo	539	585	425	424	411	365	66	72	84
Chicago	373	327	161	306	266	137	24	30	23
Cincinnati	754	523	290	628	410	286	66	51	44
Cleveland	565	486	452	482	297	413	46	41	38
Columbus	537	428	468	312	342	306	46	41	28
Dallas	446	434	335	446	434	335	44	51	35
Denver	610	587	404	568	558	401	24	34	28
Detroit	506	448	408	445	384	382	40	38	43
Ft. Worth	401	362	279	401	362	279	33	36	30
Honolulu	445	237	201	403	230	196	34	25	24
Houston	424	365	414	424	365	414	36	30	32
Indianapolis	236	299	284	236	299	284	19	28	25
Kansas City	709	565	376	681	551	374	54	64	38
Long Beach	110	274	160	110	269	160	9	19	16
Los Angeles	564	634	465	533	614	457	30	27	273
Louisville	725	754	549	544	594	515	70	39	24
Memphis	694	666	507	694	628	506	51	52	62
Milwaukee	428	295	259	398	263	244	51	36	35
Minneapolis	242	320	527	242	320	527	32	38	57
Newark	350	346	267	283	319	267	41	43	44
New Orleans	499	361	391	499	360	372	32	32	42
New York	1281	1576	949	1140	1056	914	113	167	391
Oakland	297	344	355	214	277	348	16	26	26
Oklahoma City	904	779	596	903	705	579	56	61	54

220

Omaha	165	277	230	160	277	226	22	36	29
Philadelphia	637	571	586	554	504	586	45	75	57
Phoenix	383	367	323	383	365	315	27	21	12
Pittsburgh	340	232	203	217	187	194	43	26	26
Portland	234	96	264	178	74	258	20	10	17
San Antonio	363	390	636	338	374	629	21	18	23
San Diego	234	145	86	234	145	86	15	12	8
San Francisco	568	575	703	487	458	658	93	54	72
Seattle	637	737	622	630	695	615	37	36	35
St. Louis	320	252	213	320	252	213	24	36	24
Toledo	223	248	265	120	121	144	14	27	26

City	Average Ratio of Short-Term/Gross Debt		Average Ratio of Capital/General Spending		Unrestricted Net-Cash Reserves/ Annual Operating Expenditures	
	FY 1969–75	FY 1975–79	FY 1969–75	FY 1975–79	FY 1975	FY 1979
Atlanta	0.0%	0.0%	36.7%	33.1%	156%	225%
Baltimore	7.6	4.6	18.9	21.8	42	31
Boston	25.0	15.1	14.6	11.8	–1	9
Buffalo	26.2	19.9	15.1	18.3	9	22
Chicago	19.4	16.6	17.4	11.5	9	11
Cincinnati	16.1	11.4	20.1	18.4	66	84
Cleveland	21.6	22.7	19.2	17.1	12	24
Columbus	31.6	25.3	20.9	17.6	39	20
Dallas	0.0	0.0	34.2	23.5	117	94
Denver	6.2	2.7	17.9	18.6	108	67
Detroit	12.6	11.5	18.4	17.2	21	21
Ft. Worth	0.6	0.0	33.5	29.9	90	64
Honolulu	11.9	4.9	27.4	24.8	37	36
Houston	0.0	0.0	26.0	25.4	130	162
Indianapolis	0.1	0.0	22.5	17.4	47	51

(continued on next page)

TABLE 5.12 *(cont'd)*

City	Average Ratio of Short-Term/Gross Debt		Average Ratio of Capital/General Spending		Unrestricted Net-Cash Reserves/Annual Operating Expenditures	
	FY 1969–75	FY 1975–79	FY 1969–75	FY 1975–79	FY 1975	FY 1979
Kansas City	3.8	1.4	28.9	26.7	99	67
Long Beach	1.2	0.4	23.5	20.2	142	105
Los Angeles	4.3	2.3	24.1	15.2	84	69
Louisville	22.1	10.5	36.9	25.5	105	55
Memphis	1.3	1.1	18.0	16.2	29	46
Milwaukee	9.4	7.3	23.3	16.5	53	42
Minneapolis	0.0	0.0	25.6	22.4	82	78
Newark	9.8	5.9	7.0	4.1	4	22
New Orleans	0.1	2.7	20.5	18.5	75	46
New York	24.4	13.3	12.0	5.7	−28	15
Oakland	23.3	9.8	28.8	20.4	49	79
Oklahoma City	3.2	6.4	31.0	31.0	144	171
Omaha	2.9	1.5	37.9	35.6	61	32
Philadelphia	10.4	5.0	18.9	16.5	0	35
Phoenix	0.6	1.3	29.0	27.5	28	55
Pittsburgh	26.2	11.5	19.2	17.0	83	62
Portland	22.3	10.1	20.6	14.9	68	90
San Antonio	6.0	2.3	21.7	23.5	147	66
San Diego	0.1	0.0	22.5	19.1	78	100
San Francisco	22.0	10.7	12.1	15.9	56	105
Seattle	4.1	3.7	25.6	18.4	93	104
St. Louis	0.0	0.0	9.9	10.9	51	42
Toledo	53.0	48.6	24.4	18.2	−37	−26

Source: Computations based on Census Bureau data.

declined from one fiscal period to the other. In Atlanta, Louisville, Dallas, Ft. Worth, and Omaha, where the average ratio of capital-to-general spending was at least 30% during the fiscal 1969–75 period, the decline probably reflects the completion of desired capital facilities. However, in older cities like New York, Boston, Newark, and Chicago, where the average ratio of capital-to-general spending ranged from only 7% to 17% between fiscal 1969 and 1975, this seems less likely.

The analysis also indicates that many cities improved their liquidity positions during the latter part of the 1970s. Between fiscal 1975 and 1979, the ratio of unrestricted net-cash reserves-to-annual operating expenditures improved in 20 of the 38 cities. This ratio increased from −28% to 15% in New York, from 0% to 35% in Philadelphia, from 12% to 24% in Cleveland, from 9% to 22% in Buffalo, from 4% to 22% in Newark, and from 9% to 11% in Chicago.

These findings are summarized in Figure 5.5 and Table 5.12.

INDEXES OF FISCAL STRESS: DEBT AND LIQUIDITY

Based on the foregoing analysis, two stress indexes, one for debt and one for liquidity, were developed. The debt index incorporates twelve variables grouped under three broad categories: debt levels, capital spending, and debt burdens. The composite indicator for debt levels includes the following variables: per capita gross debt in fiscal 1979, percent change in gross debt between fiscal 1969 and 1979, the average ratio of short-term debt-to-gross debt during the fiscal 1969–79 period, and the level of guaranteed debt issued between fiscal 1969 and 1979. The composite indicator for capital spending includes two variables: per capita capital spending in fiscal 1979 and the average ratio of capital-to-general spending for the fiscal 1969–79 period. The composite indicator for debt burdens incorporates six variables: per capita debt-service in fiscal 1979, percent change in debt-service between fiscal 1969 and 1979, the ratio of debt-service-to-general spending in fiscal 1979, the percent change in this ratio between fiscal 1969 and 1979, the ratio of long-term general debt-to-income in fiscal 1979, and the percent change in this ratio between fiscal 1969 and 1979. The liquidity index reflects each city's unrestricted net-cash reserves as a proportion of annual operating expenditures in fiscal 1979. The measures used are summarized in Figure 5.6.

The raw scores for each variable were first converted to standard (z) scores. The composite z scores represent a simple average of the variables within each major category. The composite z scores were then averaged to develop an overall stress measure. A z score of −.675 or less includes the bottom 25% of the distribution and was interpreted as a sign of stress. Scores

Debt Levels	Capital Spending	Debt Burdens	Liquidity
1. Per Capita Gross Debt, FY 1979	5. Per Capita Capital Expenditures, FY 1979	7. Per Capita Debt-Service Payments, FY 1979	12. Unrestricted Net-Cash Reserves/ Annual Operating Expenditures, FY 1979
2. Percent Change in Gross Debt, FYs 1969–79	6. Capital Spending/Total General Spending, FYs 1969–79 Average	8. Percent Change in Debt-Service Payments, FYs 1969–79	
3. Short-Term/Gross Debt, FYs 1969–79 Average		9. Debt-Service/General Expenditures, FY 1979	
4. Per Capita Guaranteed Debt Issued, FYs 1969–79		10. Percent Change, Debt-Service/ General Expenditures, FYs 1969–79	
		11. Long-Term General Debt/Income, 1979	
		12. Percent Change, Long-Term General Debt/Income, FYs 1969–79	

FIGURE 5.6. Debt, Capital Spending, and Liquidity Measures Used to Denote Fiscal Stress

TABLE 5.13. Indexes of Debt and Liquidity Stress For Large Cities

Rank	City	The Index of Debt Stress	Debt Levels	Capital Spending	Debt Burdens	Rank	City	The Index of Liquidity Stress
				Composite z Score for				
1	New York	-1.72	-1.82	-1.16	-2.17	1	Toledo	-1.87
2	Boston	-0.67	-1.01	-0.18	-0.82	2	Boston	-1.13
3	Minneapolis	-0.64	-1.02	-0.12	-0.77	3	Chicago	-1.09
4	Newark	-0.52	+0.25	-1.86	+0.04	4	New York	-1.01
5	Toledo	-0.50	-0.79	-0.46	-0.26	5	Columbus	-0.90
6	Los Angeles	-0.43	+0.40	-0.62	-1.07	6	Detroit	-0.88
7	Philadelphia	-0.25	-0.28	-0.01	-0.47	7	Buffalo	-0.86
8	San Francisco	-0.23	-1.09	+0.76	-0.35	8	Newark	-0.86
9	Memphis	-0.22	+0.09	-0.58	-0.18	9	Cleveland	-0.82
10	Buffalo	-0.19	-0.40	+0.06	-0.24	10	Baltimore	-0.67
11	Cleveland	-0.15	-0.18	-0.58	+0.30	11	Omaha	-0.65
12	Seattle	-0.10	-0.09	-0.36	+0.16	12	Philadelphia	-0.59
13	San Antonio	-0.08	-0.46	-0.14	+0.35	13	Honolulu	-0.57
14	Oakland	-0.05	+0.01	+0.32	-0.48	14	St. Louis	-0.44
15	Columbus	-0.02	-0.46	-0.18	+0.58	15	Milwaukee	-0.44
16	Chicago	-0.01	+0.53	-1.08	+0.52	16	Memphis	-0.36
17	St. Louis	+0.03	+0.81	-1.16	+0.45	17	New Orleans	-0.36
18	Atlanta	+0.03	-1.26	+3.03	-1.68	18	Indianapolis	-0.25
19	Indianapolis	+0.04	+0.24	-0.39	+0.26	19	Louisville	-0.17
20	New Orleans	+0.08	+0.42	-0.21	+0.04	20	Phoenix	-0.17

(continued next page)

225

TABLE 5.13 (cont'd)

		Composite z Score for			
Rank	City	The Index of Debt Stress	Debt Levels	Capital Spending	Debt Burdens
21	Portland	+0.09	-0.01	-0.32	+0.61
22	Detroit	+0.10	+0.14	-0.02	+0.17
23	Long Beach	+0.13	+0.44	+0.22	-0.27
24	Pittsburgh	+0.13	+0.25	-0.30	+0.45
25	Milwaukee	+0.14	+0.45	-0.32	+0.28
26	Baltimore	+0.22	+0.27	+0.20	+0.18
27	Houston	+0.24	+0.24	+0.16	+0.31
28	Denver	+0.25	+0.19	+0.18	+0.37
29	Cincinnati	+0.30	+0.40	+0.18	+0.32
30	Dallas	+0.34	+0.38	+0.30	+0.33
31	Kansas City	+0.36	+0.59	+0.26	+0.23
32	Honolulu	+0.37	+0.61	-0.03	+0.52
33	Omaha	+0.44	+0.12	+1.09	+0.11
34	Oklahoma City	+0.46	+0.08	+1.43	-0.14
35	Ft. Worth	+0.49	+0.55	+0.58	+0.34
36	San Diego	+0.53	+1.16	-0.44	+0.86
37	Phoenix	+0.54	+0.28	+0.62	+0.72
38	Louisville	+0.55	+0.03	+1.02	+0.59

Rank	City	The Index of Liquidity Stress
21	Pittsburgh	-0.02
22	Ft. Worth	+0.02
23	San Antonio	+0.06
24	Denver	+0.08
25	Kansas City	+0.08
26	Los Angeles	+0.13
27	Minneapolis	+0.31
28	Oakland	+0.34
29	Cincinnati	+0.44
30	Portland	+0.57
31	Dallas	+0.65
32	San Diego	+0.78
33	Seattle	+0.86
34	Long Beach	+0.88
35	San Francisco	+0.88
36	Houston	+2.08
37	Oklahoma City	+2.26
38	Atlanta	+3.40

Source: Computations based on Census Bureau data

of +.675 or more include the top 25% of the distribution and indicated the relative absence of stress. Scores between −.675 and +.675 were interpreted as indicating a moderate amount of stress.

New York City was the only city to rank as distressed in terms of debt. Its overall z score was −1.72, which reflected the combination of disproportionately high debt levels and debt burdens and relatively low levels of capital spending.

Nine cities—Toledo, Boston, Chicago, New York, Columbus, Detroit, Buffalo, Newark, and Cleveland—ranked as distressed in terms of their z scores for liquidity. Some of these cities issue short-term debt for capital purposes and this was included in the measure of liquidity. Seven cities—Atlanta, Oklahoma City, Houston, San Francisco, Long Beach, Seattle, and San Diego—ranked as not distressed in terms of liquidity.

The findings regarding debt and liquidity stress in large U.S. cities are summarized in Table 5.13.

NOTES

1. See U.S. Bureau of the Census, *City Government Finances in 1980–81* Series GF 81, No. 4, (U.S. Government Printing Office, Washington, D.C., 1982) p. 111.

2. Ibid., p. 114.

3. See George E. Peterson, Henry L. Mortimer, Brian Cooper, Elizabeth Dickson, and George A. Riegeluth, *Urban Fiscal Monitoring* Draft report (Washington: The Urban Institute, 1978).

4. Alan Walter Steiss, *Local Government Finance* (Lexington, Mass: Lexington Books, 1975.)

5. See George E. Kaufman, "Debt Management," in *Management Policies in Local Government Finance*, eds. J. Richard Aronson and Eli Schwartz (Washington: International City Management Association, 1981), p. 304.

6. John E. Petersen, "State and Local Government Debt Policy and Management," in *Essays in Public Finance and Financial Management, State and Local Perspectives*, eds. John E. Petersen and Catherine Lavigne Spain (Chatham, N.J.: Chatham House Publishers, 1978), p. 68.

7. U.S. Bureau of the Census, "Taxable Property Values and Assessment/Sales Price Ratios," *1977 Census of Governments*, Vol. 2, GC 77(2), (Washington: U.S. Government Printing Office, November, 1978.)

6

The Dimensions of the Crisis in Urban Public Finance

Previous chapters analyzed the demographic and economic basis for fiscal stress in large cities and developed various fiscal measures for each city. This chapter integrates these findings into overall stress measures for each city as of fiscal 1979. More recent evidence concerning fiscal retrenchment during the fiscal 1979–81 period is introduced to determine to what extent trends observed during the late 1970s carried over into the 1980s. Recent survey information concerning the fiscal status of the nation's cities is also evaluated. The chapter concludes with a discussion of the economic and fiscal outlook for large cities in the context of Reaganomics and the "new federalism."

STRESS MEASURES FOR LARGE U.S. CITIES

There is no generally agreed upon definition of fiscal stress. According to David Stanley, troubled cities are defined as "those in which the fiscal situation is so unfavorable as to impair borrowing ability, require reductions in municipal services, pose a threat to public health and safety, and thus diminish the quality and satisfaction of urban life."[1] Although a strong economic base is generally regarded as an asset in preventing fiscal difficulties, there is no guarantee that fiscal problems will be averted just because a city has a relatively strong private-sector economy.

Given the elusiveness of a definition of fiscal stress, the full array of socio-economic and financial variables developed in this study was used to identify distressed cities. The overall z scores for revenues, expenditures, debt, and liquidity were first averaged to develop a comprehensive measure of fiscal stress for each city. This fiscal indicator and that for socio-economic stress were then averaged to develop composite stress measures for each city. The methodology gives equal weight to the socio-economic and fiscal variables in determining overall stress. There were instances in which a different weighting system would have yielded substantially different results. For example, New York City was characterized by an extremely favorable z score for the socio-economic variables and by an equally unfavorable z score for the fiscal variables. Had the fiscal variables been given greater weight, New York City would have fared much worse in the final rankings than it actually did. In most instances, however, cities that scored well in terms of the fiscal variables also scored well in terms of the socio-economic variables and vice versa. For these cities, the weighting system used was much less critical to the final results.

The findings indicate that Newark, Atlanta, St. Louis, Detroit, Boston, Minneapolis, and Oakland were distressed in terms of the socio-economic measures. New York, Boston and Newark were distressed in terms of the fiscal measures. Each of these cities was characterized by a z score of $-.675$ or lower. By contrast, San Antonio, New York, Indianapolis, Honolulu, Memphis, Omaha, Oklahoma City, and Houston ranked as not distressed in terms of the socio-economic variables. Houston, Atlanta, Oklahoma City, and Long Beach were not distressed in terms of the fiscal variables. The z scores for these cities were $+.675$ or greater. When the composite z scores for fiscal and socio-economic stress were averaged to develop a composite stress measure, Newark, Boston, Detroit, and St. Louis were found to be distressed and San Antonio, Houston, and Oklahoma City ranked as not distressed. Most sample cities clustered between the 25th and 75th percentiles in terms of relative stress. The explanation seems to be that the fiscal disadvantages of cities with high revenues, expenditures, and outstanding debt were somewhat mitigated by evidence of retrenchment during the latter part of the 1970s. By the same token, growing fiscal pressures were evident in a number of growing, sunbelt cities. In effect, during the 1970s, a process of fiscal convergence, albeit an extremely modest one, was underway.

Relative stress levels varied widely for those cities described as moderately distressed. Within this group, Baltimore, Buffalo, Minneapolis, and Cleveland, with z scores between -0.38 and -0.55, were among the more distressed cities. Honolulu, San Diego, Omaha, Memphis, Long Beach, Indianapolis, and Phoenix, with z scores ranging from $+0.44$ to $+0.62$ were among the less distressed cities.

It is also of interest that fiscal stress and socio-economic stress did not necessarily go hand-in-hand. Newark, Boston, Detroit, Buffalo, and Baltimore scored unfavorably in terms of both the fiscal and socio-economic stress measures. Houston, Oklahoma City, and San Diego scored favorably in terms of both stress measures. However, a significant number of cities scored relatively favorably on one measure and unfavorably on the other. For example, Atlanta, Pittsburgh, and Oakland scored unfavorably in terms of socio-economic stress but favorably in terms of fiscal stress. New York and Memphis scored favorably in terms of socio-economic stress but unfavorably in terms of fiscal stress. During the 1980s, certain cities may well enjoy a thriving private-sector economy despite the existence of an impoverished public-sector. Other cities may be characterized by weak private-sector economies, but may nevertheless maintain a relatively sound fiscal position.

The findings regarding relative levels of socio-economic and fiscal stress in large U.S. cities for the fiscal 1969–79 decade are summarized in Table 6.1.

The foregoing findings closely parallel those of other researchers. The results would have been even closer to those of other researchers had the same sample of cities been used in each study.

In this study, the 10 most distressed cities, as shown by the composite stress indicator, were: Newark, Boston, Detroit, St. Louis, Baltimore, Buffalo, Minneapolis, Cleveland, Atlanta, and Philadelphia. Newark, Cleveland, St. Louis, Detroit, Buffalo, and Baltimore were among the "top ten" as measured by the Congressional Budget Office (CBO) index of social need. Newark, Cleveland, Buffalo, St. Louis, and Boston were among the 10 most distressed cities in terms of the CBO index of economic need. Boston, Newark, St. Louis, Philadelphia, Baltimore, and Detroit were among the 10 most distressed cities as measured by the CBO index of fiscal need.[2]

Newark, Buffalo, Cleveland, Detroit, and Boston were among the 10 most distressed cities according to a recent Treasury Department study.[3] St. Louis, Newark, Buffalo, Cleveland, Boston, and Baltimore were among the 10 most distressed cities as measured by the Brookings Institution urban conditions index.[4] Newark, St. Louis, Baltimore, Cleveland, Detroit, and Buffalo were among the 10 most distressed cities in terms of the Brookings Institution hardship index.[5] Detroit, Philadelphia, Boston, Cleveland, Newark, and Minneapolis were among the 10 most distressed cities as measured by the Urban Institute Index.[6]

The findings of this study are compared with those of related studies in figure 6.1.

RETRENCHMENT DURING THE 1980s

The latest available fiscal data from the U.S. Bureau of the Census suggests that the process of fiscal retrenchment, first evident during the latter part of the 1970s, carried over into the 1980s.[7] Between fiscal 1979 and

TABLE 6.1. Stress Rankings for Large Cities

	The Composite Stress Measure			The Socio-Economic Stress Measure			The Fiscal Stress Measure	
Rank	City	z Score	Rank	City	z Score	Rank	City	z Score
1	Newark	-1.26	1	Newark	-1.74	1	New York	-1.22
2	Boston	-1.07	2	Atlanta	-1.39	2	Boston	-1.02
3	Detroit	-0.76	3	St. Louis	-1.30	3	Newark	-0.79
4	St. Louis	-0.76	4	Detroit	-1.17			
5	Baltimore	-0.55	5	Boston	-1.12	4	Buffalo	-0.62
6	Buffalo	-0.52	6	Minneapolis	-0.76	5	Baltimore	-0.54
7	Minneapolis	-0.42	7	Oakland	-0.74			
8	Cleveland	-0.38	8	Pittsburgh	-0.66	6	Toledo	-0.45
9	Atlanta	-0.28	9	Cleveland	-0.62	7	Indianapolis	-0.37
10	Philadelphia	-0.25	10	Baltimore	-0.56	8	Detroit	-0.36
						9	Philadelphia	-0.34
11	Oakland	-0.21	11	Buffalo	-0.43	10	Chicago	-0.28
12	Pittsburgh	-0.21	12	Cincinnati	-0.43			
13	Denver	-0.16	13	Denver	-0.36	11	Memphis	-0.26
14	New Orleans	-0.12	14	Kansas City	-0.29	12	St. Louis	-0.23
15	Chicago	-0.12	15	San Francisco	-0.22	13	Cleveland	-0.15
						14	Omaha	-0.14
						15	New Orleans	-0.13
16	Kansas City	-0.08	16	Philadelphia	-0.16	16	Minneapolis	-0.09
17	Toledo	-0.06	17	Portland	-0.12	17	Columbus	-0.09

#			#			#		
18	San Francisco	−0.04	18	New Orleans	−0.11	18	Milwaukee	+0.02
19	Cincinnati	−0.02	19	Seattle	−0.09	19	Honolulu	+0.03
20	New York	+0.03	20	Chicago	+0.04	20	Los Angeles	+0.05
21	Los Angeles	+0.06	21	Los Angeles	+0.06	21	Denver	+0.05
22	Portland	+0.11	22	Louisville	+0.07	22	San Antonio	+0.06
23	Seattle	+0.12	23	Ft. Worth	+0.11	23	Kansas City	+0.13
24	Louisville	+0.14	24	Dallas	+0.12	24	San Francisco	+0.13
25	Ft. Worth	+0.14	25	Long Beach	+0.19	25	Ft. Worth	+0.18
26	Columbus	+0.16	26	Milwaukee	+0.33	26	Louisville	+0.20
27	Milwaukee	+0.18	27	Toledo	+0.33	27	Pittsburgh	+0.24
28	Dallas	+0.30	28	Columbus	+0.41	28	Phoenix	+0.30
29	Phoenix	+0.44	29	Phoenix	+0.58	29	Oakland	+0.32
30	Indianapolis	+0.45	30	San Diego	+0.64	30	Portland	+0.34
31	Long Beach	+0.46	31	Houston	+0.76	31	Seattle	+0.34
32	Memphis	+0.47	32	Oklahoma City	+0.79	32	Cincinnati	+0.38
33	Omaha	+0.50	33	Omaha	+1.14	33	Dallas	+0.49
34	San Diego	+0.57	34	Memphis	+1.20	34	San Diego	+0.50
35	Honolulu	+0.62	35	Honolulu	+1.22	35	Long Beach	+0.74
36	Oklahoma City	+0.80	36	Indianapolis	+1.27	36	Oklahoma City	+0.81
37	Houston	+0.80	37	New York	+1.28	37	Atlanta	+0.83
38	San Antonio	+0.85	38	San Antonio	+1.64	38	Houston	+0.85

Source: Computations based on Census Bureau data.

233

	This Study				
Rank	Composite Stress Measure	Socio-Economic Stress Measure	Fiscal Stress Measure	Treasury Study	Urban Institute Index
1	Newark	Newark	New York	New York	Detroit
2	Boston	Atlanta	Boston	Newark	Toledo
3	Detroit	St. Louis	Newark	Los Angeles	Philadelphia
4	St. Louis	Detroit	Buffalo	Buffalo	Boston
5	Baltimore	Boston	Baltimore	Cleveland	New Orleans
6	Buffalo	Minneapolis	Toledo	Long Beach	New York
7	Minneapoiis	Oakland	Indianapolis	Oakland	Cleveland
8	Cleveland	Pittsburgh	Detroit	Chicago	Newark
9	Atlanta	Cleveland	Philadelphia	Detroit	Milwaukee
10	Philadelphia	Baltimore	Chicago	Boston	Minneapolis

	Congressional Budget Office Study			Brookings Institution Indicators	
Rank	Social Need	Economic Need	Fiscal Need	Urban Conditions Index	Hardship Index
1	Newark	Newark	Washington, D.C.	St. Louis	Newark
2	Cleveland	New York	Boston	Newark	St. Louis
3	St. Louis	Jersey City	New York	Buffalo	New Orleans
4	Detroit	Cleveland	Newark	Cleveland	Miami
5	New Orleans	Buffalo	St. Louis	New Orleans	Birmingham
6	Buffalo	Chicago	Philadelphia	Pittsburgh	Baltimore
7	Miami	St. Louis	Baltimore	Boston	Cleveland
8	Gary	Boston	Jersey City	Cincinnati	Detroit
9	Baltimore	Paterson	Detroit	Baltimore	Buffalo
10	Tampa	Pittsburgh	Birmingham	Birmingham	Louisville

FIGURE 6.1. The Ten Most Distressed Cities as Indicated by Selected Studies of Urban Stress

fiscal 1981, general revenues, expressed in constant 1972 dollars, declined in 21 of the 38 sample cities; 19 cities experienced real declines in general spending; 24 were characterized by real declines in outstanding debt.

Retrenchment in large U.S. cities was apparently spurred by significant reductions in intergovernmental aid between fiscal 1979 and 1981. Such aid declined in constant dollars in 27 of the 38 cities. Declines exceeded 10% in Boston, Buffalo, Cleveland, Atlanta, Oakland, Denver, New Orleans, San Francisco, Los Angeles, Portland, Louisville, Ft. Worth, Columbus, Dallas, Phoenix, Omaha, San Diego, Honolulu, and Oklahoma City. Between fiscal

1979 and 1981, 19 cities experienced real declines in state aid; 29 of them experienced real declines in Federal aid.

Declines in outside aid apparently forced many cities to fall back upon their own resources. Between fiscal 1979 and 1981, own-source revenues increased in constant dollars in 22 of the sample cities; tax revenues increased in 14 of them. It is interesting to note that own-source revenue declined in constant dollars between fiscal 1979 and 1981 in those cities that were defined in this study as most distressed. The ten most distressed cities, as identified in this study were: Newark, Boston, Detroit, St. Louis, Baltimore, Buffalo, Minneapolis, Cleveland, Atlanta, and Philadelphia. Own-source revenue declined in real terms in each of them except Cleveland and Atlanta.

As a result of the substitution of own-source revenues for intergovernmental aid in most large cities, the ratio of intergovernmental revenue-to-total general revenue declined in 26 of the 38 sample cities between fiscal 1979 and fiscal 1981: from 42% to 37% in Boston, from 43% to 28% in Cleveland, from 33% to 27% in Atlanta, from 40% to 30% in Oakland, and from 45% to 38% in New Orleans.

Declines in the ratio of intergovernmental aid-to-total general revenue were accompanied by increases in the ratio of taxes-to-total general revenue. That ratio increased in 22 of the 38 cities between fiscal 1979 and 1981. However, the relative importance of property taxes continued to diminish in most of the sample cities, indicating that they had come to rely more heavily on general sales and income taxes. The ratio of property taxes-to-total taxes increased between fiscal 1979 and 1981 in only nine of the sample cities: Newark, Detroit, Oakland, Pittsburgh, Chicago, San Francisco, Los Angeles, Long Beach, and San Diego.

Between fiscal 1979 and 1981, operating expenditures declined in constant dollars in 28 of the 38 cities. There were also real declines in wage and salary spending in 29 cities. This, in turn, reflected reductions in municipal employment. Between October, 1979 and October, 1981, the number of full-time equivalent employees per 10,000 residents declined in 26 of the 38 cities: from 389 to 373 in Newark, from 204 to 170 in Detroit, from 297 to 253 in St. Louis, from 527 to 426 in Baltimore, from 193 to 160 in Cleveland, from 201 to 180 in Atlanta, from 224 to 171 in New Orleans, from 371 to 327 in Memphis, and from 152 to 128 in San Antonio.

These findings are summarized in Table 6.2.

RECENT SURVEY EVIDENCE: IS THE FISCAL CRISIS REAL?

Several recent surveys underscore the worsening fiscal plight of large cities and raise the specter of more drastic retrenchment ahead. In February,

TABLE 6.2. Retrenchment in Large Cities, Fiscal 1979–81 (Per Capita Constant 1972 Dollars)

Distress Rank	City	General Revenue		Revenue Intergovernmental Revenue		Own-Source Revenue		Taxes	
		FY 1979	FY 1981	FY 1979	FY 1981	FY 1979	FY 1981	FY 1979	FY 1981
1	Newark	675	594	431	415	244	179	215	139
2	Boston	949	840	395	308	554	532	449	423
3	Detroit	503	518	247	305	256	213	165	144
4	St. Louis	443	467	139	184	304	283	231	208
5	Baltimore	706	806	408	509	298	297	225	212
6	Buffalo	626	572	428	379	198	193	139	131
7	Minneapolis	357	334	181	166	176	168	120	91
8	Cleveland	339	320	145	89	194	231	110	131
9	Atlanta	414	419	136	112	277	307	135	138
10	Philadelphia	474	445	148	137	326	308	251	240
11	Oakland	341	370	138	110	203	260	101	113
12	Pittsburgh	245	274	101	108	144	166	121	139
13	Denver	533	513	168	141	365	372	198	195
14	New Orleans	348	374	158	141	190	233	117	134
15	Chicago	271	282	101	113	170	169	139	126
16	Kansas City	383	377	104	95	279	282	196	194

#	City								
17	Toledo	242	239	99	103	143	136	89	82
18	San Francisco	859	867	441	362	418	505	235	265
19	Cincinnati	421	414	170	162	251	252	165	161
20	New York	1175	1139	530	479	646	660	505	506
21	Los Angeles	284	274	104	69	180	205	110	122
22	Portland	305	294	110	82	195	212	118	116
23	Seattle	327	339	101	114	226	225	129	127
24	Louisville	385	287	155	125	230	162	127	119
25	Ft. Worth	213	194	64	42	149	152	92	87
26	Columbus	236	237	85	72	151	165	86	85
27	Milwaukee	278	273	139	146	140	127	92	60
28	Dallas	228	216	39	33	189	183	130	125
29	Phoenix	238	248	115	103	123	145	81	75
30	Indianapolis	302	313	143	165	159	148	94	86
31	Long Beach	337	440	113	125	224	315	83	97
32	Memphis	388	380	235	221	153	159	88	89
33	Omaha	263	224	109	71	154	153	116	112
34	San Diego	212	214	89	67	123	147	66	74
35	Honolulu	250	235	94	67	156	168	130	133
36	Oklahoma City	291	278	92	74	199	204	121	123
37	Houston	220	227	36	37	184	190	121	122
38	San Antonio	163	168	62	60	101	108	53	51

(continued next page)

TABLE 6.2 *(cont'd)*

Expenditures and Debt

Distress Rank	City	General Expenditures		Operating Expenditures		Wage & Salary Expenditures		Gross Debt	
		FY 1979	FY 1981	FY 1979	FY 1981	FY 1979	FY 1981	FY 1979	FY 1981
1	Newark	646	601	559	509	340	340	267	230
2	Boston	919	746	723	601	500	412	603	491
3	Detroit	472	468	367	336	241	203	408	352
4	St. Louis	405	429	321	315	222	208	213	158
5	Baltimore	691	702	581	499	369	334	404	438
6	Buffalo	613	562	499	463	279	257	425	333
7	Minneapolis	323	315	225	204	147	139	527	632
8	Cleveland	370	305	239	223	161	146	452	341
9	Atlanta	484	467	216	200	146	140	1223	1147
10	Philadelphia	482	464	349	336	208	190	586	529
11	Oakland	307	352	226	226	124	125	355	516
12	Pittsburgh	267	272	197	181	111	114	203	254
13	Denver	492	444	342	333	239	225	404	419
14	New Orleans	321	334	241	255	143	135	391	457
15	Chicago	253	293	211	217	165	132	161	192
16	Kansas City	346	331	253	229	123	116	376	281

17	Toledo	266	251	219	193	112	101	265	220
18	San Francisco	693	672	446	430	342	350	703	627
19	Cincinnati	381	380	262	252	172	158	290	219
20	New York	984	978	693	734	497	467	949	672
21	Los Angeles	217	217	175	173	157	156	465	463
22	Portland	296	297	225	214	135	126	264	457
23	Seattle	288	336	219	228	188	219	622	474
24	Louisville	379	278	249	213	139	119	549	405
25	Ft. Worth	203	207	144	128	106	87	279	256
26	Columbus	290	277	212	184	123	104	468	540
27	Milwaukee	252	256	184	175	140	134	259	278
28	Dallas	226	241	166	144	126	118	335	333
29	Phoenix	246	252	163	158	103	89	323	338
30	Indianapolis	295	318	211	191	117	114	284	213
31	Long Beach	340	415	247	255	131	135	160	249
32	Memphis	373	374	298	299	239	243	507	431
33	Omaha	247	220	161	159	102	96	230	216
34	San Diego	164	178	116	122	84	78	86	73
35	Honolulu	211	198	160	147	107	95	201	125
36	Oklahoma City	274	274	145	135	96	97	596	470
37	Houston	207	231	132	142	92	99	414	423
38	San Antonio	178	169	117	121	99	100	636	710

(continued next page)

TABLE 6.2 *(cont'd)*

Selected Fiscal Ratios (percents)

Distress Rank	City	Intergovernmental Revenue/General Revenue		Property Taxes/Total Taxes		Capital Spending/General Spending		Debt-Service/General Spending	
		FY 1979	FY 1981	FY 1979	FY 1981	FY 1969–79[a]	FY 1981	FY 1979	FY 1981
1	Newark	64	70	71	80	6	5	7	2
2	Boston	42	37	99	99	13	6	12	5
3	Detroit	49	59	47	50	18	23	9	4
4	St. Louis	31	39	18	16	10	14	6	2
5	Baltimore	58	63	66	64	20	24	7	3
6	Buffalo	68	66	94	93	17	14	14	4
7	Minneapolis	51	50	84	80	23	18	18	7
8	Cleveland	43	28	36	29	18	7	10	6
9	Atlanta	33	27	59	54	35	44	18	12
10	Philadelphia	31	31	25	24	18	19	12	6
11	Oakland	40	30	28	34	25	25	8	11
12	Pittsburgh	41	39	53	56	18	28	10	5
13	Denver	32	28	37	34	18	12	6	3
14	New Orleans	45	38	30	30	19	17	13	6
15	Chicago	37	40	43	44	14	22	9	3
16	Kansas City	27	25	17	15	28	19	11	4
17	Toledo	41	43	16	15	21	19	10	3

240

18	San Francisco	51	42	46	48	14	21	10	5
19	Cincinnati	40	39	22	21	20	24	12	3
20	New York	45	42	52	45	8	8	40	4
21	Los Angeles	37	25	32	37	19	14	13	4
22	Portland	36	28	73	73	18	20	6	8
23	Seattle	31	34	35	33	22	24	12	3
24	Louisville	40	44	31	30	30	11	6	4
25	Ft. Worth	30	22	59	56	32	32	15	6
26	Columbus	36	30	11	11	19	24	10	8
27	Milwaukee	50	53	96	94	20	21	14	4
28	Dallas	17	15	59	55	28	29	16	4
29	Phoenix	48	42	34	33	28	31	5	5
30	Indianapolis	47	53	96	96	20	27	8	4
31	Long Beach	34	28	23	30	22	33	5	4
32	Memphis	61	58	72	71	17	14	17	4
33	Omaha	41	32	56	47	34	20	12	5
34	San Diego	42	31	29	33	21	24	5	2
35	Honolulu	38	28	81	79	26	21	11	3
36	Oklahoma City	32	27	30	26	32	43	20	7
37	Houston	16	16	57	55	25	30	15	7
38	San Antonio	38	35	57	54	23	22	13	3

[a]Represents the average for the fiscal 1969–79 period.

(continued next page)

241

TABLE 6.2 *(cont'd)*

Municipal Employment
Full-Time Equivalent Employment/10,000 Residents

Distress Rank	City	October 1979	October 1981
1	Newark	389	373
2	Boston	431	444
3	Detroit	204	170
4	St. Louis	297	253
5	Baltimore	527	426
6	Buffalo	303	313
7	Minneapolis	134	130
8	Cleveland	193	160
9	Atlanta	201	180
10	Philadelphia	205	198
11	Oakland	116	102
12	Pittsburgh	132	135
13	Denver	253	240
14	New Orleans	224	171
15	Chicago	158	141
16	Kansas City	150	173
17	Toledo	102	96
18	San Francisco	314	306

No.	City		
19	Cincinnati	162	167
20	New York	459	462
21	Los Angeles	138	137
22	Portland	110	118
23	Seattle	177	172
24	Louisville	201	145
25	Ft. Worth	121	122
26	Columbus	123	122
27	Milwaukee	140	140
28	Dallas	154	148
29	Phoenix	112	109
30	Indianapolis	161	171
31	Long Beach	124	126
32	Memphis	371	327
33	Omaha	94	88
34	San Diego	81	75
35	Honolulu	120	110
36	Oklahoma City	107	104
37	Houston	103	114
38	San Antonio	152	128

Source: Computations based on Census Bureau data.

243

1983, the U.S. Conference of Mayors released its evaluation of the impact of the President's fiscal 1984 budget on urban areas. They concluded:

"Despite the Administration's call for a 'freeze' on spending for domestic programs, the FY 84 budget proposes major reductions in a wide range of programs which serve cities and the poor. . . . The result of the additional FY 84 reductions will be further layoffs, tax increases and service cuts at the local level, and the continued inability of cities to meet the needs of the unemployed and the poor."[8]

"Over the last two years, cities have absorbed immense cuts in urban aid, which have led to tax increases and service cuts across the country. These reductions together with the continued deterioration of our urban infrastructure, threaten to drive businesses and jobs in record numbers out of our cities."[9]

In January, 1982, the Joint Economic Committee of Congress released its survey of fiscal conditions in 48 large cities, 36 of which are profiled in this study.[10] Some 40% of the cities surveyed reported recent tax increases; most had raised property or sales taxes. Approximately 60% of the respondents reported having increased user charges and fees between 1981 and 1982; 93% of them anticipated declines in Federal aid during the coming year. The survey confirmed that own-source revenues were being substituted for intergovernmental aid, and that as a result, municipal taxes were once again increasing. The Joint Economic Committee report came to the following conclusion.

"In general, city governments simply do not have the financial resources to undertake the enormous fiscal and administrative responsibilities being imposed on them by the Federal government."[11]

The report goes on to say:

"The outlook for cities is bleak. In the declining cities, where capital deferrals are accompanied by reductions in service levels and large tax increases, it appears that crises cannot long be avoided."[12]

A 100-city survey conducted between November 3rd and November 10th, 1981 by the U.S. Conference of Mayors came to a similar set of conclusions.[13] Approximately 60% of the respondents replied that they were laying off workers, 41% said that they had raised or will raise taxes and fees, and a majority said that they had reduced services and/or deferred capital spending plans in order to absorb recent Federal funding cuts. The employee layoffs apparently affected cities in all regions. Baltimore reported furloughing 1000 workers, Buffalo 1400, Los Angeles 2100, Louisville 796, and St. Louis 1068. Cities that had reduced or planned to reduce municipal services generally targeted parks and recreation, health and human services, public works and sanitation for the cutbacks. More than 60% of the respondents reported that they had already delayed planned capital projects or expected to do so. Street and bridge projects, parks and recreational facilities, police and fire stations, water projects, and libraries were most affected by such deferrals.

The Federal cutbacks also had repercussions in terms of municipal employment. The Conference of Mayors survey found that the elimination of all public-service jobs under CETA Titles IID and VI resulted in an aggregate loss of 300,000 jobs in the 100 cities surveyed. This, in turn, was expected to boost municipal expenditures for unemployment compensation and welfare. Baltimore estimated that the CETA layoffs would cause a loss of $27 million in direct wages which, through the multiplier process, would ultimately cause a $60 million drain on the City's economy.

Clearly the urban fiscal crisis is real and appears to be intensifying.

THE NEW FEDERALISM AND THE CITIES

Recent reductions in Federal aid to state and local governments are part of a "new federalism" which, as envisioned by the Reagan Administration, would drastically alter relationships between the Federal government and the states and cities. The President's National Urban Policy Report, released in July, 1982, provided the philosophical underpinnings for the new federalism and indicated the context in which future decisions regarding urban matters would be made.[14] It says:

> "It is the policy of this Administration to return maximum authority and discretion over the use of resources to State and local governments. The Administration believes that State and local government have amply demonstrated that, properly unfettered, they will make better decisions than the Federal Government acting for them. The President has thus proposed an historic, major realignment of responsibilities in the American Federal system. . . . The Administration is convinced that the time is ripe for a more rational division of responsibilities among the Federal, State and local governments. . . ."[15]

The report goes on to say:

> "It is the position of this Administration that the Nation's individuals, businesses, and communities will realize greater and longer-lasting benefits if the Federal Government creates the conditions under which all can productively pursue their own interests."[16]

The proposed readjustment in Federal–state–local relationships was a long time in coming and reflects the confluence of several forces. Susannah Calkins and John Shannon have identified four recent "shocks" to the state–local system that helped to set the stage for the new federalism.[17] They include: the 1973–75 national recession and its attendant economic dislocations; New York City's fiscal crisis, which underscored the risks of "creative accounting" and caused a fundamental reassessment of the proper role of municipal government; California's Proposition 13, which warned state and local officials of mounting taxpayer discontent; and, the 1980 election in which a more conservative president and congress was elected. Calkins and Shannon note that these shocks were particularly traumatic because they were superimposed on three long-run socio-economic changes: the transition from a "high-growth, low inflation" economy to a "low-growth, high inflation" economy; the transition from a high rate of population growth to a low rate of population growth; and the general loss of public confidence in the ability of government to resolve existing social and economic problems.

Taxes appeared more onerous once the economic pie stopped growing. Slower population growth and the concomitant aging of the population imposed greater economic burdens on the working-age population and on the social security system. Moreover, by 1980, entitlement programs such as social security, food stamps, civilian and military retirement pay, welfare, and revenue sharing, which obligate the Federal government to pay benefits automatically to those who meet certain eligibility requirements, were causing Federal spending to become uncontrollable. One of every 11 Federal dollars was being spent just to service the Federal debt. The composition of Federal spending had also changed drastically in recent decades. Defense spending had declined from 58% of the Federal budget in 1955 to less than 25% in 1980. During the same period, Federal spending for human resource programs had increased from 20% to more than 50%.

After 1980, slower economic growth, the urgent need to balance the Federal budget, and the need to modernize the nation's defense capability finally ended the drift toward human resource programs and other urban programs. They were scaled back and earmarked for an early return to the states as part of the new federalism.

Block Grants: A First Step Toward the New Federalism

The Omnibus Reconciliation Act of 1981 (PL97–35), which became effective on October 1, 1981, was the first step in the eventual return to the states of functional and financial responsibility for most domestic social programs. Under the Act, 77 categorical grant programs were consolidated into nine new block grants, bringing the total number of Federal block grant programs to 11.* Some 46 categoricals not included in the blocks were left intact, but the Administration terminated or withheld funding for 62 other categorical programs.

Of the nine new block grants, four were for health services, three for social services and cash payments to the poor, one for education, and one for community development. All go directly to the states but certain funds are designated for pass-through to local government. The block grants seek to minimize Federal regulations and paperwork. They make funds available for a broad spectrum of purposes rather than for a narrow range of activities. They are also designed to assure neutrality on the part of the Federal executive branch in determining local program priorities, to make the distribution of funds less subject to the whims of Federal program administrators, and to assure greater accountability by state governments to their citizens. The states are still subject to a Federal fiscal audit and to an evalutation of effectiveness, and they must make available to the public a plan for using the funds. By cutting through red tape, administration planners projected a 25% cost savings in these programs. Proposed fiscal 1982 funding for the consolidated programs was therefore slashed by 25%, from $8153 million to $6092 million. A brief description of each of the new block grant programs appears below.[18]

State Community Development. This grant was to be distributed to the states on the basis of a weighted average of population, poverty, and overcrowded housing in non-entitlement areas, or on the basis of a weighted average of population, poverty, and age of housing.

Elementary and Secondary Education. This block grant encompassed thirty-seven former categorical programs including alcohol and drug abuse education, community education, consumer education, elementary and secondary school education in the arts, and law-related education, among others. Funds were distributed on the basis of the school-age population in each state. States must pass through at least 80% of all funds to local education agencies based on relative enrollment adjusted for the relative number of higher cost children.

Preventive Health and Health Services. This block grant encompassed six former categorical grant programs: urban rat control, emergency medical services, the high-blood-pressure control program, home health services, preventive health services (flouridation), and health education.

---

*The two existing block grant programs were the Comprehensive Employment and Training Act and the Community Development Block Grant Program.

Funds were distributed in proportion to what each state and its entities would have received under the predecessor programs.

Alcohol, Drug Abuse, and Mental Health. This block grant encompassed ten former categorical programs: drug abuse community service, alcoholism treatment and rehabilitation/occupational services, drug abuse demonstration programs, alcohol formula grants, drug abuse preventive programs, community mental health centers—comprehensive services support, alcohol demonstration/evaluation, alcohol abuse prevention demonstration/evaluation, drug abuse prevention formula grants, and special alcoholism projects. Funds were distributed according to what each state and its entities would have received under the previous mental health law.

Maternal and Child Health Services. This block grant combined nine former categorical programs: crippled children's services, maternal and child health research, maternal and child health services, maternal and child health training, childhood lead-based paint poisoning prevention, sudden infant death syndrome information and counseling program, comprehensive hemophilia diagnostic and treatment centers, genetic diseases testing and counseling, and adolescent pregnancy prevention and services. Funds were distributed in proportion to what was received in previous years under the predecessor programs. States are required to provide $3 in matching funds for every $4 of Federal aid.

Primary Care. This block grant combined two former categorical programs: community health centers and hospital-affiliated care centers. Funds were distributed in proportion to each state's share under the predecessor programs. There is a local matching provision of 20% in fiscal 1983 and 33.5% in fiscal 1984.

Social Services. This block grant replaced one former block grant, social services for low income and public assistance recipients, and one categorical grant, social services training. Funds were distributed on the basis of relative population and up to 10% of all funds may be transferred to the four health block grants or to the low-income home energy assistance block grant.

Community Services. This block grant encompassed seven former categorical programs: community action, community food and nutrition, older persons opportunities and services, community economic development, state economic opportunity offices, national youth sports program and housing and community development. Ninety percent of all funds were dispersed according to the number of individuals and families below the poverty line.

Low-Income Home Energy Assistance. This block grant replaced one former categorical program, the low-income energy assistance program. Up to 10% of all funds may be transferred to other block grant programs.

The new block grants substantially expanded the role of the states and reduced the Federal role in the overall Federal system. They were well accepted by the nation's governors who had been espousing the "new states' rights" in recent years. Only California, New Hampshire, and New York failed to assume responsibility for some or all of the new block grants on October 1, 1981.

The Big Swap: Second Stage in the New Federalism

The President dropped the other shoe in January 1982 when, in his State of the Union Message, he proposed a "financially equal swap" under which the Federal government would assume responsibility for the cost of the Medicaid program, and the states would take over Aid to Families with Dependent Children (AFDC) and the food stamp program beginning in fiscal 1984. The Federal government currently pays the entire cost of the food stamp program but shares the cost of welfare and medicaid with the states. The Federal share of these programs ranges from 50% to 78%, with the Federal government bearing a larger proportion of total costs in states with lower per capita incomes. Beginning in 1984, 43 other Federal programs in areas such as job training, health, education, transportation, and child welfare were to be turned over to the states to be financed and administered as each state saw fit. Initially, the states would be assisted by grants from a $28 billion Federal trust fund to be financed from the proceeds of the oil windfall profits tax and from Federal excise taxes on items such as gasoline, liquor, cigarettes, and telephones. In fiscal 1987, the Federal government was to begin phasing out the trust fund and the excise taxes, a process to be completed in four years. Under the initial proposal, the only excise tax which the Federal government would impose after fiscal 1991 is a 2¢ per gallon tax on gasoline to help finance the interstate highway system. After fiscal 1991, the states could choose whether or not to continue the programs transferred to them and at what level of funding. They would also have the option of imposing the excise taxes no longer used by Washington to finance the inherited programs. The proposed swap was designed to reduce Federal aid to states and cities by approximately two-thirds by fiscal 1991.

This second stage was not well-received by the nation's governors and mayors who feared that they would be accepting costly new responsibilities without adequate financial help from the Federal government and without sufficient resources of their own to do the job. The nation's mayors and city managers in turn feared that their states would not be as generous to their "municipal offspring" as the Federal government had been. Many states are known to be philosophically opposed to major public social programs. Moreover, major interstate inequities in fiscal capacity would result if Federal taxes were returned to the states based solely on place of origin. States with mineral reserves are in an infinitely better fiscal position than states without such resources.

Largely on the basis of this opposition, the Administration has since revised its initial proposals. In July, 1982, the Administration agreed to have the Federal government assume almost all of the cost of the Medicaid program, which provides health care for the poor. The Federal government would also continue to pay for the food stamp program in its entirety, a major reversal. In exchange, the states would take over Aid to Families with Dependent Children and some 35 other programs costing almost $31 billion. To pay for these programs, the states would be given almost $39 billion in Federal and freed state revenues.

Even this scaled down version has since been modified. According to the latest proposal, the Administration plans to turn over even fewer programs to the states and cities and would agree to guarantee the same level of financing for at least five years. There would be no decision at present about the Federal tax sources to be turned over to the states after 1988. In addition, plans to have the states take over the welfare program would also be held in abeyance.

The Fiscal Status of the States: Achilles Heel of the New Federalism

The reluctance of states to assume the added responsibilities implicit in the new federalism proposals reflects their own deepening fiscal difficulties. The recent recession has severely eroded state tax revenues. Many states are also faced with massive outlays to rehabilitate their neglected public infrastructures. About the only bright spot in an otherwise gloomy picture is that the states appear better prepared administratively to assume new responsibilities than ever before.

The Advisory Commission on Intergovernmental Relations has documented the following administrative changes that have made states better able to assume new functional responsibilities. Since 1950, four-fifths of the states have modernized their constitutions. Many states have also strengthened the office of the chief executive, unified the court system, enhanced the capacity of the state legislature, and extended home rule and taxing authority to local government.[19] The authority of the nation's governors has been strengthened by lengthening their terms of office, allowing them to succeed themselves, and giving them greater budget authority and stronger powers of appointment. Most state legislatures were reapportioned pursuant to the U.S. Supreme Court's decision in Baker versus Carr (1962) and they now give better representation to minorities, women, and urban interests. The state court structure has been streamlined and efforts made to improve the administration of the court system and the quality of judges. All states now require open meetings of public bodies; 35 have some form of sunset legislation; many have strong conflict of interest laws on the books.

Although the states may be better prepared administratively to assume greater responsibility for domestic social programs, few are financially able to do so. As of 1981, 36 states used both sales and personal income taxes, thereby reducing their dependence on the property tax. In addition, most states currently impose corporate income taxes. The automatic growth of revenues from these auxiliary taxes would normally allow most states to make up any shortfall caused by reductions in Federal aid. However, this did not occur because the cuts were deeper than expected and because most states were weakened by a deep recession, by a long-simmering tax revolt and by concomitant changes in Federal tax laws.

Walter Heller has demonstrated the impact of these changes on state and local finances.[20] For example, although state and local governments account for only one-seventh of the Federal budget, they absorbed nearly one-third of the cuts in fiscal 1982 Federal spending. In real terms, Federal support for state governments was about 26% lower in fiscal 1982 than in fiscal 1981 and 37% lower in fiscal 1982 than in fiscal 1980. Heller also notes that state revenues have been affected by recent changes in Federal tax laws. For example, the availability of "all savers" certificates and universal individual retirement accounts and the reduction in the top bracket on investment income from 70% to 50% made it more difficult for states to borrow money.* Investors who would normally use state bonds as a tax shelter no longer found them as attractive. Banks and other financial institutions can no longer be counted upon to "prop up" the market for state and local securities. They currently favor floating over fixed-rate investments so that they have some protection against fluctuating interest rates. Enactment of the Accelerated Cost Recovery System (ACRS) in 1981 could potentially reduce state corporate income tax receipts in states that conform to Federal tax depreciation laws. Many states have already moved to decouple their tax systems from the Federal system to avoid such losses.

The finances of some states have also been impaired by the recent tax revolt. Between January 1976 and January 1980, 17 states enacted constitutional or statutory revenue and/or expenditure limitations. Six states also imposed limits on their local governments.

However, the recession is at the heart of the current fiscal difficulties of most states. It boosted welfare-related expenditures while curtailing the growth of locally-generated revenues. A recent survey of 41 states conducted

*With permission of *The Wall Street Journal*, January 22, 1982.

by the National Governors' Association and the National Association of State Budget Officers during the Fall of 1982 found that these states expected to incur an aggregate budget deficit of almost $2 billion in fiscal 1983.[21] This compares with a surplus of $2.35 billion in fiscal 1982 and a surplus of $4.77 billion in fiscal 1981. Moreover, states in all regions were affected. California projected a fiscal 1983 deficit of $1.65 million while New York and Wisconsin expected deficits of $530 million and $266 million respectively. Pennsylvania, Virginia, and New Jersey anticipated deficits of $164 million, $83 million, and $77 million respectively. Some 32 states indicated that they had reduced state spending, 22 had increased taxes or user fees on either a permanent or temporary basis, 33 had imposed hiring limitations, and 18 had laid off state employees. The survey found that growing state budget gaps were caused by the recession, by reduced Federal aid, and by the winding down of inflation, which affected revenues more than expenditures.*

Since states must, by law, balance their budgets, a wave of tax increases and general belt tightening is almost certain to occur. Given this situation, it is difficult to envision how the states could assume the responsibilities implicit in the new federalism proposals. An exceptionally strong economic rebound would be needed to replenish state coffers by October 1984, the target date for the start of the proposed transfer of programs.

URBAN ENTERPRISE ZONES: HOW MUCH HELP FOR THE CITIES?

In the immediate future, the nation's cities will be called upon to generate the revenues they need with much less Federal and state assistance. In order to do so, they must develop and maintain healthy local economies. The Administration's "enterprise zone" proposal, introduced in March 1982, seeks to stimulate private-sector activity in distressed inner cities by providing relief from taxes, government regulations, and other government burdens.[22] Attempts would also be made to improve local public services. The overall goal is to remove bureaucratic impediments to the expansion of private-sector economic activity.

The Federal tax incentives would include: a 3% to 5% investment tax credit for capital investments in personal property within the enterprise zone; a 10% tax credit for construction or rehabilitation of commercial, industrial, or rental housing properties; a 50% income tax credit to employers for wages

*© 1983 by The New York Times Company. Reprinted by permission.

paid to zone employees who were "disadvantaged" when hired;* and elimination of capital gains taxes for qualified properties in the zone.

Suitable enterprise zones could also be designated as foreign-trade zones, thereby giving businesses in the zone relief from tariff and import duties. Industrial development bonds would continue to be available to small businesses located within enterprise zones even if such bonds were abolished for use elsewhere. Firms located within enterprise zones would be permitted to carry over operating losses for the life of the zone or 15 years, whichever is longer. Other Federal regulations would also be relaxed, but minimum wage legislation would still apply to zone employers. The Administration anticipates that these benefits would make it easier for employers within enterprise zones to obtain the start-up capital they need. Moreover, by removing tax and regulatory burdens rather than providing government subsidies to stimulate economic activity, the drain on the Federal budget would be minimized. The proposal seeks to establish a maximum of 25 enterprise zones nationally during each of the first three years of the program. It is estimated that $310 million in Federal revenues would be foregone for every 25 zones established.

In order to be designated as an enterprise zone, an area must be nominated by local government with a confirming nomination by the state or vice versa. The strength of the incentives to be offered by state and local government would weigh heavily in the selection process. States and localities would be expected to offer tax and regulatory relief and to improve the quantity and quality of local public services, possibly through experimentation with private-sector providers. State and local tax relief could take the form of reduced income, property, or sales taxes for businesses, employees, or residents of the zone. Local regulatory relief could take the form of less restrictive planning and zoning regulations and building codes. Local governments could also fund job training projects, infrastructure improvements, and similar projects that contribute to economic development. It is also envisioned that neighborhood and community groups would become involved in plans for the zone.

Proposed areas must satisfy the criteria for Urban Development Action Grants plus one or more additional criteria. Urban Development Action Grants are awarded on the basis of extent of poverty and unemployment, direction of population change, age of housing, changes in per capita personal income, retail jobs and manufacturing jobs, and a city's track record in providing low- and moderate-income housing and in creating equal opportunity in housing and employment. Proposed enterprise zones must also meet

*A disadvantaged individual is defined as a recipient of AFDC, SSI, or general assistance, a foster child receiving payments from state or local government, or a handicapped person or one referred through vocational rehabilitation.

one of four additional criteria: the average annual unemployment rate in the area, as shown in the 1980 census, must be at least 1.5 times the national average; the area must have a poverty rate of 20% or more; at least 70% of the households in the area must have incomes below 80% of the median income of households in the jurisdiction that nominates the area; and, the population of the area must have declined by at least 20% between 1970 and 1980. In addition, the boundary of the zone must be continuous and, if located within an SMSA, the zone must contain a population of at least 4000. About 2000 communities would be eligible for designation as urban enterprise zones. However, the enterprise zone program is not an entitlement program and not all eligible areas would automatically become enterprise zones.

Enterprise zones have already been tried elsewhere. Great Britain has been experimenting with such zones since 1980. Congressmen Jack F. Kemp and Robert Garcia introduced urban enterprise zone legislation in 1980 and the current Administration proposal includes several features of the Kemp–Garcia bill. Eight states have already passed urban enterprise zone bills and several more are considering them.

Its supporters claim that enterprise zones target benefits to the most needy areas while at the same time putting the onus for success on the private-sector where it belongs. Its detractors claim that the tax incentives offered would be insufficient to offset the risk and inconvenience of doing business in distressed areas, that the proposal ignores the capital needs of new businesses, and that it does not offer sufficient job training incentives. The need for job training may be critical. Depressed areas within older, industrial cities are no longer competitive for traditional blue-collar manu-facturing jobs and lack the trained labor force needed to support high-technology manufacturing or emerging service jobs. Some analysts have also criticized the incentives as excessive. In evaluating the original Kemp–Garcia proposal, George Sternlieb suggested that the tax subsidy is so sweeping that the Federal government would be paying for 35% to 40% of any capital improvements within the zones through foregone taxes.[23]

The limited number of zones to be created and the formidable obstacles that confront businesses choosing to locate within the zones suggest that at best the proposal will have a limited impact on economic activity within distressed inner-city neighborhoods.

THE ECONOMIC OUTLOOK FOR LARGE CITIES

The economic outlook for the nation's cities depends in part on the economic outlook for the nation as a whole. In this respect, opinion is divided. Robert Reischauer has concluded that "the 1980s will be characterized by relatively slow economic growth, extremely high rates of inflation, high levels of unemployment, rapid nominal wage growth, and high interest rates."[24] Other economists believe that the "shakeout" in the economy precipitated by the 1980 and 1981–82 recessions will pave the way for resumption of stable economic growth. There are a number of optimists and pessimists regarding the economic future of large cities.

The Optimistic View

The optimists hold that changing demographic patterns and growing energy constraints will once again make cities viable as places in which to live and work. They cite the ongoing process of "gentrification" and the extensive commercial development currently occurring within the core areas of many large cities as proof that there is a sound basis for an economic and social renaissance within these cities.

Optimists note that the large-scale migration of blacks from the rural south to the urban north has ended and that the black majority has already taken control of the political and social machinery in a number of large cities. It is anticipated that this will lead to the creation of a better urban environment. Changing lifestyles would also seem to favor a central city renaissance. The nuclear family is no longer the norm. As the number of single adults, childless couples, and single-parent families increases, so will the demand for high-rise apartments and townhouses within central cities. There has already been a flurry of housing rehabilitation and new residential construction adjacent to the central business districts of large cities. This, in turn, has lured some middle-class residents back to the cities in a process known as "gentrification." The optimists suggest that high and rising energy costs will ultimately turn the gentrification trickle into a flood. The argument is that growing energy constraints will favor the cities at the expense of the suburbs, because cities, by virtue of their relatively high population densities, are energy-efficient.

The growth of offices in the core of large cities during the 1970s has also been cited as proof that these cities remain economically viable. A survey of central business district office space by the Urban Land Institute found that between 1970 and 1978, office space in the core areas of 20 selected cities expanded from 313 million to 433 million square feet, an increase of more than 38%.[25] The findings of the survey are summarized in Table 6.3.

William Baumol's outlook for the nation's cities typifies the thinking of the optimists. He foresees that the poor will leave the central cities because the housing stock suitable for them will continue to deteriorate and disappear, and because the types of jobs for which they qualify will also diminish. Nevertheless, he believes that cities still possess residual economic

TABLE 6.3. Expansion of Office Space in the Core Areas of Selected Cities, 1970–78 (millions of square feet)

City	Office Space		Percent Increase
	1970	1978	
Atlanta	10.8	16.9	56
Baltimore	8.0	10.0	25
Boston	28.5	38.0	33
Chicago	57.8	77.8	35
Cincinnati	10.1	10.5	4
Cleveland	16.5	18.7	13
Dallas	15.0	20.4	36
Denver	7.8	15.8	103
Detroit	11.5	18.0	56
Houston	13.9	22.2	60
Indianapolis	10.4	12.4	19
Los Angeles	33.0	45.0	36
Milwaukee	9.0	11.5	28
Minneapolis	10.0	14.8	48
Newark	2.8	4.6	64
New Orleans	5.5	8.5	54
Philadelphia	24.1	32.2	34
Pittsburgh	8.7	13.2	52
San Francisco	25.0	35.0	40
Seattle	4.5	7.2	60
Total	312.9	432.7	38

Source: J. Thomas Black, "The Changing Economic Role of Central Cities and Suburbs," in *The Prospective City,* ed. Arthur P. Solomon (Copyright © 1980 by The MIT Press), Table 4.16, p. 109.

advantages for activities that require face-to-face communications, for specialty retailing and for cultural activity and restaurants. He says:

"After a painful transition process, cities will emerge significantly smaller but economically viable and even prosperous, with an even balance of the different income groups in its resident population. The social ills that have escalated in recent years can be expected to abate. Economic activity will consist far more heavily than before of service and administrative activities and manufacturing will play a considerably smaller role."[26]

The Pessimistic View

There are at least an equal number of pessimists as optimists concerning the economic and social future of the nation's large cities. George Sternlieb and James Hughes note:

"The urban crisis is not over—it is rather entering on its most fearful challenge. The demographic shifts within our society have left major urban areas increasingly the focal point for the distressed—not merely the impoverished, but the increasingly impoverished. A thin facade of office structures, of new, swinging singles groups, distracts the eye from the functional reality."[27]

The pessimists allege that the suburban dream is still very much alive. Those born during the height of the post-war baby boom are now within the prime home-buying ages and recent surveys seem to suggest that they prefer live in the suburbs. In fact, the entire process of gentrification seems to be overshadowed by continued movement to the suburbs. George Sternlieb and Kristina Ford conducted 502 interviews in a sample of converted loft buildings and new apartment buildings in New York City to determine who was returning to the City and what their long-term plans were.[28] They found that the former suburbanites were relatively young and affluent. The median age of the household heads interviewed was 28 years in the converted buildings and almost 33 years in the new buildings. Their median income was $21,000 as compared with a citywide average of about $8,400. Moreover, they did not plan to remain indefinitely and talked about a home in the suburbs once they had children. Sternlieb and Ford concluded:

" . . . we do not see signs of a substantial middle-class population rebirth within central cities. Rather, we see the rising of selected areas dedicated to the relatively youthful sophisticated groups with high disposable income and an inclination for high current expenditures."[29]

Thomas Muller found that by and large, cities were not attracting young, above-average income households, thereby offsetting the outmigration of other families. His research indicated that the average male moving to central cities between 1975 and 1978 had a median income of $9,574, slightly below that for the base population, $9,766. By contrast, the average male leaving these cities between 1975 and 1978 was characterized by a median income of $12,031, which was 23% above the median for the base population.[30]

Martin Abravanel and Paul Mancini came to a similar set of conclusions based on their analysis of a 1978 HUD survey that dealt with the quality of community life.[31] The survey consisted of in-person interviews with a national, cross-section sample of 7074 Americans, age 18 and older, living in cities, suburbs, and non-metropolitan areas. Based on their analysis, the authors concluded:

"There is little evidence on a national scale of a net shift in population into cities, and there is little evidence that such a shift can be expected in the near future. Based on people's reported moving intentions, central cities will continue to lose population through migration."[32]

Abravanel and Mancini found that crime, drug addiction, teenage gangs, poor housing, dirty streets, poor schools, and high unemployment were major impediments to any significant movement back to the cities.

Results from the 1980 decennial census of population and housing provide additional evidence that housing rehabilitation adjacent to the downtowns of large cities has not stemmed the population losses that contributed to the decline of those cities. Daphne Spain of the Census Bureau evaluated 1970–80 population changes in census tracts located within a three-mile radius of the downtowns of ten large cities: Atlanta, Baltimore, Columbus, Dallas, New Orleans, Philadelphia, St. Paul, San Francisco, Seattle, and Washington, D.C.[33] The tracts analyzed included virtually all areas of gentrification within these cities. She found that the gentrifying tracts were characterized by above-average population losses affecting both blacks and whites. Whereas the nation's central cities lost 7% of their white population between 1970 and 1980, the loss of whites averaged 20% in the sample cities and 23% in the gentrifying tracts. Whereas the black population in central cities grew by more than 15% between 1970 and 1980, the gentrifying tracts lost 20% of their black populations. In effect, the loss of blacks in gentrifying tracts was almost as rapid as the loss of whites. Spain therefore concluded that gentrification has not been a vehicle for population growth in declining cities.

The pessimists also doubt that energy contraints will force any substantial return to the cities as long as opportunities for factor substitution exist. For example, suburban families can reduce energy consumption by driving smaller cars, by carpooling, by combining trips to save transportation energy, by buying more efficient furnaces, by adding storm windows and insulation, and by reducing the amount of space to be heated. Only when these opportunities are exhausted will locational choices be modified to any extent.

The pessimists also point to the competitive disadvantages of large cities for traditional types of manufacturing activities. David Birch recently examined the behavior of several million business establishments and the places in which they chose to start up or expand during the 1970s.[34] He found that manufacturing firms were migrating to "young, remote areas" which were dominated by the service sector. He concluded:

"They are avoiding the older, industrial-revolution communities where they once flourished. . . . The urban amenities that once made cities an attractive place to manufacture things that are no longer of great value to manufacturers."[35]

The Outlook for Sunbelt versus Snowbelt Cities

Even within their overall framework of optimism or pessimism, most analysts expect that some cities will fare better than others during the coming decade. Proponents of the convergence theory expect a turnaround that will benefit northern cities. According to this theory, any forces that disturb the system will eventually be offset by equal and opposite countervailing pressures. This implies the existence of a self-regulating market mechanism that will restore the competitive equilibrium between north and south and cause a narrowing of interregional growth disparities. For example, if high unemployment rates in northern cities hold down wage costs while southern prosperity and growth push up wage costs, northern cities could, in theory, again become competitive for labor-intensive industry. Or, if energy costs continue to rise, the absence of energy-saving public transportation in southern cities could reduce their competitive advantages vis-à-vis northern cities.

David Perry and Alfred Watkins disagree with the theory of convergence and suggest that growth disparities between regions are likely to be self-reenforcing.[36] They foresee a process of divergence rather than convergence. Their theory of uneven development is based on the fact that the location of rapidly-growing industries is not evenly dispersed throughout the nation. This, in turn, creates prosperous and depressed regions.

> "Once a certain critical mass is achieved, growth in the favored region proceeds in accordance with Myrdal's theory of cumulative causation. This, in turn, produces regional polarization or divergent development, i.e. the rich region prospers to the detriment of the poor area."[37]

Peter Lupsha and William Siembieda reject the convergence theory because it fails to take account of the south's unique political and cultural environment.[38] They contend that the south's political outlook is conservative, and that southerners do not value a high level of public services. They also suggest that northerners who migrate to the south do not wish to recreate the high tax environment which they left behind them.

> " . . . the political culture and organization forms of the Sunbelt are not conducive to meeting material demands . . . a belief that a high level of public services is an obligation of government . . . [has] yet to gain a major foothold in the Sunbelt cities."[39]

The general conclusion seems to be that older, declining cities can expect a difficult time. James Fossett and Richard Nathan concluded:

> "By almost any reasonable measure of the prosperity of places—levels of population, income, employment, economic activity, and concentration of

low income households—more distressed cities were apparently worse off in the late 1970s than they were ten years earlier, and more prosperous cities were apparently better off."[40]

Ira Lowry concludes:

"It is hard to be cheerful about the future of our large cities, particularly the older ones. The loss of jobs and residents, the deterioration of housing and public services, the civil tensions, the erosion of public order, and the depletion of municipal treasuries are mutually reenforcing rather than self-correcting trends."[41]

There is, nevertheless, sufficient evidence to indicate that not all northern cities will fare poorly and not all southern cities will do well during the 1980s. Norman and Susan Fainstein have identified a number of large cities, including several in the north, that are "converting" in the sense that their core areas are experiencing massive new public and private investment.[42] New York, Boston, Chicago, Minneapolis, Pittsburgh, Denver, and San Francisco are in this category. Cities that are converting have the following characteristics: The poor are being displaced from the core, not by urban renewal as in the past, but by private market forces. Rental housing is gradually disappearing and the switch to coops and condominiums is in full swing. Growing concentrations of upper-income residents are creating additional demand for specialty shops, restaurants, and theaters, but the market for "mass consumables" is softening. In effect, a process of gentrification is in progress. However, Fainstein and Fainstein go one step further. They also suggest that the nature of core area production is changing in cities that are converting. There is large scale office construction; the influx of corporate headquarters has created a booming market for corporate service firms—legal and accounting firms, banks and other financial institutions—and for services such as restaurants and hotels. The result is a vibrant urban core.

David Birch, in his research concerning the locational preferences of business establishments, also found that some large, northern cities have become highly competitive for the more sophisticated types of service activities.

"Places that grew through manufacturing during the past 150 years are now no longer attractive as places to make things, but are suddenly becoming centers for the creation of intelligence-based service firms . . . thinking per se can become a very valuable export good upon which healthy local economies can be built."[43]

Just as some northern cities may perform quite well economically during the 1980s, some southern and western cities may be subject to growing constraints on their economic progress. Robert Firestine argues that the sunbelt's initial expansion was predicated on the existence of a skilled, well-educated, upper-income labor force who prefer to live in the suburbs.[44] He underscores the fact that jobs are suburbanizing in the south as well as in the north. He therefore concludes:

> "To the extent that Sunbelt central cities and, for that matter, some of their surrounding suburbs may reach a pause in the economic development process, these same sorts of fiscal ills which are becoming rather commonplace in the industrial Northeast may well make themselves more evident in the Sunbelt as well."[45]

Gurney Breckenfeld also concluded that sunbelt cities like Atlanta, New Orleans, Houston, and Dallas could find themselves with the same kinds of problems that are currently plaguing cities like Detroit and St. Louis.[46] He notes that Atlanta's core contains a black majority and that its suburbs remain almost exclusively white. New Orleans, by virtue of deficiencies in its system of public education, now has a large "unskilled underclass" composed primarily of blacks. Cities like Houston and Dallas have developed growth patterns that segregate whites from blacks and rich from poor.

> "In short, some Sunbelt cities are beginning to repeat the misfortune of Northern cities by acquiring an increasing population of unskilled poor at a time when the industrial jobs those people need are moving out of town. . . . It would not be surprising if, in a few decades, some Sunbelt cities develop large wastelands in which few will choose to live."[47]

In the west and southwest, a lack of water may impede the further growth of population and jobs. Urban areas in California and Texas are particularly at risk.

It would appear that certain "first tier" cities, whether located in the north or the south, are likely to grow and prosper during the 1980s. However, most large cities may not be as fortunate. Moreover, the process of decline in northern cities may not relieve municipal expenditure pressures because declines in public spending are not generally proportionate to declines in population and economic activity. As population declines, the population mix tilts toward residents who consume more public services but who have less taxpaying ability. Moreover, population declines are not spatially uniform. Residents who continue to reside in declining neighborhoods are fiercely resistant both to service cutbacks and to programs of planned shrinkage that relocate them to areas in which they can be better served by existing public facilities.[48]

The southern cities have their own problems. Above-average gains in worker productivity may be difficult to sustain once unionization spreads.

Most sunbelt cities have virtually no public transportation facilities and rising energy costs would severely erode their competitive position in terms of moving people and goods. Their rapid population and job growth has also left them with a large backlog of unfilled infrastructure needs and they can expect little help from the Federal government in meeting those needs.

The nation's troubled cities, whether located in the north or south, will be required to adjust to gradually diminishing Federal and state aid. The current watchwords in Washington are "private initiative" and "self help." The 1980s will undoubtedly be a period of retrenchment in northern and southern cities alike. What lies ahead is a searching reassessment of what functions cities can reasonably perform with the resources available to them and how these services can be delivered in a cost-effective manner. Chapter 7 deals with these issues.

NOTES

1. David T. Stanley, *Cities in Trouble* (Columbus, Ohio: Academy for Contemporary Problems, December, 1976), pp. iii.

2. Peggy Cuciti, *City Need and the Responsiveness of Federal Grant Programs* Report for the U.S. House of Representatives Committee on Banking, Finance and Urban Affairs, Subcommittee on the City, 95th Congress, 2nd Session, 1978.

3. U.S. Treasury Department, Office of State and Local Finance, *Report on the Fiscal Impact of the Economic Stimulus Package on 48 Large Urban Governments* (Washington: U.S. Government Printing Office, January 1978.)

4. Richard P. Nathan, et al., "Decentralizing Community Development," Report to the Department of Housing and Urban Development (Washington: Brookings Institution, January 1978.)

5. Richard P. Nathan and Charles Adams, "Understanding Central City Hardship," *Political Science Quarterly* 91 (Spring, 1976):47–62.

6. Harry A. Garn, Thomas Muller, et al., *A Framework for National Urban Policy*, (Washington: The Urban Institute, December 1977.)

7. See U.S. Bureau of the Census, *City Government Finances in 1980–81*, Series GF 81, No. 4 (Washington: U.S. Government Printing Office, 1982.)

8. U.S. Conference of Mayors, *The Federal Budget and the Cities, A Review of the President's Budget in the Light of Urban Needs and National Priorities* (Washington: February 1983) p. ii.

9. Ibid., p. v.

10. Congress of the United States, Joint Economic Committee, *Emergency Interim Study: Fiscal Condition of 48 Large Cities* (Washington: U.S. Government Printing Office, January 14, 1982.)

11. Ibid., pp. x.

12. Ibid., p. xii.

13. U.S. Conference of Mayors, *The FY 82 Budget and the Cities, A Hundred City Survey* (Washington: November 20, 1981.)

14. U.S. Department of Housing and Urban Development, *The President's National Urban Policy Report* (Washington: U.S. Government Printing Office, July 1982.)

15. Ibid., p. 2.

16. Ibid., p. 17.

17. Susannah Calkins and John Shannon, "The New Formula for Fiscal Federalism: Austerity Equals Decentralization," *Intergovernmental Perspective* 8(Winter, 1982):23–9.

18. Wayne F. Anderson, *Memorandum: Block Grants and the Budget Reconciliation Act of 1981* (Washington: Advisory Commission on Intergovernmental Relations, January 7, 1982.)

19. Advisory Commission on Intergovernmental Relations, *In Brief, State and Local Roles in the Federal System* (Washington: U.S. Government Printing Office, November 1981.)

20. Walter W. Heller, "Federalism and the State–Local Fiscal Crisis" *The Wall St. Journal*, January 22, 1982, p. 30.

21. Robert Pear, "States Report Recession is Squeezing Budgets" *The New York Times*, January 9, 1983, p. 20.

22. The White House, Office of the Press Secretary, *The Administration's Enterprise Zone Proposal*, March 23, 1982.

23. George Sternlieb, "Kemp–Garcia Act: An Initial Evaluation," in *New Tools for Economic Development: The Enterprise Zone, Development Bank and RFC*, eds. George Sternlieb and David Listokin (Piscataway, N.J.: Rutgers University Center for Urban and Policy Research, 1981), pp. 42–83.

24. Robert Reischauer, "The Economy and the Federal Budget in the 1980s: Implications for the State and Local Sector," in *Urban Government Finance, Emerging Trends*, ed. Roy Bahl (Beverly Hills, CA: Sage Publications, 1981), p. 18.

25. J. Thomas Black, "The Changing Economic Role of Central Cities and Suburbs," in *The Prospective City*, ed. Arthur P. Solomon (Cambridge, Mass: The MIT Press, 1980), pp. 80–123.

26. William J. Baumol, "Technological Change and the New Urban Equilibrium," in *Cities Under Stress, The Fiscal Crisis of Urban America*, eds. Robert W. Burchell and David Listokin (Piscataway, N.J.: Rutgers University Center for Urban Policy Research, 1981), p. 10.

27. George Sternlieb and James W. Hughes, "New Dimensions of the Urban Crisis," in *Cities Under Stress*, p. 75.

28. George Sternlieb and Kristina Ford, "The Future of the Return-to-the-City Movement," in *Revitalizing Cities*, ed. Herrington J. Bryce (Lexington, Mass: Lexington Books, 1979), pp. 77–104.

29. Ibid., p. 103.

30. Thomas Muller, "Changing Expenditures and Service Demand Patterns of Stressed Cities," in *Cities Under Stress*, pp. 277–99.

31. Martin D. Abravanel and Paul K. Mancini, "Attitudinal and Demographic Constraints," in *Urban Revitalization*, ed. Donald B. Rosenthal, Volume 18, Urban Affairs Annual Reviews (Beverly Hills, CA: Sage Publications, 1980), pp. 27–47.

32. Ibid., p. 45.

33. Daphne Spain, "A Gentrification Scorecard," *American Demographics* (November, 1981):14–20.

34. David L. Birch, *Choosing a Place to Grow: Business Location Decisions in the 1970s*, (Cambridge, Mass: MIT Program on Neighborhood and Regional Change, January 1981).

35. Ibid., p. 29.

36. David C. Perry and Alfred J. Watkins, "Regional Change and the Impact of Uneven Urban Development," in *The Rise of the Sunbelt Cities*, eds. David C. Perry and Alfred J. Watkins, Vol. 14, Urban Affairs Annual Reviews (Beverly Hills, CA: Sage Publications, 1977), pp. 19–54.

37. Ibid., p. 24.

38. Peter A. Lupsha and William J. Siembieda, "The Poverty of Public Services in the Land of Plenty: An Analysis and Interpretation," in *The Rise of the Sunbelt Cities*, pp. 169–89.

39. Ibid., p. 188.

40. James W. Fossett and Richard P. Nathan, "The Prospects for Urban Revival," in *Urban Government Finance, Emerging Trends*, p. 84.

41. Ira S. Lowry, "The Dismal Future of Central Cities," in *The Prospective City*, p. 196.

42. Norman I. Fainstein and Susan S. Fainstein, "Restructuring the American City: A Comparative Perspective," in *Urban Policy Under Capitalism*, eds. Norman I. Fainstein and Susan S. Fainstein, Vol. 22, Urban Affairs Annual Reviews (Beverly Hills, CA: Sage Publications, 1982), pp. 161–89.

43. David L. Birch, *Choosing a Place to Grow: Business Location Decisions in the 1970s*, p. 42.

44. Robert E. Firestine, "Economic Growth and Inequality, Demographic Change and the Public Sector Response," in *The Rise of the Sunbelt Cities*, pp. 191–210.

45. Ibid., p. 207.

46. Gurney Breckenfeld, "Refilling the Metropolitan Doughnut," in *The Rise of the Sunbelt Cities*, pp. 231–58.

47. Ibid., pp. 239–40.

48. For a discussion of the relationship between population decline and municipal spending see Roy Bahl, *The New York State Economy: 1960–78 and Outlook* (Syracuse: Metropolitan Studies Program, Maxwell School of Citizenship and Public Affairs, October, 1979).

7

Policy Options for Fiscal Survival During the 1980s

During the past decade, urban areas have increasingly come to depend on the public-sector, and particularly on the Federal government, to satisfy their needs. Today, this situation is changing and the Federal government is attempting to disentangle itself from a host of urban programs. Local government, in turn, must find ways to fill this vacuum. The Committee for Economic Development suggests that:

"Local governments will need to define their role and manage their operations in new ways. They will require active assistance and appropriate legal, financial, and administrative tools from their state governments. To make full use of the private sector's potential, local governments will need to adopt an entrepreneurial approach that anticipates needs, seeks out opportunities, and encourages an effective coalition of public and private efforts."[1]

This chapter develops a menu of policy options designed to ensure urban fiscal survival during the 1980s. On the revenue side, options such as restructuring the local tax system, greater utilization of current charges and fees, and metropolitan tax base sharing will be discussed. On the expenditure side, the analysis focuses on opportunities for turning over selected municipal functions to the private-sector, on better management of cities, and on joint public–private ventures.

Structural changes in government within metropolitan areas, including city–county consolidation or metropolitan government, might also alleviate the fiscal problems of large cities. However, these options are not considered because they are unlikely to be implemented. The option of shifting given functions to higher levels of government is also omitted because it appears unrealistic, given current "new federalism" proposals.

THE REVENUE OPTIONS

Most analysts agree that restructuring the local tax system and diversifying the local revenue base offer some potential for fiscal relief in large cities. However, as Thomas Galloway notes, the cities are creatures of their states.

> "As local governments were created by the State, their power is derived from the state, and this power is typically limited and constrained by state legislative processes. Whether the power concerns taxation, bonding limits, annexation, incorporation, or local developmental controls, the cities and other substate entities must look to the state for modification and expansion of their powers."[2]

Therefore, the first step may be to loosen state-imposed constraints and give the nation's cities the tools they need to help themselves. In recent years, just the opposite has occurred; state controls on local governments have actually intensified. These controls include both state-imposed tax and expenditure limitations and additional state-imposed, non-reimbursable mandated costs.

Restructuring the Local Tax System

Once state-imposed barriers are lifted, the nation's large cities still face the difficult task of overhauling their local tax systems. A prime target is the real-property tax.

A number of measures can be taken to relieve property tax burdens. Robert Ebel has evaluated four of these measures: a tax freeze, deferral of current taxes, the use of homestead exemptions, and the implementation of circuit breakers.[3] He criticizes a tax freeze because it is both vertically inequitable and inefficient. He suggests that the homestead exemption violates the criteria for horizontal and vertical equity because it cannot be well targeted. However, Ebel regards the deferral of taxes as equitable because all deferred taxes come due when the property is sold; such deferrals are also "neutral" in the sense that they minimize government intrusion into the private housing market. Ebel also favors the circuit breaker because it can be easily targeted to low-income households.

Wisconsin enacted the first circuit breaker law in 1964, and currently,

30 states and the District of Columbia have circuit breaker legislation on 'their books. The circuit breaker is a mechanism that allows tax relief to vary inversely with income. Under the threshold formula, the maximum property tax payable is defined as some percentage of household income. Any tax in excess of that amount automatically qualifies for circuit breaker relief. Under the sliding scale formula, taxpayers within a given income class are relieved of a fixed proportion of the property tax. John Bowman favors the use of circuit breakers because they allow people to remain in their homes despite a decline in income.[4] Circuit breakers thereby promote neighborhood stability.

Current circuit breaker laws differ in terms of their coverage, their formulas for calculating benefits, their benefit limits, and their means of administration. There is wide latitude in terms of coverage. For example, circuit breakers may apply to persons of all ages or just to the elderly, to home owners or to both owners and renters, to all income groups or just to the poor. Circuit breaker benefits can take the form of refundable state income tax credits or direct reductions in property taxes.

Property tax circuit breakers are not without their problems. For example, there is a need to measure personal ability-to-pay and to establish what constitutes an excessive tax burden. Bowman suggests that ability-to-pay be measured in terms of current income because calculations of net worth would entail substantially higher administrative and compliance costs.

Property tax relief can also be achieved in a number of other ways. For example, it is estimated that about one-third of all property in the United States is currently exempt from real-property taxes and that this proportion is even higher in urban areas. By reducing the amount of tax exempt property, property tax burdens in large cities could be stabilized or even reduced. Better administration of the property tax in its current form is another alternative. Suggested improvements include more frequent and more accurate property assessments, assessments that reflect full market value rather than varying fractions of market value, and an accessible appeals process.

There are also a number of alternatives to the property tax in its present form. One alternative is a site value or land value tax. In its purest form, this tax would be levied on bare land values but would not apply to improvements. Critics of the property tax argue that by taxing buildings and other improvements at the same rate as land values, the property tax discourages the maintenance and rehabilitation of existing structures and the construction of new ones and thereby impedes the redevelopment of older cities. Moreover, it is alleged that a tax on improvements as well as land motivates homeowners to substitute land for capital. That is, they tend to choose smaller houses on larger lots, thereby perpetuating low-density development and urban sprawl. Proponents of a land value tax note that land is immobile so that the tax cannot be avoided. Moreover, if cities increase taxes on bare land, landowners would be motivated to develop their properties to the fullest and most profitable uses.

If a land value tax were imposed at the beginning of development, the public-sector would capture the private windfall gains that would otherwise accrue to landowners. However, a land value tax imposed at a later date, the most likely situation in large, developed cities, could impose windfall losses on current owners. There is also some question as to the accuracy with which site values can be determined in large cities because so few vacant lots exist.

Even these obstacles can be overcome. In order to avoid windfall gains and losses in converting from a general property tax to a site value tax, cities could offer only partial tax reductions for existing improvements. Pittsburgh currently has such a "graded" tax plan in operation. For municipal tax purposes, real estate improvements in Pittsburgh are assessed at half the percentage used for site value. Another variation is to use a site value tax solely to fund increases in municipal spending. William Oakland views this variation as a promising option for municipal government.

> "While it would not eliminate existing disparities in metropolitan general property tax rates, such a policy could help insure that these disparities do not widen in the future."[5]

Another variation of the real-property tax, the classified real-property tax, has fewer benefits. Under a classified real-property tax, different types of property are taxed at different effective rates. That is, each class of property is assessed at a different fraction of market value; different tax rates may also be applied to each class of property. Thus, business property can be taxed more heavily than residential property. This is an inefficient mechanism for residential property tax relief. It is also administratively cumbersome because assessors must determine the current use(s) of all properties.

Tom Bradley suggests that the current property tax system be converted to a "functional" tax system that explicitly recognizes that property taxes should finance only property-related services, such as police and fire protection, street work, sewers, and garbage collection.[6] Other municipal functions would be financed differently, possibly through local income or general sales taxes.

Implementing User Charges

Some public services can be shifted from general tax support to user charges. User charges are levied for the voluntary consumption of selected public services and facilities such as swimming pools and golf courses. User charges put public prices on public products. They are favored by economists not only because they provide an additional source of revenue, but also because they can lead to a more efficient allocation of resources and a more equitable distribution of public services. User charges are the most direct way of getting people to reveal their true preferences for public goods.

Selma Mushkin and Charles Vehorn cite several examples of how user charges could influence public-sector production.[7] Consumers could register their preferences for more frequent trash collection via user charges; additional days of collection would be offered at a specified price. Or, consumers could buy extra police patrol services from the public-sector as they currently do from the private-sector. User charges might also reveal a market for more frequent street cleaning or snow removal or for additional street lighting or off-street parking. If properly applied, user charges can also discourage suburban development. For example, cities that have a monopoly over metropolitan water and sewer services can sell such services to adjacent suburbs and impose graduated charges with distance from the central city. The Illinois Department of Commerce and Community Affairs recommends that user charges be set higher for "high demanders" of service and for residents who live in areas that are expensive to service. The level at which charges are set should cover the full cost of providing the service.[8]

Robert Poole believes that many public services are amenable to user charges. He says:

"When we look closely at garbage collection, recreation programs, paramedic service, water and sewer systems, and even many aspects of police and fire protection, we don't find classic examples of public goods. . . . If most public services are not really public goods, there is no theoretical case for them to be provided exclusively by government or funded by compulsory taxation of all residents."[9]

Metropolitan Tax Base Sharing

Metropolitan tax base sharing has been proposed as a solution to the fiscal problems of declining cities. Tax base sharing was originally conceived as a vehicle for moderating the incentives for fiscal zoning. Under such a plan, the entire metropolitan area shares in the fiscal surpluses that result from rapid business growth in some parts of the area. There are currently regional tax base sharing programs in New Jersey, Maryland, and Minnesota.

The Minnesota statute was passed in 1971 and became effective for taxes payable in 1975. It is being used in the seven-county Minneapolis–St. Paul metropolitan area. The law applies to all local taxing units including cities, townships, school districts, counties, and special districts. Paul Gilje has evaluated how tax base sharing works in the Minneapolis–St. Paul area.[10] Under the pooling formula 40% of the net growth in the assessed value of commercial and industrial property since 1971 is placed in a regional pool. The local mill rate is applied to that portion of assessed value that remains local and the areawide mill rate is applied to the portion in the regional pool. Each locality is assigned a share of that pool based on a formula that considers population and the per capita market value of property. Localities with above-average property values receive a slightly smaller share and vice versa. In effect, the entire metropolitan area legally shares 40% of the net growth of commercial–industrial valuation, regardless of where that growth occurred physically. Since pooling is limited to a fraction of the growth of the non-residential tax base, its impact on the total tax base will be gradual.

In order for metropolitan tax base sharing to work, the shared portion must be high enough to capture a significant portion of the growth surplus, but low enough so that developing communities will not be motivated to prohibit new development. Gilje found that tax base sharing has worked satisfactorily in Minneapolis–St. Paul, that intrametropolitan tax base differentials were narrowing, and that incentives for fiscal zoning had been reduced. For example, assessed values in localities with the most new commercial–industrial development were not growing as rapidly as they otherwise would. Localities with slow growth were nevertheless able to keep tax rates below what they would otherwise have been without the law. Gilje also found that tax base sharing did not appear to be influencing business location decisions in the Minneapolis–St. Paul area. He likened the law to an insurance policy for which every metropolitan jurisdiction pays a premium.

Metropolitan tax base sharing has a number of other advantages. It is more acceptable than metropolitan government because it allows local governments to retain their own structural identities and to respond to the unique requirements of their constituents. Tax base sharing can also be a potent force for more rational land use planning. It can channel new development into areas with adequate public facilities and away from areas with fragile environmental resources. Tax base sharing was incorporated into the Hackensack Meadowlands Act in New Jersey for precisely this purpose. Tax base sharing has also been proposed by Alberta, Canada and by the State of Maine as part of plans to exploit local mineral resources.

However, tax base sharing does not appear to be a panacea for the fiscal problems of declining cities. Katharine Lyall evaluated the Minneapolis–St. Paul experience and found that tax base sharing did not reduce the average tax burden of low- and moderate-income residents.[11] Nor was it effective in diverting revenues from the suburbs to the twin cities of Minneapolis and St.

Paul. Lyall found that between 1974 and 1975, for example, the tax base of Minneapolis–St. Paul increased by 2.5%, largely as a result of efforts at central business district renewal during the previous decade and not as a result of tax base sharing.

W. Patrick Beaton also analyzed the ability of current tax base sharing formulas to restore the fiscal structure of older, declining cities.[12] He found that the formulas failed to recognize that new development entails service costs as well as benefits and that "It is more a matter of serendipity than purposefulness that certain municipalities have been able to improve their basic business-related expenditure–revenue balance."[13]

Roy Bahl and David Puryear have also criticized regional tax base sharing because local tax systems, particularly those in the suburbs, tend to be regressive.

"The net equity effect of regional sales or property taxation . . . is a likely increase in the regressivity of the tax system accompanied by a likely (small) decrease in central city–suburban fiscal disparities. Thus, the case for fiscal regionalism is ambiguous on equity grounds as well as on efficiency grounds."[14]

THE EXPENDITURE OPTIONS

Revenues and expenditures can be brought into balance by increasing revenues, by reducing the scope and quality of public services, and/or by providing those services in a more cost-effective manner. This section explores the latter alternative. It discusses the shifting of selected municipal functions to the private-sector, the application of private-sector management techniques to government operations, and the implementation of joint public–private ventures.

In evaluating the options for expenditure retrenchment, it is important to recognize that public organizations differ significantly from their private-sector counterparts. For example, public organizations are particularly resistant to change. Harold Wolman examined the response patterns of 23 cities and three counties to increased fiscal pressure.[15] He found that the initial response to fiscal stress was to stall for time and attempt to raise additional revenues rather than to address expenditure problems directly. When cutbacks become inevitable, he found that they were generally made on the basis of expediency rather than after scientific program evaluation. This tends to make a deteriorating situation even worse. Wolman found that locally-funded programs are much more vulnerable to cutbacks than programs that receive outside funding. He also found that spending cuts are made in those areas in which they are least visible.

Charles Levine has cited a number of paradoxes that tend to impede rational cutbacks in the public-sector.[16] These include the paradox of irreducible wholes, the management science paradox, the participation paradox, the forgotten deal paradox, the productivity paradox and the efficiency paradox. The paradox of irreducible wholes refers to the fact that an organization cannot be reduced simply by reversing the sequence of events upon which it was built, because organizations are complex organisms and cutbacks can have unanticipated results. The management science paradox refers to the fact that in a situation of decline, municipal-management analysts are among the first to find better jobs. This, in turn, hinders rational cutbacks. The participation paradox refers to the incompatibility between organization theory and reductions in force. Organization theory suggests that participation is needed to manage change. However, in situations involving cutbacks, managers who participate display protective behavior, thereby impeding the reduction process. The forgotten deal paradox describes why public managers are reluctant to engage in long-term bargaining, particularly in situations of decline. If cuts are made with the provision that they will then be restored, they fear that the other party to the agreement may not be around to restore those cuts. The productivity paradox refers to the fact that an additional "up-front" investment is often needed to ultimately save money. For example, additional training and equipment may be needed to improve worker productivity. In situations of decline, it is difficult to find the resources to finance such expenses. The efficiency paradox suggests that it is easier to cut an inefficient organization than an efficiently-run organization. In well-run organizations, budget-cutters must slash bone and muscle; in poorly-run organizations, there is generally some fat to cut.

Based on his observations, Levine came to the following conclusions:

> "So great is our enthusiasm for growth that even when an organizational decline seems inevitable and irreversible, it is nearly impossible to get elected officials, public managers, citizens, or management theorists to confront cutback and decremental planning situations as anything more than temporary slowdowns . . . management and public policy theory must be expanded to incorporate nongrowth as an initial condition that applies in some cases."[17]

The U.S. Chamber of Commerce has noted several distinctions between public- and private-sector managers that can complicate the management of public-sector cutbacks.[18] They note that public officials work in a "fishbowl" and that their actions are constantly subject to public scrutiny, that government organizations suffer from diffusion of power, that middle management can thwart the policy decisions of their superiors simply by withholding pertinent information, and that there are few rewards for effective performance or penalties for ineffective performance in the public-sector. Moreover, unlike their private-sector counterparts, public managers have relatively short terms of office and consequently function with relatively short time horizons. They therefore tend to ignore solutions with short-term costs but long-term benefits.

These circumstances make it more difficult to manage change in public organizations. However, change is inevitable. One of the more promising vehicles for change is the turning over of selected municipal functions to the private-sector.

Turning Over Selected Functions to the Private-Sector

Attempts to control spending in large cities have generally focused on personnel cuts and deferral of capital spending. The International City Management Association notes:

> "The greatest temptation when trying to get by with less is to defer costs. Some might call this mortgaging the future to pay for the present. . . . The infrastructures of urban areas are prime candidates for such deferrals. . . . But the costs will balloon and become unavoidable. . . . Maintenance is an annual process that should not be deferred, even in the face of stern pressures to get by with less now."[19]

David Stanley found that only 10% to 15% of the operating budget can be saved by reducing municipal employment and holding down pay and benefit increases. He also notes that such cutbacks often make cities less safe and less attractive.[20]

By contrast, turning over services to the private-sector can improve service delivery while at the same time resulting in substantial savings. Services are turned over through performance contracts under which local government retains control of the service while enjoying the competitive aspects of private business operations. Contracts can also be negotiated with other governmental bodies. Donald Fisk, Herbert Kiesling, and Thomas Muller justify performance contracts as follows:

> "The premise is that when services are provided by government, not only is the choice available to the consumer reduced, but competition in the production of the service is largely absent. Since there is no price associated with the use of government services, it is difficult to know if the service is being provided efficiently."[21]

The International City Management Association (ICMA) lists the following advantages of "contracting out:" Performance contracts limit municipal employment and pension obligations, they assure reliable services in cities with municipal labor problems, they allow for rapid implementation of new projects that require specialized personnel and equipment or which involve high start-up costs, they provide added flexibility in "peak and valley" operations, and they promote increased objectivity because program evaluations are separated from actual operations.[22] Performance contracts are also useful when the work is dangerous or services are needed sporadically or for short intervals. The ICMA also lists the following disadvantages associated with performance contracts: the service might cost more in the long run because the contractor must make a profit and because the municipality incurs costs for contract administration and monitoring; the contractor might reduce service in order to maximize profits; a "loose" contract could weaken the city's control over the final service; contracting out displaces public employees; there may be too few qualified contractors to provide the needed competition; and, contractors can go out of business leaving the city to fend for itself.

Deciding which services to contract out and writing and negotiating the performance contract are difficult matters. Stephen Gordon and Joseph Kelley suggest a three-stage decision process: know the service, compare costs, and monitor the results.[23] For example, in order to develop an enforceable contract, a city must know the service and be able to specify its scope, frequency, and quality. This, in turn, requires that the service be subdivided into its component tasks, that performance measures be established for each task, and that procedures for monitoring performance be established. The next step is to compare the costs of internally providing the service with the costs of private-sector provision. Gordon and Kelley suggest that as part of this evaluation, the department currently responsible for providing the service should submit a sealed bid along with outside vendors. All costs including overhead, supplies, depreciation, salaries and overtime, and fringe benefits as well as needed capital investments should be considered over several years. Once an outside vendor is selected, the performance contract should be written in specific language which details the responsibilities of the city, the contractor, and the recipients of the service, and which ideally includes the equipment to be used by make, model, and year, and the work standards to be applied.

After an award has been made, the results must be closely monitored. To encourage satisfactory performance, some contracts provide for non-competitive contract renewal for an additional term. Other contracts require performance bonds or provide financial incentives for above-average performance and financial penalties for below-average performance. Still others specify that the contract will be awarded to the next-lowest bidder in case of "non-performance."

Not all public services can be successfully contracted out to private providers. The best candidates are clearly delineated services such as water supply and solid waste collection. Newer services such as day care facilities and drug abuse programs are suitable for performance contracting because there is no existing bureaucracy to block the change and because often the needed equipment and facilities are not available. Services such as road construction, street lighting, snow removal, leaf pickup, and tree trimming lend themselves to performance contracting because they are only needed sporadically. Legal, architectural, and engineering assistance may be purchased from private providers because of their specialized nature.

There are numerous examples of successful performance contracting by U.S. cities and counties. E.S. Savas has analyzed the costs of publicly-provided versus privately-provided residential refuse collection.[24] A telephone survey, conducted in 1975, obtained responses from almost 1400 communities in SMSAs with populations of less than 1.5 million. The sample was intentionally biased toward metropolitan areas because residential refuse collection poses the greatest difficulties in these areas. An in-depth study of a subset of 315 cities, with populations of 50,000 or more, was also made. Savas found that contract collection was the least costly service arrangement and that municipal collection cost 15% more per household than contract collection. The average annual cost per household was $27.82 for contract collection and $32.08 for municipal collection. Savas concluded:

> "The significantly lower cost of contract collection compared to municipal collection firmly discredits the popular but simplistic assertion that 'government can do it cheaper because it doesn't make a profit'."[25]

Savas attributed the high cost of municipal collection as compared with contract collection to "bureaucratic inefficiency." The municipal refuse collection agencies in cities with populations of 50,000 or more had higher absentee rates than the private firms, 12% versus 6.5%; they employed larger crews, 3.26 men versus 2.15 men; they served fewer households per shift, 632 versus 686; and, they spent more time serving each household, 4.35 versus 2.37 manhours per year.[26]

Fisk, Kiesling and Muller also cited case studies of successful performance contracting.[27] For example in Wichita, Kansas and St. Paul, Minnesota, the public sanitation department competes directly with private collection firms to provide residential refuse collection. Boston has contracted with private firms for residential refuse collection since the late 1940s. The city is divided into 13 geographic districts and the lowest bidder for each district is awarded a contract for a year with an option to renew for two more years. Duluth, Minnesota contracts for all its ambulance services. It provides $20,500 a year to subsidize the service and provides emergency dispatching through the police and fire departments. Ambulance users are charged on a mileage basis. The Minneapolis–St. Paul area uses a private firm to manage its bus system. Scottsdale, Arizona obtains fire protection from a private, profit-making company under a five-year renewable contract. The company is permitted to make a profit equivalent to 7% to 8% of gross receipts. Washington, D.C. contracts out for vocational rehabilitation services and for day care and nursing home care. Dade County, Florida also contracts out for day care services with private, profit-making companies.

Fisk, Kiesling and Muller estimated that as of 1975, private contracts by state and local governments totaled $36 billion or about 24% of all spending by state and local governments. This figure includes purchase-of-service agreements by state and local governments with other governmental units, with non-profit firms, and with private, for profit, suppliers.[28]

Although some large cities can undoubtedly benefit by contracting out selected public functions, many municipal services cannot readily be contracted out. For these services, better municipal management can result in significant cost savings.

Improving Municipal Management

Changing Organizational Structures. During the 1980s, the municipal decision-making process will become increasingly complex. Revenue constraints are likely to become more acute. Rising energy, labor, material, and construction costs will also limit municipal options in continuing old programs and in implementing new ones. The organizational structure of government may have to be modified to accomodate these more complex decision-making processes.

The International City Management Association (ICMA) notes that in most cities, the current organizational structure resembles a pyramid; the mayor or city manager is at the top of the pyramid and the various line departments, such as police, fire, and public works, report directly to him.[29] This type of structure achieves unity of command because there is a single leader and authority is delegated downward through the organization; there are no horizontal lines of authority. However, this form of organization cannot harness the diverse skills originating in different functional departments so as to apply them in an integrated manner to complex municipal problems. The ICMA specifies a number of "second generation" organizational models that partially circumvent this problem. They can take several forms including staff coordination, project office, project-oriented matrix, and functional-oriented matrix. The staff coordinator brings together a diverse array of personnel and resources but has no direct line authority over functional department specialists. They continue to report to their own department heads. When a project office is formed, the team members report to a designated project manager as do outside consultants and vendors. They are no longer responsible to their own line departments for the duration of the project. Under a functional-oriented matrix, line departments also assign staff to a project manager who controls the "what" and "when" of the project but leaves control over the "how" to the line manager. According to the ICMA, these second generation organization structures provide " . . . a single point of responsibility for a project, exercise centralized control over information, and permit contributions from functional organizational elements on a decentralized basis."[30] The ICMA suggests that a third-generation organizational structure, known as a "mature matrix" is also needed. This organizational model embodies a dual authority relationship. Authority over the project manager is shared equally by two bosses, each of whom represents a different aspect of local government. This arrangement violates the one-man, one-boss concept. However, it is being increasingly implemented by both the public and private sectors because it " . . . offers a method for integrating the complex requirements of today's activities, so that while traditional organizations can be maintained, proper and appropriate emphasis can be placed on activities and items of special need."[31]

First, second and third generation organizational structures are summarized in Figure 7.1.

Systematic Program Evaluation. A more responsive managerial structure can improve the quality of municipal management. However, a process to help determine which municipal programs should be modified, expanded, or dropped is also needed. Harry Hatry, Richard Winnie, and Donald Fisk have developed a series of practical program evaluation techniques.[32] They utilize performance criteria that are designed to measure program impact. For example, the authors suggest that the following performance measures be used in evaluating the effectiveness of a local recreation program: percent of user households rating recreational opportunities as good or poor; percent rating facilities as crowded or dirty; percent rating staff attitude, hours of operation, or safety as poor; number of serious accidents per 100,000 hours of use; percent of residents who used the facilities one or more times during a given period; total attendance at given facilities by hours of use; average number of programs per facility; and, proportion of residents who live within a given distance of each facility. They suggest the following criteria in evaluating local transportation facilities: percent of residents not within a given distance of public transit service and more than one hour from key destinations; percent of residents rating comfort or convenience as poor; average travel time between key origin and destination points; duration and severity of delays; rate of transportation-related deaths and injuries; cost per trip; total program cost; and, noise and

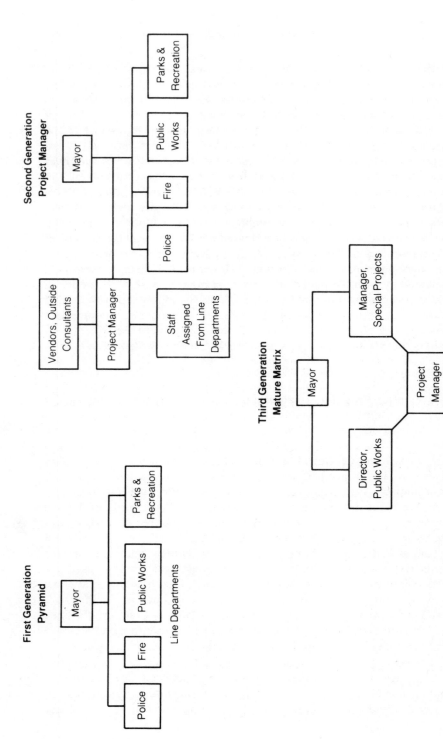

First Generation
Pyramid

Mayor

Police | Fire | Public Works | Parks & Recreation

Line Departments

Second Generation
Project Manager

Mayor

Police | Fire | Public Works | Parks & Recreation

Vendors, Outside Consultants

Project Manager

Staff Assigned From Line Departments

Third Generation
Mature Matrix

Mayor

Director, Public Works | Manager, Special Projects

Project Manager

Source: International City Management Association, "Local Government Organizational Structures for the Eighties", *Management Information Service Report* 12(March 1980).

FIGURE 7.1 Examples of First, Second, and Third Generation Organizational Structures

278

air pollution levels along transportation routes and persons at risk from such dangers.

After municipal officials assemble this information, the authors suggest that they compare what actually happened with what would have happened without the program in order to pinpoint those changes that can reasonably be attributed to the program. This is not an easy task and may well be the Achilles heel of the entire process. It can be accomplished in several ways: by comparing before and after data; by comparing pre-program data with actual post-program results; by comparing population elements served by the program with those not served; by comparing planned with actual performance; and, by systematically studying specific changes in an experimental group that is served by the program and comparing this group with a control group that is not served by the program. Hatry, Winnie, and Fisk note that systematic program evaluation allows program outcomes to be compared with the characteristics of clients and the characteristics of the workload to determine where adjustments are needed. It can also relate program outcomes to the operational characteristics of the program—to procedures, staffing, and organization—so as to identify which program characteristics should be modified to achieve greater efficiency.

Applying Private-Sector Management Techniques. Municipal management can also be improved by applying private-sector management techniques to local government operations. Loaned business executives have been a primary vehicle for private-sector management assistance to local governments. A recent Conference Board study noted:

> "Both parties benefit by this arrangement—government gains management and organizational expertise; companies benefit from a familiarity with the workings of local government; both sectors establish the contacts needed for future cooperation."[33]

The business community has begun to assume a more active role in assisting local governments in the communities in which they operate. They have come to regard such assistance as in their own self-interest. The U.S. Chamber of Commerce notes:

> " . . . a fiscally ailing community can adversely affect companies in terms of markets, tax burden, attraction and retention of employees, and protection of capital investments."[34]

The Committee for Economic Development echoes this sentiment:

> "Businesses should view the improvement of social and economic conditions in the communities in which they operate as a goal tied so

closely to their bottom line interests that it requires direct and effective action."[35]

The following are a few of the more successful attempts at transferring private management expertise to the public-sector via loaned executive programs.

New York's Economic Development Council. Founded in 1965, the Economic Development Council (EDC) is a non-profit consortium of more than 200 of the nation's largest corporations. It has attempted to reverse New York City's economic decline by means of loaned executives who provide free management consulting services. David Rogers has analyzed how the EDC program works.[36]

Executives are organized into a series of task forces, each containing from 10 to 20 executives. There is one task force for each agency with which the EDC is involved. The task forces utilize retired executives as well as executives on loan from large corporations. The latter take public-service sabbaticals but their corporations continue to pay their salaries. The task forces are advisory only. They receive assistance from the full-time EDC staff and generally submit monthly progress reports to their chairmen, to public officials, and sometimes to their own companies. Rogers notes that the EDC program is predicated on the assumption that management skills are transferable from business to government because all large organizations face similar problems, that the application of private-sector management skills can significantly improve the delivery of public services, and that improved services will result in a better quality of life in the city. He credits the EDC task forces with streamlining the city's payroll system, helping to develop a computerized management information system, and providing management assistance to criminal justice agencies at the city and state levels. Rogers concluded:

" . . . the EDC program contains components that other cities may well find useful . . . the most significant components include the task forces; the use of retired top executives as task force directors; the on-loan people from business, taking public-service sabbaticals, who do much of the consulting work; the support given them in a three-tiered structure (on-loan people, task force directors, EDC business leaders) . . . ; the strategies of the EDC task forces, in particular, their collaborative approach, their avoidance of simple solutions, and their continued emphasis on implementation . . . ; and the many outside resources EDC brought to city government—foundation and government grants, business funding, free consultant services, management training, and help with such technical matters as computerized information systems, budgeting, and accounting practices."[37]

The Committee for Progress in Allegheny County (ComPAC). One of the most ambitious efforts involving public–private cooperation took place in Allegheny County, Pennsylvania. At the request of the County, the Committee for Progress in Allegheny County was launched in April, 1976. The chief executive officers of the twelve largest corporations headquartered in Pittsburgh participated. In all, eight task forces involving ninety executives were used. Their goals were to make more effective use of taxpayer money through management reforms, to involve the business community in helping county government to operate efficiently, and to encourage joint public–private sector planning to address problems of mutual interest. ComPAC was supported by more than $250,000 from ten foundations. The Greater Pittsburgh Charitable Trust acted as agent for the receipt and disbursement of funds and maintained all financial records. The Greater Pittsburgh Chamber of Commerce also participated in this endeavor.

John Olsen notes that ComPAC stressed the practical operational types of problems for which business had the expertise to devise solutions.[38] Task forces were set up in each of the following functional areas: purchasing, cash management, personnel, computer services, management information-program budgeting, construction management, and records management. Each task force reported to a designated board member and performed between 3000 and 7000 manhours of work. Most task force members served part-time and retained their normal business responsibilities. Their employers absorbed the cost of their time and expenses while they worked for ComPAC; collectively these costs were estimated at $800,000. Monthly meetings were held with county officials to report on task force recommendations and to arrange for their implementation. County employees were involved throughout the project and their suggestions were solicited.

Task force accomplishments included the speeded up collection of funds due the county, the implementation of a centralized personnel system, the development of better information for budgeting decisions, and the development of better procedures for records management.

The Citizens Committee for Effective Government (CCEG) in Hartford. The Hartford management study was conducted between January 1979 and June 1980 by the Citizens Committee for Effective Government, a non-profit corporation formed by seven leaders from business, labor, government, and civic affairs.[39] Its purpose was to bring private management techniques to bear on public management problems. The study was funded by the Hartford business community and the Hartford Foundation for Public Giving at an estimated cost of $300,00 for the 18-month project. Sixteen task forces conducted studies in the following areas: lost time, facilities management, telecommunications, cash and revenue, social services, purchasing, management systems, streets and parks, vehicles, personnel planning, data processing, inspectional services, property management, police and fire, and housing. The task force recommendations saved an estimated $3 million to $5 million annually.

Each of the foregoing efforts involved the committment of time and resources by top corporate executives and public officials. Each emphasized practical recommendations that would yield measurable cost savings when implemented. Each sought to develop effective managerial procedures. Each was predicated on the assumption that good private management practices were transferable to the public sector and could improve public-sector efficiency and productivity.

JOINT PUBLIC–PRIVATE VENTURES

Joint public–private ventures are another vehicle for enlisting private-sector help. According to the Committee for Economic Development:

> "Roles and responsibilities are changing simultaneously among the levels of government and among the public and private organizations at each of those levels . . . the ability of local government to handle the greater responsibilities delegated to it by the federal or state governments will depend in part on what share of that responsibility is assumed by the private sector at the local level."[40]

The Committee for Economic Development has documented several joint public–private ventures that were designed to revitalize the decaying downtowns of large cities or otherwise promote economic development.

Detroit's Renaissance Center. This development, begun in 1971, encompasses 33 acres of formerly decaying industrial and commercial land along the Detroit River. Designed as a catalyst for revitalizing downtown Detroit, it includes hotel and office space as well as retail and service facilities. Ford Motor Land Development Corporation, the real estate subsidiary of the Ford Motor Company, assembled the land and formulated the development program. The project was implemented through the Renaissance City Partnership, a limited partnership consisting of the Detroit Downtown Development Corporation and fifty corporate partners. Twenty-eight banks and four life insurance companies financed the project. The City of Detroit cooperated by vacating streets and giving zoning approvals.[41]

Dallas's Reunion. This 5-acre downtown development, started in 1973, includes a Hyatt Regency Hotel, a 50-story theme tower, a municipal sports arena, the restored Union Terminal Building, parks, pedestrian walkways, a road network, and public parking. The City of Dallas and the Woodbine Development Corporation were joint participants in the project. The public sector built the sports arena, renovated Union Terminal, constructed the road network, parking facilities, and some of the utilities, and contributed 33 acres of land. The private sector provided the hotel, the theme tower, some roads and utilities and contributed 20 acres of land. The public share was financed through revenue bonds and sports arena seat options. Equitable Life and the First National Bank of Dallas financed the private share of the project. Some 425 people were employed during the construction phase and construction payrolls totaled $20 million. The sports arena opened in the Spring of 1980. The hotel opened in the Summer of 1980 and generated 800 jobs, a payroll of $3.5 million and $200,000 annually in hotel occupancy taxes. The local tax base increased by 2700% as a result of the project.[42]

St. Paul's Town Square. This development was constructed through a partnership between the City of St. Paul and Oxford Properties, Inc. It was started in the late 1960s and includes two office towers, a major retail complex and a luxury hotel. The public sector prepared design and development controls, built an indoor park, public walkways and skyways, granted building permits, and vacated a major downtown street. The private sector built the non-public structures and obtained the necessary tenant committments. The public share was financed by industrial revenue bonds sold by the St. Paul Port Authority. Private institutions financed the private-sector portion of the development.[43]

Pittsburgh's Renaissance II. This development has three components: Grand Street Plaza, PPG Place, and Vista International. Grand Street Plaza was started in 1981 and is slated for completion in 1984. It includes a 53-story office complex with shopping, restaurant, and leisure activity, and a major subway terminal. The partners in the project are U.S. Steel, Port Authority Transit, the City of Pittsburgh, and the Urban Redevelopment Authority. PPG Place consists of a 40-story office complex with six structures including shops, restaurants, and an open plaza and winter garden. The project was started in 1980 and is slated for completion in 1983. The partners are Pittsburgh Plate Glass Industries, Inc., the Urban Redevelopment Authority, and the City of Pittsburgh. Vista International includes a 20-story hotel and a 36-story office complex. Partners in the project are Vista International, the Urban Redevelopment Authority, and the City of Pittsburgh.[44]

A promising new financing mechanism, Tax Increment Financing (TIF) may result in more widespread participation by local governments in joint public–private economic development ventures.[45] It can be used to finance land acquisition and clearance in designated renewal areas. TIF works as follows: There must first be a finding that physical, social, and economic blight are present in the designated renewal area and that private initiatives are unlikely to alleviate these conditions without substantial public assistance. If the community decides that property values in the area would remain stable or decline without public intervention, they can freeze assessed values at existing levels until redevelopment is completed. Any subsequent increase in assessed values is presumed to reflect the redevelopment process. The difference in revenues from the improved property and those from the frozen assessed value is the tax increment that is attributable to the redevelopment program. All governments in the designated area receive revenues based on the frozen assessed values. However, taxpayers pay taxes based on the improved values, with the difference going to a special fund within the redevelopment authority. Upon completion of the project or when the cost of redevelopment is fully paid, the tax increments revert to local taxing authorities.

Tax increment financing is currently being used in Minnesota, Wisconsin, and California. Jonathan Davidson suggests that TIF has the following advantages:

> "When compared to the red-tape and project delays which characterize federal assistance under the urban renewal program, or the year-to-year grant process of the present federal community development program, TIF offers municipalities an alternative based on the economic merits of its redevelopment plan. The advantages include avoidance of municipal borrowing and debt limitations . . . and the ability to finance redevelopment without committing tax or grant revenues for years without prior consent of affected taxing districts."[46]

Conclusions

This study has demonstrated that the need to economize in municipal government is urgent, that it affects large cities in all regions and stages of economic development, and that it is likely to become even more pressing in the next several years. In response to these pressures, the scope of municipal services and the manner in which they are delivered will change dramatically. How these changes are implemented and the effectiveness of the resulting public-service package may well determine whether large cities remain viable as places in which to live and work.

NOTES

1. Committee for Economic Development, Research and Policy Committee, *Public–Private Partnership, An Opportunity for Urban Communities*, (New York: February 1982), p. 2.

2. Thomas D. Galloway, "State and Regional Policy and the Urban Crisis: A Continuing Question of the Will to Act," in *The Changing Structure of the City, What Happened to the Urban Crisis*, ed. Gary A. Tobin (Beverly Hills, CA: Sage Publications, 1979), p. 48.

3. Robert D. Ebel, "Research and Policy Developments: Major Types of State and Local Taxes," in *Essays in Public Finance and Financial Management, State and Local Perspectives*, eds. John E. Petersen and Catherine Lavigne Spain (Chatham, N.J.: Chatham House Publishers, 1978), pp. 1–21.

4. John H. Bowman, "Property Tax Circuit Breakers Reconsidered: Continuing Issues Surrounding a Popular Program," *The American Journal of Economics and Sociology* 39(October 1980):355–72.

5. William Oakland, *Financial Relief for Troubled Cities* (Columbus, Ohio: Academy for Contemporary Problems, January 1978), p. 6.

6. Tom Bradley, "Management Techniques and the Urban Crisis," in *The Changing Structure of the City, What Happened to the Urban Crisis*, pp. 133–56.

7. Selma J. Mushkin and Charles L. Vehorn, "User Fees and Charges," *Governmental Finance* 52(November 1977):42–4.

8. Illinois Department of Commerce and Community Affairs, *User Charges— An Overlooked Revenue Source* (Springfield, Ill: State of Illinois, October 1981), p. 8.

9. Robert W. Poole, Jr., *Cutting Back City Hall* (New York: Universe Books, 1980), p. 26.

10. Paul A. Gilje, "Sharing of Tax Growth—Redefinitions," *Governmental Finance* 52(November 1977):35–40.

11. Katharine C. Lyall, "Regional Tax Base Sharing–Nature and Potential for Success," in *Cities Under Stress, The Fiscal Crisis of Urban America*, eds. Robert W. Burchell and David Listokin (Piscataway, N.J.: Rutgers University Center for Urban Policy Research, 1981), pp. 493–500.

12. W. Patrick Beaton, "Regional Tax Base Sharing: Problems in the Distribution Function," in *Cities Under Stress*, pp. 501–26.

13. Ibid., p. 512.

14. Roy Bahl and David Puryear, "Regional Tax Base Sharing: Possibilities and Implications," *National Tax Journal* 29(September 1976):333.

15. Harold Wolman, "Local Government Strategies to Cope with Fiscal Pressure," in *Fiscal Stress and Public Policy*, eds. Charles H. Levine and Irene Rubin (Beverly Hills, CA: Sage Publications, 1980), pp. 233–47.

16. Charles H. Levine, "More on Cutback Management: Hard Questions for Hard Times," *Public Administration Review*, Vol. 39 (March/April 1979), pp. 179–83.

17. Charles H. Levine, "Organizational Decline and Cutback Management," in

Managing Fiscal Stress, The Crisis in the Public Sector, ed. Charles H. Levine (Chatham, N.J.: Chatham House Publishers, Inc., 1980), p. 14.

18. Chamber of Commerce of the United States, *Improving Local Government Fiscal Management, Action Guidelines for Business Executives* (Washington, February 1979).

19. International City Management Association, *Managing With Less*, ed. Elizabeth K. Kellar (Washington: 1979), p. 7. With permission from the International City Management Association.

20. David T. Stanley, *Cities in Trouble* (Columbus, Ohio: Academy for Contemporary Problems, December 1976), p. 12.

21. Donald Fisk, Herbert Kiesling, and Thomas Muller, *Private Provision of Public Services, an Overview* (Washington: The Urban Institute, May 1978), p. 1.
1.

22. International City Management Association, "Contracting With the Private Sector for Municipal Services: A Dialogue Between Practitioners," *Management Information Service Report* 12(April 1980).

23. Stephen B. Gordon and Joseph T. Kelley, "The Private Delivery of Public Services: A Public Service Option," *Resources in Review* (Government Finance Research Center, Municipal Finance Officers Association, November 1981), pp. 6–9.

24. E.S. Savas, "Policy Analysis for Local Government: Public vs. Private Refuse Collection," in *Managing Fiscal Stress, The Crisis in the Public Sector*, pp. 281–302.

25. Ibid., p. 296.

26. Ibid., p. 298.

27. Fisk, Kiesling and Muller, p. 14.

28. Ibid., p. 87.

29. International City Management Association, "Local Government Organizational Structures for the Eighties," *Management Information Service Report* 12(March 1980).

30. Ibid., p. 3.

31. Ibid., p. 9.

32. Harry P. Hatry, Richard E. Winnie, and Donald M. Fisk, *Practical Program Evaluation for State and Local Governments*, 2nd Edition (Washington: The Urban Institute, 1981).

33. Linda Wintner, "Business and the Cities: Programs and Practices," *Information Bulletin No. 87* (New York: The Conference Board, 1981), p. 5.

34. Chamber of Commerce of the United States, *Improving Local Government Fiscal Management, Action Guidelines for Business Executives*, p. vii.

35. Committee for Economic Development, *Public–Private Partnership, An Opportunity for Urban Communities*, p. 6.

36. David Rogers, *Can Business Management Save the Cities? The Case of New York* (New York: The Free Press, 1978), with permission.

37. Ibid., p. 247.

38. John B. Olsen, "Applying Business Management Skills to Local Governmental Operations," *Public Administration Review* 39(May/June, 1979):282–89.

39. Howard A. Schretter, *The Ultimate Business Loan, Sharing Business Expertise With Local Government to Solve City Problems* (University of Georgia: Institute of Community and Area Development, September, 1980.)

40. Committee for Economic Development, *Public–Private Partnership, An Opportunity for Urban Communities*, p. 97.

41. Ibid., p. 35.

42. Ibid., p. 37.

43. Ibid., p. 38–9.

44. Ibid., p. 41.

45. Jonathan M. Davidson, "Tax Increment Financing as a Tool for Community Redevelopment," *University of Detroit Journal of Urban Law* 56(Winter 1979):405–44.

46. Ibid., p. 443.

Glossary of Census Bureau Fiscal Terminology

The Census Bureau allocates municipal financial statistics, as shown in the official reports and records of individual cities, to given categories according to specific guidelines and definitions. Sometimes Census Bureau procedures and definitions differ from common fiscal usage. For example, the Census Bureau reports the finances of cities on an "all funds" basis so that it is not possible to determine the condition of the general fund alone.

A selected list of Census Bureau definitions and procedures follows:

Capital Outlay Direct expenditure for contract or force account construction of buildings, roads, and other improvements, and for purchases of equipment, land, and existing structures. Includes amounts for additions, replacements, and major alterations to fixed works and structures. However, expenditure for repairs to such works and structures is classified as current operating expenditure.

Cash and Security Holdings Cash, deposits, and governmental and private securities (bonds, notes, stocks, mortgages, etc.), except holdings of agency and private trust funds. Does not include interfund loans, receivables, and the value of real-property and other fixed assets.

Census Bureau Fiscal Coverage Data relate only to municipal corporations and their dependent agencies, and do not include amounts for other local governments overlying city areas. Therefore, expenditure figures for "education" do not include spending by the separate school districts that administer public schools within most municipal areas. Variations in the assignment of governmental responsibility for public assistance, health, hospitals, public housing, and other functions to a lesser degree, also have an important effect upon reported amounts of city expenditure, revenue, and debt.

Current Charges   Amounts received from the public for performance of specific services benefiting the person charged and from sales of commodities and services except by city utilities. Includes fees, assessments, and other reimbursements for current services, rents and sales derived from commodities or services furnished incident to the performance of particular functions, gross income of commercial activities, and the like. Excludes amounts received from other governments and interdepartmental charges and transfers.

Current Operation   Direct expenditure for compensation of own officers and employees and for supplies, materials, and contractual services except amounts for capital outlay.

Debt   All long-term credit obligations of the city and its agencies whether backed by the city's full faith and credit or nonguaranteed, and all interest-bearing short-term credit obligations. Includes judgments, mortgages, and revenue bonds, as well as general obligation bonds, notes, and interest-bearing warrants. Excludes noninterest-bearing short-term obligations, interfund obligations, amounts owed in a trust or agency capacity, advances and contingent loans from other governments, and rights of individuals to benefits from city employee retirement funds.

Debt Outstanding   All debt obligations remaining unpaid on the date specified.

Debt Redemption   Long-term debt redeemed—for example, amounts retired other than by refundings—plus any net decrease in short-term debt outstanding.

Direct Expenditure   Payments to employees, suppliers, contractors, beneficiaries, and other final recipients of government payments—for example, all expenditure other than Intergovernmental Expenditure.

Education   Schools and other educational facilities and services. Local schools include mainly city-operated elementary and secondary schools.

Expenditure All amounts of money paid out by a government—net of recoveries and other correcting transactions—other than for retirement of debt, investment in securities, extension of credit, or as agency transactions. Note that expenditure includes only external transactions of a government and excludes non-cash transactions such as the provision of perquisites or other payments in kind.

Financial Administration Municipal officials and agencies concerned with tax assessment and collection, accounting, auditing, budgeting, purchasing, custody of funds, and other central finance activities.

Fire Protection City fire fighting organization and auxiliary services thereof, inspection for fire hazards, and other fire prevention activities. Includes cost of fire fighting facilities such as fire hydrants and water, furnished by other agencies of the city government.

Full Faith and Credit Debt Long-term debt for which the credit of the city, implying the power of taxation, is unconditionally pledged. Includes debt payable initially from specific taxes or non-tax sources, but representing a liability payable from any other available resources if the pledged sources are insufficient.

General Control The governing body, municipal courts, office of the chief executive, and central staff services and agencies concerned with personnel administration, law, recording, planning and zoning, and the like.

General Debt All debt other than that identified as having been issued specifically for utility purposes.

General Expenditure All city expenditure other than the specifically enumerated kinds of expenditure classified as utility expenditure, liquor stores expenditure, and employee-retirement or other insurance trust expenditure.

General Revenue All city revenue except utility revenue, liquor stores revenue, and employee-retirement or other insurance trust revenue. The basis for distinction is not the fund or administrative unit receiving particular amounts, but rather the nature of the revenue sources concerned. Includes all tax collections and intergovernmental revenue, even if designated for employee retirement or local utility purposes.

Hospitals   Establishment and operation of hospital facilities, provision of hospital care, and support of other public or of private hospitals.

Housing and Urban Renewal   City housing and redevelopment projects and regulation, promotion, and support of private housing and redevelopment activities. For cities in Arizona, Kentucky, Michigan, New Mexico, New York, and Virginia, this generally includes data for municipal housing authorities. Housing authorities for other cities are usually classified as independent governments and data for them are not included in city finance statistics.

Interest Expenditure   Amounts paid for use of borrowed money.

Intergovernmental Revenue   Amounts received from other governments as fiscal aid in the form of shared revenues and grants-in-aid, as reimbursements for performance of general government functions and specific services for the paying government (for example, care of prisoners or contractual research), or in lieu of taxes. Excludes amounts received from other governments for sale of property, commodities, and utility services. All intergovernmental revenue is classified as general revenue.

Long-Term Debt   Debt payable more than 1 year after date of issue.

Long-Term Debt Issued   The par value of long-term debt obligations incurred during the fiscal period concerned, including funding and refunding obligations. Debt obligations authorized but not actually incurred during the fiscal period are not included.

Long-Term Debt Retired   The par value of long-term debt obligations liquidated by repayment or exchange, including debt retired by refunding operations.

Non-Guaranteed Debt   Long-term debt payable solely from pledged specific sources—for example, from earnings of revenue producing activities (utilities, sewage disposal plants, toll bridges, etc.), from special assessments, or from specific non-property taxes. Includes only debt that does not constitute an obligation against any other resources of the city if the pledged sources are insufficient.

Property Taxes   Taxes conditioned on ownership of property and measured by its value. Includes general property taxes relating to property as a whole, real and personal, tangible or intangible, whether taxed at a single rate or at classified rates, and taxes on selected types of property, such as motor vehicles or certain or all intangibles.

Public Welfare   Support of and assistance to needy persons contingent upon their need. Excludes pensions to former employees and other benefits not contingent on need. Expenditures under this heading include: Cash Assistance paid directly to needy persons under the categorical programs (Old Age Assistance, Aid to Families with Dependent Children, Aid to the Blind, and Aid to the Disabled) and under any other welfare programs; Vendor payments made directly to private purveyors for medical care, burials, and other commodities and services provided under welfare programs; and provision and operation by the city of welfare institutions. It also includes city payments to other governments for welfare purposes, amounts for administration, support of private welfare agencies, and other public-welfare services.

Revenue   All amounts of money received by a government from external sources—net of refunds and other correcting transactions—other than from issuance of debt, liquidation of investments, and as agency and private trust transactions. Revenue excludes non-cash transactions such as receipt of services, commodities, or other "receipts in kind."

Salaries and Wages   Amount expended for compensation of employees. Consists of gross amounts without deduction of withholdings for income tax, social security, or retirement coverage.

Sales or Gross Receipts Taxes (General)   Sales or gross receipts taxes that are applicable with only specified exceptions to all types of goods, all types of goods and services, or all gross income, whether at a single rate or at classified rates. Taxes imposed distinctively upon sales of or gross receipts from selected commodities, services, or businesses are reported separately.

Sales or Gross Receipts Taxes (Selective)   Sales and gross receipts taxes imposed on sales of particular commodities or services or gross receipts of particular businesses, separately and apart from the application of general sales and gross receipts taxes.

Short-Term Debt   Interest-bearing debt payable within one year from date of issue, such as bond anticipation notes, bank loans, and tax anticipation notes and warrants. Includes obligations having no fixed maturity date if payable from a tax levied for collection in the year of their issuance.

Sources of Data   For the 46 cities with 300,000 inhabitants or more and for a limited number of smaller cities, the basic data were compiled by Census Bureau representatives from official reports and records, with the advice and assistance of local officers and employees.

Taxes   Compulsory contributions exacted by a government for public purposes, except employee and employer assessments for retirement and social insurance purposes, which are classified as insurance trust revenue. All tax revenue is classified as general revenue and comprises amounts received (including interest and penalties but excluding protested amounts and refunds) from all taxes imposed by a government. City tax revenue excludes any amounts from shares of state-imposed and collected taxes, which are classified as intergovernmental revenue.

Utility Debt   Debt originally issued specifically to finance city-owned and operated water, electric, gas, or transit utility facilities.

Bibliography

BOOKS

Aaron, Henry J. *Who Pays the Property Tax? A New View*. Washington, D.C.: The Brookings Institution, 1975.

Abravanel, Martin D. and Paul K. Mancini. "Attitudinal and Demographic Constraints." In *Urban Revitalization*, edited by Donald B. Rosenthal, pp. 27–47. Beverly Hills, Cal: Sage, 1980.

Aronson, J. Richard and Eli Schwartz, eds. *Management Policies in Local Government Finance*. Washington, D.C.: International City Management Association, 1981.

Bahl, Roy W. *Metropolitan City Expenditures, A Comparative Analysis*. Lexington, Ky: University of Kentucky Press, 1969.

_____. *The New York State Economy: 1960–1978 and the Outlook*. Syracuse, N.Y.: Maxwell School of Citizenship and Public Affairs, 1979.

_____. "The Next Decade in State and Local Government Finance: A Period of Adjustment." In *Urban Government Finance, Emerging Trends*, edited by Roy W. Bahl, pp. 191–220. Beverly Hills, Cal: Sage, 1981.

Bahl, Roy W., Bernard Jump, Jr., and Larry Schroeder. "The Outlook for City Fiscal Performance in Declining Regions." In *The Fiscal Outlook for Cities, Implications of a National Urban Policy*, edited by Roy W. Bahl, pp. 1–47. Syracuse, N.Y.: Syracuse University Press, 1978.

Bahl, Roy W. and Walter Vogt. *Fiscal Centralization and Tax Burdens: State and Regional Financing of City Services*. Cambridge, Mass: Ballinger, 1975.

Baumol, William J. "Technological Change and the New Urban Equilibrium." In *Cities Under Stress, The Fiscal Crisis of Urban America*, edited by Robert W.

Burchell and David Listokin, pp. 3–17. Piscataway, N.J.: Rutgers Center for Urban Policy Research, 1981.

Beaton, W. Patrick. "Regional Tax Base Sharing: Problems in the Distribution Function." *In Cities Under Stress, The Fiscal Crisis of Urban America*, edited by Robert W. Burchell and David Listokin, pp. 501–26. Piscataway, N.J.: Rutgers Center for Urban Policy Research, 1981.

Birch, David L. *Choosing a Place to Grow: Business Location Decisions in the 1970s.* Cambridge, Mass: MIT Program on Neighborhood and Regional Change, 1981.

Bish, Robert L. and Hugh O. Nourse. *Urban Economics and Policy Analysis.* New York: McGraw-Hill, 1975.

Bradbury, Katharine L., Anthony Downs, and Kenneth A. Small, eds. *Urban Decline and the Future of American Cities.* Washington, D.C.: The Brookings Institution, 1982.

Bradley, Tom. "Management Techniques and the Urban Crisis." In *The Changing Structure of the City, What Happened to the Urban Crisis*, edited by Gary A. Tobin, pp. 133–56. Beverly Hills, Cal: Sage, 1979.

Break, George F. *Financing Government in a Federal System.* Washington, D.C.: The Brookings Institution, 1980.

Breckenfeld, Gurney. "Refilling the Metropolitan Doughnut." In *The Rise of the Sunbelt Cities*, edited by David C. Perry and Alfred J. Watkins, pp. 231–58. Beverly Hills, Cal: Sage, 1977.

Bryce, Herrington J. ed. *Revitalizing Cities.* Lexington, Mass: Lexington, 1979.

Burchell, Robert W., David Listokin, George Sternlieb, James W. Hughes, and Stephen C. Casey. "Measuring Urban Distress: A Summary of the Major Urban Hardship Indices and Resource Allocation Systems." In *Cities Under Stress, The Fiscal Crisis of Urban America*, edited by Robert W. Burchell and David Listokin, pp. 159–229. Piscataway, N.J.: Rutgers Center for Urban Policy Research, 1981.

Campbell, Alan K. and Seymour Sachs. *Metropolitan America, Fiscal Patterns and Governmental Systems.* New York: The Free Press, 1967.

Chamber of Commerce of the United States. *Improving Local Government Fiscal Management, Action Guidelines For Executives.* Washington, D.C.: 1979.

Chinitz, Benjamin. *Central City Economic Development.* Cambridge, Mass: Abt Books, 1979.

Choate, Pat and Susan Walter. *America in Ruins.* Washington, D.C.: The Council of State Planning Agencies, 1981.

Cohen, Robert B. "Multinational Corporations, International Finance, and the Sunbelt." In *The Rise of the Sunbelt Cities*, edited by David C. Perry and Alfred J. Watkins, pp. 211–26. Beverly Hills, Cal: Sage, 1977.

Committee for Economic Development. Research and Policy Committee. *Public–Private Partnership, An Opportunity for Urban Communities.* New York: 1982.

Courant, Paul N., Edward M. Gramlich, and Daniel L. Rubinfeld. "The Stimulative Effects of Intergovernmental Grants: Or Why Money Sticks Where It Hits." In *Fiscal Federalism and Grants-in-Aid*, edited by Peter Mieszkowski and William H. Oakland, pp. 5–21. Washington, D.C.: The Urban Institute, 1979.

Deacon, Robert T. "State and Local Government Expenditures." In *Essays in Public Finance and Financial Management, State and Local Perspectives*, edited by John E. Petersen and Catherine Lavigne Spain, pp. 22–33. Chatham, N.J.: Chatham House, 1978.

Dearborn, Philip M. "Urban Fiscal Studies." In *Essays in Public Finance and Financial Management, State and Local Perspectives*, edited by John E. Petersen and Catherine Lavigne Spain, pp. 156–64. Chatham, N.J.: Chatham House, 1978.

Dickson, Elizabeth, Harold A. Hovey, and George E. Peterson. *Public Employee Compensation, A Twelve City Comparison*. Washington, D.C.: The Urban Institute, 1980.

Fainstein, Norman I. and Susan S. Fainstein. "Restructuring the American City: A Comparative Perspective." In *Urban Policy Under Capitalism*, edited by Norman I. Fainstein and Susan S. Fainstein, pp. 161–89. Beverly Hills, Cal: Sage, 1982.

Firestine, Robert E. "Economic Growth and Inequality, Demographic Change, and the Public Sector Response." In *The Rise of the Sunbelt Cities*, edited by David C. Perry and Alfred J. Watkins, pp. 191–210. Beverly Hills, Cal: Sage, 1977.

Fisher, Glenn W. "What is the Ideal Revenue Balance—A Political View." In *Cities Under Stress, The Fiscal Crisis of Urban America*, edited by Robert W. Burchell and David Listokin, pp. 439–57. Piscataway, N.J.: Rutgers Center for Urban Policy Research, 1981.

Fisk, Donald, Herbert Kiesling, and Thomas Muller. *Private Provision of Public Services, An Overview*. Washington, D.C.: The Urban Institute, 1978.

Fossett, James W. and Richard P. Nathan. "The Prospects for Urban Revival." In *Urban Government Finance, Emerging Trends*, edited by Roy W. Bahl, pp. 63–104. Beverly Hills, Cal: Sage, 1981.

Galloway, Thomas D. "State and Regional Policy and the Urban Crisis: A Continuing Question of the Will to Act." In *The Changing Structure of the City, What Happened to the Urban Crisis*, edited by Gary A. Tobin, pp. 45–76. Beverly Hills, Cal: Sage, 1979.

Gold, Steven David. *Property Tax Relief*. Lexington, Mass: Lexington, 1979.

Gorham, William and Nathan Glazer, eds. *The Urban Predicament*. Washington, D.C.: The Urban Institute, 1976.

Greytak, David and Bernard Jump, Jr. *The Impact of Inflation on the Expenditures and Revenues of Six Local Governments, 1971–79*. Syracuse University: Maxwell School of Citizenship and Public Affairs, 1975.

Grosskopf, Shawna. "Public Employment's Impact on the Future of Urban Economies." In *Urban Government Finance, Emerging Trends*, edited by Roy W. Bahl, pp. 39–62. Beverly Hills, Cal: Sage, 1981.

Grossman, David A. *The Future of New York City's Capital Plant*. Washington, D.C.: The Urban Institute, 1979.

Gustely, Richard D. *Municipal Public Employment and Public Expenditure*. Lexington, Mass: Lexington, 1974.

Hansen, Niles M. *The Future of Nonmetropolitan America, Studies in the Reversal of Rural and Small Town Population Decline*. Lexington, Mass: Lexington, 1973.

Hatry, Harry P., Richard E. Winnie, and Donald M. Fisk. *Practical Program Evaluation for State and Local Governments*, 2nd ed. Washington, D.C.: The Urban Institute, 1981.

Hirsch, Werner Z., Philip E. Vincent, Henry S. Terrell, Donald C. Shoup, and Arthur Rosett. *Fiscal Pressures on the Central City, The Impact of Commuters, Nonwhites and Overlapping Governments*. New York: Praeger, 1971.

Humphrey, Nancy, George E. Peterson, and Peter Wilson. *The Future of Cincinnati's Capital Plant*. Washington, D.C.: The Urban Institute, 1979.

James, Franklin J. "Economic Distress in Central Cities." In *Cities Under Stress, The Fiscal Crisis of Urban America*, edited by Robert W. Burchell and David Listokin, pp. 19–49. Piscataway, N.J.: Rutgers Center for Urban Policy Research, 1981.

Jump, Bernard Jr. "Public Employment, Collective Bargaining and Employee Wages and Pensions." In *Essays in Public Finance and Financial Management, State and Local Perspectives*, edited by John E. Petersen and Catherine Lavigne Spain, pp. 74–85. Chatham, N.J.: Chatham House, 1978.

Larkey, Patrick D. *Evaluating Public Programs, The Impact of General Revenue Sharing on Municipal Government*. Princeton, N.J.: Princeton University Press, 1979.

Leveson, Irving and Jane Newitt. *The Future of the U.S. and its Regions*. Croton-on-Hudson, N.Y.: The Hudson Institute, 1978.

Levine, Charles H. "Hard Questions for Hard Times." In *Managing With Less*, edited by Elizabeth K. Kellar, pp. 8–15. Washington, D.C.: International City Management Association, 1979.

_____. "Organizational Decline and Cutback Management." In *Managing Fiscal Stress, The Crisis in the Public Sector*, edited by Charles H. Levine, pp. 13–30. Chatham, N.J.: Chatham House, 1980.

Lupsha, Peter A. and William J. Siembieda. "The Poverty of Public Services in the Land of Plenty: An Analysis and Interpretation." In *The Rise of the Sunbelt Cities*, edited by David C. Perry and Alfred J. Watkins, pp. 169–89. Beverly Hills, Cal: Sage, 1977.

Lyall, Katharine C. "Regional Tax Base Sharing—Nature and Potential for Success." In *Cities Under Stress, The Fiscal Crisis of Urban America*, edited by Robert W. Burchell and David Listokin, pp. 493–500. Piscataway, N.J.: Rutgers Center for Urban Policy Research, 1981.

MacManus, Susan A. *Revenue Patterns in U.S. Cities and Suburbs, A Comparative Analysis*. New York: Praeger, 1978.

Matz, Deborah. "The Tax and Expenditure Limitation Movement." In *Urban Government Finance, Emerging Trends*, edited by Roy W. Bahl, pp. 127–53. Beverly Hills, Cal: Sage, 1981.

Miller, Mary J., Marcy Arvin, Bonnie Berk, and George E. Peterson. *The Future of Oakland's Capital Plant*. Washington, D.C.: The Urban Institute, 1981.

Miller, Mary J., J. Chester Johnson, and George E. Peterson. *The Future of Boston's Capital Plant*. Washington, D.C.: The Urban Institute, 1981.

Mollenkopf, John H. "Paths Toward the Post-Industrial Service City: The Northeast and the Southwest." In *Cities Under Stress, The Fiscal Crisis of Urban*

America, edited by Robert W. Burchell and David Listokin, pp. 77–112. Piscataway, N.J.: Rutgers Center for Urban Policy Research, 1981.

Muller, Thomas. *Growing and Declining Urban Areas: A Fiscal Comparison.* Draft Report. Washington, D.C.: The Urban Institute, 1975.

———. "Changing Expenditures and Service Demand Patterns of Stressed Cities." *Growing and Declining Urban Areas: A Fiscal Comparison*, edited by Robert W. Burchell and David Listokin, pp. 277–99. Piscataway, N.J.: Rutgers Center for Urban Policy Research, 1981.

Muller, Thomas and Grace Dawson. *The Impact of Annexation on City Finances: A Case Study in Richmond Virginia.* Washington, D.C.: The Urban Institute, May, 1973.

Musgrave, Richard A. and Peggy B. Musgrave. *Public Finance in Theory and Practice.* 2nd ed. New York: McGraw-Hill, 1973.

Nathan, Richard P. and Charles F. Adams, Jr. *Revenue Sharing: The Second Round.* Washington, D.C.: The Brookings Institution, 1977.

Netzer, Dick. *Economics and Urban Problems.* New York: Basic, 1970.

Oakland, William. *Financial Relief For Troubled Cities.* Columbus, Ohio: Academy for Contemporary Problems, 1978.

Peters, B. Guy. "Fiscal Strains on the Welfare State: Causes and Consequences." In *Fiscal Stress and Public Policy*, edited by Charles H. Levine and Irene Rubin, pp. 43–8. Beverly Hills, Cal: Sage, 1980.

Petersen, John E. "State and Local Government Debt Policy and Management." In *Essays in Public Finance and Financial Management, State and Local Perspectives*, edited by John E. Petersen and Catherine Lavigne Spain, pp. 62–73. Chatham, N.J.: Chatham House, 1978.

Peterson, George E. *The Economic and Fiscal Accompaniments of Population Change.* Syracuse University: Maxwell School of Citizenship and Public Affairs, 1979.

———. "Transmitting the Municipal Fiscal Squeeze to a New Generation of Taxpayers: Pension Obligations and Capital Investment Needs." In *Cities Under Stress, The Fiscal Crisis of Urban America*, edited by Robert W. Burchell and David Listokin, pp. 249–76. Piscataway, N.J.: Rutgers Center for Urban Policy Research, 1981.

Peterson, George E., Henry L. Mortimer, Brian Cooper, Elizabeth Dickson, and George A. Riegeluth. *Urban Fiscal Monitoring.* Draft report. Washington, D.C.: The Urban Institute, 1978.

Poole, Robert W., Jr. *Cutting Back City Hall.* New York: Universe, 1980.

Reischauer, Robert. "The Economy and the Federal Budget in the 1980s: Implications for the State and Local Sector." In *Urban Government Finance, Emerging Trends*, edited by Roy W. Bahl, pp. 13–38. Beverly Hills, Cal: Sage, 1981.

Rogers, David. *Can Business Management Save the Cities? The Case of New York.* New York: The Free Press, 1978.

Rosenberg, Philip. *Is Your City Heading For Financial Difficulty: A Guidebook for Small Cities and Other Governmental Units.* Chicago: Municipal Finance Officers Association. 1978.

Ross, John P. and James Greenfield. "Measuring the Health of Cities." In *Fiscal Stress and Public Policy*, edited by Charles H. Levine and Irene Rubin, pp. 89–110. Beverly Hills, Cal: Sage, 1980.

Rubin, Irene S. *Running in the Red, The Political Dynamics of Urban Fiscal Stress.* Albany, N.Y.: State University of New York Press, 1982.

Savas, E.S. "Policy Analysis for Local Government: Public versus Private Refuse Collection." In *Managing Fiscal Stress, The Crisis in the Public Sector*, edited by Charles H. Levine, pp. 281–302. Chatham, N.J.: Chatham House, 1980.

Schroeder, Larry D. and David L. Sjoquist. *The Property Tax and Alternative Local Taxes, An Economic Analysis.* New York: Praeger, 1975.

Shapiro, Perry. "Popular Response to Public Spending Disequilibrium: An Analysis of the 1978 California Property Tax Limitation Initiative." In *Tax and Expenditure Limitations*, edited by Helen F. Ladd and T. Nicolaus Tideman, pp. 13–35. Washington, D.C.: The Urban Institute Press, 1981.

Solomon, Arthur P. ed. *The Prospective City.* Cambridge, Mass: The MIT Press, 1980.

Stanley, David T. *Cities in Trouble.* Columbus, Ohio: Academy for Contemporary Problems, 1976.

Steiss, Alan Walter. *Local Government Finance.* Lexington, Mass: Lexington, 1975.

Sternlieb, George. "Kemp–Garcia Act: An Initial Evaluation." In *New Tools For Economic Development: The Enterprise Zone, Development Bank and RFC*, edited by George Sternlieb and David Listokin, pp. 42–83. Piscataway, N.J.: Rutgers Center for Urban Policy Research, 1981.

Sternlieb, George and James W. Hughes. "New Dimensions of the Urban Crisis." In *Cities Under Stress, The Fiscal Crisis of Urban America*, edited by Robert W. Burchell and David Listokin, pp. 51–75. Piscataway, N.J.: Rutgers Center for Urban Policy Research, 1981.

Stillwell, Lee J. "The Niagara Falls Experiment." In *Managing With Less*, edited by Elizabeth K. Kellar, pp. 52–6. Washington, D.C.: International City Management Association, 1979.

Stocker, Frederick D. and Dan Crippen. *Fiscal and Governmental Reform Options for Cities in the Industrial Midwest.* Columbus, Ohio: Academy for Contemporary Problems, 1979.

United States Conference of Mayors. *General Revenue Sharing (State and Local Share) and the Fiscal Condition of Cities.* Washington, D.C.: 1980.

_____. *The FY 82 Budget and the Cities, A Hundred City Survey.* Washington, D.C.: 1981.

_____. *The Federal Budget and the Cities, A Review of the President's Budget in the Light of Urban Needs and National Priorities.* Washington, D.C.: 1983.

Watkins, Alfred J. and David C. Perry. "Regional Change and the Impact of Uneven Urban Development." In *The Rise of the Sunbelt Cities*, edited by David C. Perry and Alfred J. Watkins, pp. 19–54. Beverly Hills, Cal: Sage, 1977.

Weinstein, Bernard L. and Robert J. Clark. "The Fiscal Outlook For Growing Cities." In *Urban Government Finance, Emerging Trends*, edited by Roy W. Bahl, pp. 105–25. Beverly Hills, Cal: Sage, 1981.

Wilson, Peter. *The Future of Dallas's Capital Plant*. Washington, D.C.: The Urban Institute, 1980.

Wolman, Harold. "Local Government Strategies to Cope with Fiscal Pressure." In *Fiscal Stress and Public Policy*, edited by Charles H. Levine and Irene Rubin, pp. 233–47. Beverly Hills, Cal.: Sage, 1980.

ARTICLES

Aronson, J. Richard and A.E. King. 'Is There a Fiscal Crisis Outside of New York." *National Tax Journal* 31(1978):135–55.

Bahl, Roy W. and David Greytak. "The Response of City Government Revenues to Changes in Employment Structure." *Land Economics* 52(November 1976): 415–34.

Bahl, Roy and David Puryear. "Regional Tax Base Sharing: Possibilities and Implications." *National Tax Journal* 29(September 1976):328–35.

Beaton, W. Patrick. "The Determinants of Police Protection Expenditures." *National Tax Journal* 27(June 1974):335–49.

Blaydon, Colin C. and Steven R. Gilford. "Financing the Cities: An Issue Agenda." *Duke Law Journal* 1976(January 1976):1057–117.

Booth, Douglas E. "The Differential Impact of Manufacturing and Mercantile Activity on Local Government Expenditures and Revenues." *National Tax Journal* 30(1978):33–43.

Bowman, John H. "Property Tax Circuit Breakers Reconsidered: Continuing Issues Surrounding a Popular Program." *American Journal of Economics and Sociology* 39(October 1980):355–72.

Bradbury, Katharine, Anthony Downs, and Kenneth A. Small. "Some Dynamics of Central City–Suburban Interactions." *The American Economic Review* 70(May 1980):410–14.

Browne, Lynn E. and Richard F. Syron. "Cities, Suburbs and Regions." *New England Economic Review* No. 5103 (January/February 1979):41–61.

Calkins, Susannah and John Shannon, "The New Formula For Fiscal Federalism: Austerity Equals Decentralization." *Intergovernmental Perspective* 8(Winter 1982):23–29.

Carey, Hugh L. "New Federalism, 'Yes', But Reagan's Proposal Needs Major Revision." *New York Times*, March 14, 1982, p. 23.

Conte, Christopher. "Reagan Rejects Tax Rises to Curb Deficits, Offers Welfare Program Swap With States." *Wall St. Journal*, January 27, 1982, p. 3.

Daken, James B. "The Ultimate Corporate Loan." *Public Management* 59(August 1977):11–13.

Davidson, Jonathan M. "Tax Increment Financing as a Tool For Community Redevelopment." *University of Detroit Journal of Urban Law* 56(Winter 1979):405–44.

"Dislocations That May Deepen." *Business Week*, Special Issue No. 2690, June 1, 1981, pp. 62–64.

Gilje, Paul A. "Sharing of Tax Growth—Redefinitions." *Governmental Finance* 52(November 1977):35–40.

Herbers, John. "Shift to Block Grants Raising Issue of States' Competence." *New York Times*, September 27, 1981, p. 1.

———. "U.S. Cities, in Fiscal Squeeze, Turn to Private Sector for Aid." *New York Times*, October 1, 1981, p. 1.

Concepts and Programs." *Management Information Service Report* 12(January 1980).

———. "Local Government Organizational Structures for the Eighties." *Management Information Service Report* 12(March 1980).

———. "Contracting with the Private Sector for Municipal Services: A Dialogue Between Practitioners." *Management Information Service Report* 12(April 1980).

Klein, Frederick C. "Born Again? Big Old Cities of East, Midwest are Reviving After Years of Decline." *Wall St. Journal*, May 19, 1980, p. 1.

Lund, Leonard. "Business Involvement With Local Government." *The Conference Board Information Bulletin No. 30*. New York: The Conference Board, 1977.

Mushkin, Selma J. and Charles L. Vehorn. "User Fees and Charges." *Governmental Finance* 52(November 1977):42–44.

Myers, Will and John Shannon. "Revenue Sharing for States: An Endangered Species." *Intergovernmental Perspective* 5(Summer 1979):10–18.

Nathan, Richard P. and Charles F. Adams, Jr. "Understanding Central City Hardship." *Political Science Quarterly* 91(Spring 1976):47–62.

Oates, Wallace E. "On Local Finance and the Tiebout Model." *American Economic Review* 71(May 1981):93–8.

Olsen, John B. "Applying Business Management Skills to Local Governmental Operations." *Public Administration Review* 39(May/June 1979):282–89.

Pack, Janet Rothenberg. "Frostbelt and Sunbelt, Convergence Over Time." *Intergovernmental Perspective* 4(Fall 1978):8–15.

Pear, Robert. "States Report Recession is Squeezing Budgets." *New York Times*, January 9, 1983, p. 20.

Shannon, John and L. Richard Gabler, "Tax Lids and Expenditure Mandates: The Case for Fiscal Fair Play." *Intergovernmental Perspective* 3(Summer 1977):7–12.

Solomon, Rod. "New Urban Economic Development Initiatives: History, Problems and Potential." *Harvard Journal on Legislation* 16(1979):811–51.

Tiebout, Charles M. "A Pure Theory of Local Expenditures." *Journal of Political Economy* 64(1956):416–24.

Wintner, Linda. "Business and the Cities: Programs and Practices." *The Conference Board Information Bulletin No. 87*. New York: The Conference Board, 1981.

PUBLIC DOCUMENTS

Advisory Commission on Intergovernmental Relations. *Measures of State and Local Fiscal Capacity and Tax Effort*. Washington, D.C. Government Printing Office, 1962.

————. *City Financial Emergencies: The Intergovernmental Dimension.* Washington, D.C.: Government Printing Office, 1973.

————. *Categorical Grants: Their Role and Design.* Washington, D.C.: Government Printing Office, 1977.

————. *Community Development: The Workings of a Federal–Local Block Grant.* Washington, D.C.: Government Printing Office, 1977.

————. *Federal Grants: Their Effects on State–Local Expenditures, Employment Levels, Wage Rates.* Washington, D.C.: Government Printing Office, 1977.

————. *The Comprehensive Employment and Training Act: Early Readings from a Hybrid Block Grant.* Washington, D.C.: Government Printing Office, 1977.

————. *Trends in Metropolitan America.* Washington, D.C.: Government Printing Office, 1977.

————. *Countercyclical Aid and Economic Stabilization.* Washington, D.C.: Government Printing Office, 1978.

————. *Significant Features of Fiscal Federalism.* 1978–89 Edition. Washington, D.C.: Government Printing Office, 1979.

————. *Central City–Suburban Fiscal Disparity and City Distress 1977.* Washington, D.C.: Government Printing Office, 1980.

————. *State and Local Roles in the Federal System.* Washington, D.C.: Government Printing Office, 1981.

Anderson, Wayne F. *Block Grants and the Budget Reconciliation Act of 1981,* Memorandum to Members of the Advisory Commission on Intergovernmental Relations. Washington, D.C.: ACIR, January 7, 1982.

Aronson, J. Richard. *Municipal Fiscal Indicators.* Washington, D.C.: U.S. Department of Housing and Urban Development, 1980.

————. *A Catalog of Municipal Cost-Cutting Techniques.* Springfield, Ill: Cost Cutters Project, June, 1981.

Illinois Department of Commerce and Community Affairs. *A Catalog of Municipal Cost-Cutting Techniques.* Springfield, Ill: Cost Cutters Project, June, 1981.

————. *A Blueprint for Controlling Workers Compensation and Unemployment Insurance Costs.* Springfield, Ill: Cost Cutters Project, October, 1981.

————. *Cost Reduction Through Better Work Force Utilization.* Springfield, Ill: Cost Cutters Project, October, 1981.

————. *Municipal Cash Management.* Springfield, Ill: Cost Cutters Project, October, 1981.

Jusenius, Carol L. and Larry C. Ledebur. *Where Have All the Firms Gone? An Analysis of the New England Economy.* Washington, D.C.: U.S. Department of Commerce, Economic Development Administration, September, 1977.

————. *Documenting the "Decline" of the North.* Washington, D.C.: U.S. Department of Commerce, Economic Development Administration, June, 1978.

League of California Cities. *More California Cutback Management.* Sacramento, Cal: League of California Cities, Innovation Exchange Program, November, 1981.

U.S. Congress, Congressional Budget Office. *Barriers to Urban Economic Development.* Washington, D.C.: Government Printing Office, May 1978.

————. *Proposition 13: Its Impact on the Nation's Economy, Federal Revenues, and Federal Expenditures.* Washington, D.C.: Government Printing Office, July, 1978.

U.S. Congress. *Hearings Before the Subcommittee on Urban Affairs of the Joint Economic Committee.* 94th Cong., 2nd Sess., January 22nd and 23rd, 1976. Washington, D.C.: Government Printing Office, 1977.

U.S. Congress, Joint Economic Committee. *Central City Businesses—Plans and Problems.* Washington, D.C.: Government Printing Office, 1979.

_____. *Trends in the Fiscal Condition of Cities: 1978–80.* Washington, D.C.: Government Printing Office, 1980.

_____. *Emergency Interim Study: Fiscal Condition of 48 Large Cities.* Washington, D.C.: Government Printing Office, January 14, 1982.

U.S. Department of Agriculture. *Size Economies in Local Government Services.* Rural Development Research Report No. 22. Washington, D.C.: Government Printing Office, 1980.

U.S. Department of Commerce, Bureau of Census. "Taxable Property Values and Assessment/Sales Price Ratios." *1977 Census of Governments.* GC77(2), Vol. 2, Washington, D.C.: Government Printing Office, November, 1978.

_____. *Property Values Subject to Local General Property Taxation in the United States, 1978.* Washington, D.C.: Government Printing Office, 1979.

_____. *Boundary and Annexation Survey 1970–1979.* GE-30-4. Washington, D.C.: Government Printing Office, 1980.

_____. *Expenditures of General Revenue Sharing and Anti-Recession Fiscal Assistance Funds, 1977–78.* Washington, D.C.: Government Printing Office, 1980.

_____. *1980 Census of Population, Standard Metropolitan Statistical Areas and Standard Consolidated Statistical Areas: 1980.* PC 80-S1-5. Washington, D.C.: Government Printing Office, October 1981.

_____. *City Employment in 1981,* Series GE 81, No. 2. Washington, D.C.: Government Printing Office, 1982.

_____. *City Government Finances in 1980–81,* Series GF 81, No. 4. Washington, D.C.: Government Printing Office, 1982.

U.S. Department of Housing and Urban Development. *The President's National Urban Policy Report.* Washington, D.C.: Government Printing Office, July, 1982.

U.S. Department of Labor, Bureau of Labor Statistics, *Wage Differences Among Large City Governments and Comparisons With Industry and Federal Pay, 1975–76.* Report 520. Washington, D.C.: Government Printing Office, 1978.

_____. "Moving to the Sun: Regional Job Growth, 1968 to 1978." *Monthly Labor Review* March, 1980, pp. 12–19.

_____. *Wage Differences Among Large City Governments and Comparisons With Industry and Federal Pay, 1978–79.* Report 633. Washington, D.C.: Government Printing Office, 1981.

U.S. Department of the Treasury. *Report on the Fiscal Impact of the Economic Stimulus Package on 48 Large Urban Governments.* Washington, D.C.: Government Printing Office, 1978.

Index

About the Author

PEARL M. KAMER is Chief Economist, Long Island Regional Planning Board, and Associate Professor, part-time, Harriman College of Urban and Policy Sciences, State University of New York at Stony Brook.

Dr. Kamer has published widely in the areas of economic development, urban and regional economics, and public finance. Her articles have appeared in the *Journal of the American Real Estate and Urban Economics Association, The New York Statistician*, and *Socio-Economic Planning Sciences*. She is currently President of the New York Regional Economists Society, Vice-President of the Metropolitan Economic Association and editor of *The Regional Economic Digest*.

Dr. Kamer has taught at New York University and Hofstra University, has served as a consultant to several financial institutions and more recently as a consultant to the New York State Governor's Council on State Priorities.

Dr. Kamer holds a B.A. from Queens College and an M.B.A. and Ph.D. from New York University. She is a member of Phi Beta Kappa.